CULTURAL POLITICS

Gender, race, Renaissance drama

Gender, race, Renaissance drama

Ania Loomba

Delhi
Oxford University Press
Bombay Calcutta Madras
1992

Oxford University Press, Walton Street, Oxford OX2 6DP

New York Toronto
Delhi Bombay Calcutta Madras Karachi
Kuala Lumpur Singapore Hong Kong Tokyo
Nairobi Dar es Salaam
Melbourne Auckland

and associates in
Berlin Ibadan

First published in India 1992
Reprinted by arrangement with the original publisher

SBN 0 19 563004 1

Printed at Crescent Printing Works (P) Ltd., New Delhi-110001
and published by S. K. Mookerjee, Oxford University Press
YMCA Library Building, Jai Singh Road, New Delhi 110001

Contents

Acknowledgements

I am happy to acknowledge the many people whose support, criticism and own work has made this book possible – especially Jonathan Dollimore, who supervised the thesis on which the present project is based and encouraged me to write it, and Alan Sinfield, whose comments and editing have been invaluable. I would also like to thank John Drakakis for his suggestions and criticism, and for sending me material; Jacqueline Rose for her consistent support; Martin Orkin for giving me his stimulating book; Rajeswari Sunder Rajan for generously sharing her own work and ideas; Ahmer N. Anwar and Pradip Datta for their suggestions; Pratap Rughani and Deepa Grover for sending material I could not find in India. To Suvir Kaul I owe one rare book, and a very stimulating friendship.

The solidarity of Primla Loomba, Nayanjot and Kishore Lahiri, Gayatri Thapar and my son, Tariq, made it possible to write in chaotic circumstances. My main debt, as usual, is to Rajiv Thapar, Kerys Murrell, and above all, my sister, Bindia Thapar.

Foreword: **Cultural politics**

The break-up of consensus in British political life during the 1970s was accompanied by the break-up of traditional assumptions about the values and goals of literary culture. Initially at specialised conferences and in committed journals, but increasingly in the mainstream of intellectual life, literary texts have been related to the new and challenging discourses of Marxism, feminism, structuralism, psychoanalysis and poststructuralism, and juxtaposed with work not customarily accorded literary or artistic standing.

Some recent developments offer a significant alternative to traditional practice; others are little more than realignments of familiar positions. But our belief is that a combination of historical and cultural context, theoretical method, political commitment and textual analysis offers the strongest challenge and has already contributed substantial work. We call this *cultural materialism*.

There are (at least) two ways of using the word 'culture'. The evaluative use has been more common when we are thinking about 'the arts' and 'literature': to be 'cultured' is to be the possessor of superior values and a refined sensibility, both of which are manifested through a positive and fulfilling engagement with 'good' literature, art, music and so on. The analytic one is used in the social sciences and especially anthropology: it seeks to describe the whole system of significations by which a society or a section of it understands itself and its relations with the world. Cultural materialism draws upon the latter, analytic sense, and therefore studies 'high' culture alongside work in popular culture, in other media and from subordinated groups.

'Materialism' is opposed to 'idealism': it insists that culture does not (cannot) transcend the material forces and relations of production. Culture is not simply a reflection of the economic and political system, but nor can it be independent of it. Cultural materialism therefore sees texts as inseparable from the conditions of their production and reception in history; and as involved, necessarily in the making of cultural meanings which are always, finally, political meanings. Hence the series title: Cultural Politics.

Finally, cultural materialism does not pretend to political neutrality. It does not, like much established literary criticism, attempt to mystify its perspective as the natural or obvious interpretation of an allegedly given textual fact. On the contrary, it registers its commitment to the transformation of a social order that exploits people on grounds of race, gender, sexuality and class.

The Cultural Politics Series seeks to develop this kind of understanding in a sequence of volumes that has intellectual coherence, but no restrictive format. The books will be both introductory and innovatory: introductory in that they will be clear and accessible; innovatory in their application of distinctive perspectives both to established topics and to new ones. In the tradition of Shelley, Arnold, Eliot, the Leavises and Williams, though often in terms very different from theirs, culture and politics are again at the centre of important intellectual debates.

Jonathan Dollimore
Alan Sinfield
University of Sussex

For Bindia, Rajiv and Kerys

Introduction

Sensitivity to race, class and gender in feminist criticism, despite being on its agenda for some time, is still in its infancy. Renaissance studies (especially feminist ones) are only beginning to address not just the coexistence, but the interlocking of these various structures of oppression. The absence of 'class' in the title of this project might then be surprising; it is not intended as a statement of its omission in my analysis. But whereas Renaissance historiography and criticism have increasingly been concerned with the interlinking of sexual and class politics in the period, racial difference, *especially as it affects our analysis of women and class*, is still largely missing as a theoretical and analytical category.[1] The recurrent confrontation between independent or disorderly women and public and private authority in the drama of the period has been the subject of much Renaissance criticism lately. By and large, it has been read as indicative of *either* a radical female assertiveness implying a proto-feminist theatre, *or* a punishment of female deviancy which aligns the drama with patriarchal ideologies. Each of these positions has included a variety of feminist approaches, ranging from the liberal and essentialist to materialist and historicist. This book will examine the sexual politics of these plays by setting it alongside an analysis of racial difference in two distinct but connected ways; hence its subject is race and gender (rather than class, but both used as related to class) in Renaissance drama.[2]

Firstly, it will focus upon the black presence in some texts in order to interrupt recent debates and to lift the theatrical 'punishment' of the rebellious woman out from the options laid out by current criticism. 'Patriarchy', at best a functional term useful for referring to those social structures and ideologies that contribute to the subordination of women, has lately been dislodged from the status of a transhistorical and unitary phenomenon which was accorded it by varieties of essentialist feminism – the ongoing (and by no means conclusive) attempts to combine class and gender analysis have dismantled it into a histori-cally and culturally variable, complex and even contradictory amalgam of institutions and attitudes.[3] But a sensitivity to race calls for the tripling of what Joan Kelly had termed 'the doubled vision of feminist theory' (p. 51).[4] In the drama, attention to racial difference has at least two important implications. One, it becomes obvious that each hierarchical structure of domination is analogous to and linked with the others. The processes by which women and black people are constructed as the 'others' of white patriarchal society are similar and connected, and they also reflect upon other sorts of exclusion such as that based on class. Two, race further problematises feminist efforts to make analogies between or interwine different aspects of women's subordination; the *specificity* of each emerges more clearly.[5]

The difficulty in combining race, class and gender only confirms that neither women nor their opponents can be considered homogeneous. Renaissance patriarchy, like any other, is not a monolith but a shifting alignment of various power structures which are also in conflict with one another. Women, black people and other oppressed subjects are both constituted by and subversive of this authority. It seemed to me crucial for feminist criticism to acknowledge rather than to efface contradictions in the female subject of this drama, and not to duplicate the idealist search for a perfect revolutionary by demanding a unified 'heroine' capable of providing a distilled opposition to a monolithic patriarchy as a prerequisite for a 'subversive' text. This will involve historicising the repeated theatrical foregrounding of duplicitous women in terms of Renaissance politics and society, the position of women and contemporary discourses about them, and the rather complex position occupied by the popular theatre itself. Also, real women and their literary representations (especially by men) are not identical. All this must lead us to situate the text among its various 'con-texts'.[6]

But what are the contexts of this, or any other, literature? If 'cultural production occurs all the time and at every point where meaning is communicated' (Sinfield, 'Reproductions', p. 131), then these are not limited to the ideological and material conditions of the inception of the text but must include its subsequent deployments. Textual meaning is not communicated solely by the discursive strategies of the text; it is not even explained by extending the discussion to its origins because it is created also by 'the use to which a particular text is put, its function within a particular conjecture, in particular institutional spaces, and in relation to particular audiences' (Steve Neale, quoted Morley, pp. 170-1). The reader of the text cannot be assumed to be a neutral or unchanging category.

This leads to my *second* usage of race and gender to map aspects of the history of the plays themselves. The export of English literature was a crucial component in establishing the ideological hegemony of the British Empire in Asia and Africa. English literature was strategically employed in the service of colonial education and had a role to play in what Spivak has termed the worlding of the Third World ('The Rani of

Sirmur', p. 247). The fact that my position as a teacher of English literature
in Delhi University is shared with more than 700 others is some indication of the massive presence of the subject in colonial education and
its tenacity in the post-colonial situation. But Spivak's phrase implies a
passive colonial subject. The presence of the English canon or the pre-
valence of these readings in the Indian classroom does not only make
a straightforward and by now tired statement about colonial hegemony.
English literature as a formal discipline of study in British institutions
both fulfilled the demands of colonial rule and was itself shaped by
what happened overseas. At both ends of the imperial connection,
women were implicated in the project. As the next chapter shows, the
encounter between Western text and Indian readers has been and is
the site of a complex drama where imperialism, colonialism, post-
colonialism and patriarchy interact.

What does this imply for Renaissance criticism? If it is the 'task of the
oppositional critic to re-read culture so as to amplify and strategically
position the marginalised voices of the ruled, exploited, oppressed and
excluded' (Lentricchia, quoted Dollimore, 'Shakespeare', p. 14), then
s/he must be sensitive to how textual usage, or the conditions of textual
reception, may contribute to such marginalisation and also provide the
space from which to question it. I will consider the question of disorderly women and racial 'others' in Renaissance drama also, though not
exclusively, from the perspective of its encounter with non-European
and female readers in the Indian classroom, where English literature
and its established canon have acquired specific political and ideological
connotations. I am of course drawing on my experience, shared with
many others, of teaching this drama in India, but I am not subscribing
to what Baldick has characterised as 'a cult of raw experience' privileged
by the English literary-critical tradition from Arnold through to the
Leavises and beyond (p. 203). Rather I hope to break my own position
into its historically determined components in order to examine the
impact of 'disorderly women' as it has been mediated by our existing
critical practice, as it might be negotiated by an alternative criticism, and
as it allows us to see what is missing in current Western debates. The
volatile and violent nature of Indian sexual politics; the heterogeneous
nature of Indian society; the acceleration of social and political fissures
in recent years as well as the consolidation of the bourgeois state at
another level; the revealed contingency of law and its manipulation by
political and religious authority; – these all provide a material basis from
which to approach the diverse constituents of Renaissance sexual politics.

The two ways of employing racial and sexual difference overlap with each other. Both together contest what 'preferred readings' have made of Renaissance history and drama and also offer an alternative position on the political and ideological effect of female disobedience.[7] The history of Western sexual politics and the contemporary situation of women in Europe and America are only one standpoint from which to evaluate such an effect. Moreover, it is a standpoint that has been moulded by a long history of the exclusion of racial difference in Western criticism and social thought. I don't just mean that the black presence in the plays has been overwhelmingly neglected, but that certain generalisations about 'the female subject' or women's resistance have crept in. I am suggesting that the introduction of racial difference is useful beyond analysing the representation of blacks; it also allows for a more complex perspective on the question of authority itself, even where colour differentiation either appears to be, or actually is, absent. It can be argued, for example, that the gender politics of a pre-Freudian society have been generally interpreted on the basis of assumptions derived from the very Eurocentric models of sexuality predominant in post-Freudian Western thought, and that this may be interrogated both by historicising the relationship between patriarchalism and racism and from the perspective allowed by a different culture.

Both these ways of correlating race and gender, then, alert us to what Lentricchia has called 'the multiplicity of histories' – both within the text and of the text. This perspective, of course, can be seen as drawing upon a great deal of post-modern theoretical work, spanning various disciplines and '-isms', which has been increasingly concerned with dismantling the unifying intellectual traditions of dominant Western thought. Its effect on cultural analysis and literary studies generally, and Renaissance studies particularly, has been invigorating, and has contributed enormously to the shaping of a critical practice which is firmly committed to political transformation.[8] But, on the other hand, I need to acknowledge the warning (which has been voiced especially often by colleagues in Delhi) that there may be political dangers in privileging fragmentation and heterogeneity to the extent that the very possibility of understanding, formulation and therefore resistance and change is questioned. As Perry Anderson has cautioned, history may then dissolve into 'an antinomy' of structural determinism and destructured contingency' (see Montrose, 'Renaissance literary studies', p. 5). What Allon White has called 'a carnival of scepticism' (p. 138) then becomes a new and equally paralysing orthodoxy, which has specific and particularly dangerous implications for the Third World whose intelligentsia was initially persuaded to adopt dominant Western paradigms of linearity, coherence and development, to block out its own rich heritages in favour of the coloniser's monologue. Now an *uncritical* play on the complexity of power structures and resistances can serve to disguise the control, consolidation and unification of neo-colonial and imperialist, as well as indigenous, power structures especially in Asian, African or Latin American societies.[9]

We can see, however, that this itself involves a particular interpretation of otherwise useful perspectives; for example, Doraiswamy points out that much Western work on Bakhtin 'is an appropriative discourse based on silences, misrepresentations and reductions, that have forestalled a genuine dialogue on Bakhtin and his contribution to thinking on culture' (p. 110). Allon White has shown, indeed, how Bakhtin's work offers a critique of much deconstructionist practice (pp. 123-46). No theory is globally valid, and it is up to us to utilise critically what we can (see also Bhatnagar, 'Uses and limits of Foucault').

Discussing diversity in feminist theories and politics, Newton and Rosenfelt point out that it may be argued that provisionality of knowledge, the historical determination of our own attempts at understanding and the relative coherence of human vision deny the very possibility of either understanding and theorising about, or changing, reality. But as they go on to argue, none of these have historically precluded political transformation and change; moreover, 'seeing knowledge as a form of historical practice does not mean we cannot lay claim to degrees of its relative coherency and completeness while maintaining all the while a vision of its inescapable provisionality, its ongoing process of being transformed' (p. xxix; see also Ryan, pp. 19, 213).

Therefore to resist the closure effected by unifying ideologies and criticisms is not *necessarily* to slide into political and academic impotence. My emphasis on the plurality of voices in Renaissance drama does not also mean to replace 'preferred readings' with a simple pluralism, but to indicate the sites of struggle and resistance in the plays which our own contradictions as readers and critics may amplify. Following Raymond Williams' crucial and useful distinction between residual, dominant and emergent aspects of culture, contradictions can be acknowledged as an indication that dominant ideologies are potentially unstable and never totally effective; hence they may provide the space for radical intervention and change (see Sinfield, 'Shakespeare and education', pp. 134-5). Authoritative discourses, past traditions and institutions within which the text is deployed, form and structure its effect and frame its 'successive new encounters' but do not completely determine these (see Dave Morley, pp. 163-73). Firstly, dominant discourses themselves are not monolithic, uniform or homogeneous and therefore contain a potential for divergent readings; the discourse, as Volosinov insists, can become 'an arena of struggle' because it is 'multi-accentual'. For example, as Homi Bhabha has suggested, the stereotypes of colonial discourse connote 'rigidity and an unchanging order as well as disorder, degeneracy and demonic repetition', indicating the insecurity as well as power of this discourse ('The other question', p. 18). Similarly, the patriarchal notion of woman as witch acknowledges female power even as it seeks to demonise it. Therefore, these stereotypes are not entirely contained, or harnessed by and useful to, those who produce them. Moreover, in certain literary texts, this ambivalence may be even more pronounced. It has been shown that Shakespeare's The Tempest exemplifies the operation of colonialism in 'a moment of historical crisis' and therefore simultaneously contains 'the apotheosis, mystification and potential erosion of the colonialist discourse' (Brown, 'This thing of darkness', pp. 48-69). My own analysis of Webster's The Duchess of Malfi will suggest a radical instability in the patriarchal stereotype of the duplicitous woman (see chapters 3-5).

While locating the radical instability of contradictions, it is equally important to recognise the nature and power of the preferred and institutionalised readings, which seek precisely to efface contradiction by claiming universality, naturalness and an objective and therefore true representation of 'facts'. But a second undermining of their effect occurs via the important distinction made by Paul Willemen between the subject 'constructed and marked in and by the text' and the social subject: 'Real readers are subjects in history, living in social formations, rather than mere subjects of a single text. The two types of subject are not commensurate' (cited Morley, p. 169). More generally, dominant discourses are not the sum total of the reality experienced by the subject/reader. The disjunction between the two may become impossible for the former to efface, hence further space for radical readings is opened up. As Morley says, 'the text may be contradicted by the subject's position(s) in relation to other texts, problematics, institutions, discursive formations' (p. 167).[10]

These clashes render the text potentially volatile; it can become a space from which to question and even subvert its dominant educational deployment. Preferred readings emerging from European institutions have had a particular role to play overseas. The female reader in the sub-continent is the recipient of texts that are the products of another culture and employed in the service of colonial and neo-colonial attitudes; written by men and made to speak on behalf of anti-feminism; brought in for specific purposes but projected as universally valid and true. But precisely these alienations, as I hope to show, can be useful in formulating an alternative reading and teaching practice.

As Barker and Hulme acknowledge in their essay on *The Tempest*, there are real difficulties in combining the historical conditions of the 'originating moment' of the production of a text and 'the successive inscriptions of a text during the course of its history' (pp. 192-3), as I will attempt to do. Firstly, the discussion expands to include many new areas, each of which demands far more detailed examination than is possible in a study like this. For example, it is almost impossible to generalise the 'Indian situation'. The nexus of colonialist, patriarchalist and elitist attitudes in post-colonialist education is further complicated by the diversity of Indian social structures, and my own perspective is shaped by a limited and specific positioning within all of these. Secondly, there are many dangers inherent in any cross-cultural analysis – of oversimplifications and generalisations, of lapsing into the universalisations of dominant criticism, of adopting the paradigms of modernisation theories, whereby the Third World is seen to be replicating the histories of Western 'progression'.

Finally, much as I would like to suggest that opening out the discussion on Renaissance tragedy and offering a critique of post-colonial English studies are not contradictory enterprises, and are even collateral, they are inconsistent to the extent that I am offering ways of reading texts whose very presence in our classrooms is questionable. Reinterpreting Shakespeare is not likely to solve all the problems arising from his privileged position in our curricula, but it is a strategy that we may employ while still negotiating the future of English studies.

Perhaps as what Spivak calls a 'diasporic Indian, a post-colonial intellectual', one cannot avoid such oscillations between contexts and cultures.[11] I will still suggest, however, that connections between alternative textual readings and teaching practices are not just an unfortunate result of our position. The ways in which interpretations of texts spill over into a critique of the institutions of literature are important for those seeking to make a political intervention in contemporary cultural studies, and I hope both together will identify the grounds for anti-racist, materialist and feminist appropriations of the plays.

As Chris Baldick argues, English criticism from Dryden onwards 'passes from the subordinate position of defender of poetry to a position of self-appointed authority from which it can turn to the offensive, in social as well as literary comment: since Arnold in particular, English literary criticism has, as Patrick Parrinder has put it, lost its innocence' (p. 6). Our own re-appropriations then, need not be apologetic about their partisanship.

Notes

1 Since Joan Kelly made her seminal proposition that our notions of historical change and progress can look very different with the introduction of gender as an analytical category (pp. 19-50), Renaissance scholarship (cultural, historical, literary and inter-disciplinary) has been rich in sensitivity to the interlacing of class and gender. A comprehensive list of such work is not possible here but one may mention the studies of Joan Kelly, Alison Heisch, Natalie Zemon Davis, Keith Thomas, Lawrence Stone, Catherine Belsey, Jonathan Dollimore, Stephen Greenblatt, Louis Montrose, Lisa Jardine, Ann Rosalind Jones, Alan Sinfield, Leonard Tennenhouse and Linda Woodbridge as having richly contributed to this approach (see bibliography for details).

2 For example, Irene Dash, *Wooing, Wedding and Power* finds that Shakespeare's heroines are able to learn 'the meaning of self-sovereignty for women in a patriarchal society' (p. 1). Marilyn French comes to the opposite conclusion that Shakespeare was a misogynist with almost a pathological fear of women and sex (*Shakespeare's Division of Experience*). Both these books adopt transcendental definitions of patriarchy and do not attempt to contextualise the plays in terms of Renaissance culture. Linda Bamber, *Comic women, Tragic men* differentiates between a feminist Shakespeare who writes comedies and a misogynist tragic bard; she defines the feminine as 'some general principle' of 'simple difference, . . . that which exists on the other side of a barrier' (pp. 4-5). On the other hand, Juliet Dusinberre's *Shakespeare and the Nature of Women* traces an emergent feminism in the plays to 'radical' Puritan sexual politics. Lisa Jardine disputes this and argues that the drama confirms patriarchal prejudice; she is rigorously historical and her view to me seems to be in conformity with the results of some feminist historiography of the period, such as Joan Kelly's 'Did women have a Renaissance?' (see Kelly, *Women, History, Theory*). Leonard Tennenhouse confirms and extends this opinion (*Power on Display*) whereas Catherine Belsey (*The Subject of Tragedy*) shifts emphasis by seeing the plays moving towards liberal humanist ideals. I will return to the debate in later chapters.

3 The material generated by contemporary feminist debates is enormous. For a discussion of these see chapter one of my 'Disorderly Women'. Kate Millett's *Sexual Politics* and Shulamith Firestone's *The Dialectic of Sex* remain classic articulations of the radical feminist definition of patriarchy. Kuhn and Wolpe, *Feminism and Materialism*; Barrett, *Women's Oppression Today*; Jaggar, *Feminist Politics*; Eisenstein, *Capitalist Patriarchy*; and Sargant, *Women and Revolution* provide accessible refutations of this position; they point out its transcendental and ahistorical premises and discuss alternatives to it.

4 The ways in which race problematises and critiques white feminist theory has also been widely discussed; useful examples are Carby, 'White woman listen'; Bhavani and Coulson, 'Transforming socialist-feminism'; Joseph, 'The incompatible *ménage à trois*'; Parmar, 'Gender, race and class'; Davis, *Women, Race and Class* and Spivak, *In Other Worlds*.

5 Representative positions in the class-gender debate can be found in *Feminist Review* no. 23 (Summer, 1986, pp. 3-58); Hartmann, 'The unhappy marriage'; Weir and Wilson, 'The British women's movement'; Young, 'Beyond the unhappy marriage'; Lown, 'Not so much a factory' and the second group of books in n. 2 above, especially Jaggar, *Feminist Politics*.

6 The term is so used by Barker and Hulme, whose discussion of what it has come to imply in alternative criticism is useful (pp. 191-205); for this also see Dollimore, 'Shakespeare, cultural materialism' (pp. 2-15).

7 Dave Morley suggests 'that a text of the dominant discourse does privilege or prefer a certain reading' (p. 167).

8 It can be argued that Marxist dialectics provided the basis for such work, which however effected a critique of the mechanical reductionism of much Marxist theory. The ques-

tions of the relation of base and superstructure, of ideology, and the relationship of the individual to social formation, especially after Althusser, opened up the question the what is submerged, marginalised, hidden by dominant culture. Structuralism, different post-structuralisms, psychoanalysis, certain feminisms, as well as the work of individuals such as Gramsci, Foucault and Macheray have all interrupted previous social thought in the sense of formulating a different conception of social totality, one in which unity is the 'result of many determinations' (to use a phrase from Marx). For programmes of a literary criticism committed to social change see Newton and Rosenfelt, Dollimore and Sinfield, and the Literature and Society Group.

9 Kumkum Sangari warns that postmodern scepticism, itself 'the complex product of a historical conjuncture', 'becomes authoritative because it is inscribed within continuing power relations, and as a mode of "aquisitive cognition" is deeply implicated in the structure of institutions . . . (it) occurs in the academies at a time when usable knowledge is gathered and processed with growing certainity and control though technologies of information retrieval from the rest of the world' ('Marquez', pp. 56-7).

10 I am indebted to Morley's article for its discussion of the interrelation between texts and their readers.

11 'Interview with Gayatri Chakravorty Spivak', Book Review, Vol. XI, no. 3 (May June 1987), pp. 16-22. She suggests also that the teaching of English literature and the women's movement have been historically discontinuous and continually bring each other to 'crisis' which may explain some of our added contradictions as feminist critics.

Imperialism, patriarchy and post-colonial English studies

And who in time knowes wither we may vent
The treasure of our tongue, to what strange shores
This gaine of our best glorie shal be sent
T'enrich vnknowing Nations with our stores?
What worlds in th'yet vnformed Occident
May come refin'd with th' accents that are ours?

Samuel Daniel, *Musophilus* (1599)

Contradictions and consolidations

More students probably read *Othello* in the University of Delhi every year than in all British universities combined. A large proportion of them are women. But the politics of English teaching as it developed in colonised countries have largely been excluded from considerations of its current 'crisis'. This is indicative both of the insular nature of even radical and alternative Western criticism, and of the difficulty, for the post-colonial critic, of interrogating a pedagogy whose most successful strategy has been to project the English literary text as an amalgam of universal value, morality, truth and rationality. Inquiries into the histories and ideologies of English literary study in India are only beginning now, and it is clear that they will have to range over a formidably large canvas and involve various methodological skills – from archival work to discourse analysis.[1] My own concern here is to outline some aspects of the institution of English studies as it exists today, particularly the relative stability of the discipline and its growing feminisation. These are the contexts in which the process of 'unlearning' can be initiated (see Williams, *Culture and Society*, p. 376).

Gayatri Chakravorty Spivak suggests that

'great works' of literature cannot easily flourish in the fracture or discontinuity which is covered over by an alien legal system masquerading as law as such, an alien ideology established as the only truth, and a set of human sciences busy establishing the 'native' as self-consolidating other ... For the early part of the nineteenth century in India, the literary critic must turn to the archives of imperial governance as her text. ('Rani', p. 250)

But conversely, it may be proposed that the enterprise of English literature teaching in India can be read as one of the texts of imperial governance. In a pioneering essay, Gauri Viswanathan has pointed out that 'humanistic functions traditionally associated with the study of literature – for example, the shaping of character or the development of the esthetic sense or the disciplines of ethical thinking – are also essential to the process of sociopolitical control (p. 2)'. In England, literary education was a participant in the creation of a paternalistic, elitist culture, designed to contain the challenges variously posed to the status quo by the middle and working classes as well as women. In India, it not only responded to the exigencies, ideologies as well as the contradictions of colonial rule, but was crucial to imperialist strategy. But, in both cases, it needs to be added that we are not speaking of an already given, well defined disciplinary formation. English literary study was shaped by the same political processes in which it actively participated. In other words, it did not have some inherent claim to, but *was invested with* humanistic and moral attributes. The history of this investment is interlaced with what Chris Baldick has called the civilising mission of English literature in relation to various subordinate classes and groups.

Two further observations will indicate the complexity of the formation of this discipline. Firstly, the colonial history of English teaching shaped its development in the metropolis, and the two pedagogic traditions can be seen as interlaced. Secondly, English literature, like British education in general, was not inserted upon a colonial vacuum, but entered into a complex interaction with indigenous education, the native intelligentsia and Indian nationalism. Therefore its study has to be sensitive to what we may demarcate as three interpenetrating cultures – British, Anglo Indian (i.e. the British in India) and Indian.

One recurring issue in theories of colonial discourse is the *effectiveness* of imperialist strategy. Edward Said's work has analysed Orientalism as a body of European discourses which offered a certain construction of the East, facilitated the hegemonic control of colonised cultures and peoples and, indeed, deeply affected their self-conception as well. As Benita Parry discusses in a recent essay, Said's emphasis on the power of colonial discourse has been criticised on the grounds that it renders the colonial subject mute, and disallows an oppositional culture and the spaces from which the hegemony of the imperialist construction can be questioned (pp. 35-55). But while both the consolidation of and the resistance to authority should be discussed, a desire to locate opposition is not sufficient; it is possible to romanticise the colonial subject and the site of his/her struggle against imperialism. In order to understand the authority of the English text in the Indian classroom and its

durability , we will have to differentiate between various colonial subjects and acknowledge stances which are double-edged. For example,
it is possible to argue that Indian nationalists received the European text
contrary to the intentions of their colonial masters, since the independence struggle was paradoxically led by Indians schooled in Britain and
in the British system here. But although Indian nationalism resisted
colonial rule it also consolidated its own hierarchy, and as I will discuss
shortly, this complicates the nationalist interaction with English literature. From the position of bourgeois nationalism, the humanistic claims
of institionalised English education could not, and in fact did not need
to be subverted.

Again, despite their differences, both colonial and post-independence
educationists shared certain attitudes to literature, women and modernisation. As a result, the enormous political and social upheavals of independence notwithstanding, dominant patriarchal and literary ideologies
were adapted to the exigencies of the new situation in ways that only
deepened the contradictions of all those involved with English literature
in India, and especially women. It becomes necessary, then, to note the
ways in which colonial, nationalist and post-colonial discourses on both
literature and women interlink. Lata Mani's explanation of discourse
analysis as something which 'focuses on that which is stable and persistent in the ordering of social reality . . . (and) point(s) to assumptions
shared by those who claim to be opposed to each other' is relevant
here (p. WS 32).

In a recent discussion which followed a lecture given at Delhi University by Marilyn Butler on 'Revising the English Canon', opinion was
divided about how canons are shaped in the first place.[2] While receptive
to the speaker's analysis of the complex politics involved in the formation of the hierarchy of 'great authors', and sympathetic also to her
argument that this was more than a power 'conspiracy', sections of the
audience felt that in as much as canons are institionalised, and supported
by vast structures of teaching, job market and publishing, they are not
simply the oblique results of cultural norms. The two positions are not
irreconcilable, but the fact is that the Indian reader especially cannot
assume that the English canon has been firmly placed in the Indian
curriculum without a great deal of consolidation and alliances between
otherwise divergent positions; it is with this in mind that I will trace a
complicity between indigenous and imperial power structures and not
in order to imply a simple collaboration between them. This also
suggests that the dominant asumptions of English studies or colonial
education cannot be challenged in a uniform way in all colonised
societies, or by a monolithic and undifferentiated 'colonised subject'

but particular sections of colonised peoples are, for very specific reasons at different periods, in a postion to dismantle the edifice.

'The treasure of our tongue'

As far back as 1492, Antonio de Nebrija, author of one of the first modern grammars, recognised that 'language is the perfect instrument of empire' (Barker and Hulme, p. 197). India was the first site for British experimentation with this early colonialist perception (see Basu, p. 53). The formal decision to introduce English education was taken only in 1835 upon the advice of Lord Thomas Babington Macaulay, who arrived to serve on the Supreme Council of Lord William Bentinck, Governor-General of India, as the Fourth Member specifically in charge of legislation. But as Gauri Viswanathan shows, the introduction of English education and literature was the result of a wide range of economic, political and religious motives; it 'represented an embattled response to historical and political pressures: to tensions between the English Parliament and the East India company, between Parliament and the missionaries, between the East India company and the native elite classes' (p. 24).

Despite the growing military strength of the Empire, colonial pronouncements on education register both confidence and anxiety in relation to their native subjects. For example, Charles Grant's 'Scheme for the Intellectual, Moral and Social Regeneration of the People of India' (1792-97) marks out the stability of the Raj as a justification imparting education in English:

In general, when foreign teachers have proposed to instruct the inhabitants of any country, they have used the vernacular tongue of that people, for a natural and necessary reason that they could not hope to make any other means of communication intelligible to them. This is not our case in respect of our Eastern dependencies. *They are our own, we have possessed them long.* (Mahmood, p. 11. Emphasis added)

In spite of his aggressive posture, Macaulay departs from the certainty expressed in Grant's document regarding the willing subjection of the Indian people to the Raj. His 'Minute on Indian Education' betrays an uneasiness about their natural loyalty to the English, indicating the need for 'interpreters between us and the millions whom we govern'. But this class was to be marshalled by the same policy advocated by Grant. English education was to ensure that 'a class of persons Indian in blood and colour but English in tastes, in opinion, in morals and intellect' would negotiate the ideological gap between the colonisers and the colonised (p. 729).

On the other hand, this strategy of a Filtration Theory, involving the cooperation of the native elite, could also be advanced from an opposite position of educating Indians in their own languages. This is one of the various points at which the apparently different views of the Orientalists, who advocated education through the vernacular, and the Anglicists, who supported English, can be seen to converge. Although the Orientalist passion for Sanskrit, for example, contradicted the premises of English teaching at one level, at another, 'it was as a dead language, far removed from the backwardness of modern Indians that its value accrued' (Said, 'Raymond Schwab', p. 164). Many Sanskrit lovers, such as Schlegel, completely ignored the 'living, contemporary Orient', which could then be devalued in comparison with its own glorious past and the European present (Said, Orientalism, p. 98). Moreover, as Viswanathan says, 'Anglicism was dependent upon Orientalism for its ideological programme. Through its government-supported researches and scholarly investigations, Orientalism had produced a vast body of knowledge about the native subjects which the Anglicists subsequently drew upon to mount their attack on the culture as a whole' (p. 7).

Both Anglicism and Orientalism consolidated the native allies of imperial rule. The former catalysed the wide-scale emergence of what Said identifies as the 'native informant' (Orientalism, p. 324) i.e. the colonised intellectual. The reformer Raja Ram Mohan Roy, for example, expressed disappointment at the establishment of Sanskrit schools in Calcutta and urged the British government to allocate funds for 'employing European gentlemen of talent and education to instruct the natives of India in mathematics, natural philosophy, chemistry, anatomy and other useful sciences, which the natives of Europe have carried to a degree of perfection that has raised them above the inhabitants of the other parts of the world' (Bailey and Gorlach, p. 354-5). It is not surprising that Roy also gave 'thanks to the Supreme Disposer . . . for having unexpectedly delivered this country from the long-continuing tyranny of its former rulers and placed it under the government of the English' (Moorhouse, pp. 85-6). Such intellectuals ultimately reconciled their conflicts by resorting to notions of a universal humanism (Sunder Rajan, p. 32).

Veneration of Sanskrit, on the other hand, tied in with a revivalism of Aryan India, which served several purposes. It was used politically to endorse the claims of Hindu princes (see Spivak, 'Rani', pp. 264-5). It also established brahmins as the custodians and true representatives of a varied and heterogeneous Indian tradition and customs, thus repressing the claims of those excluded by brahminical hegemony, such as the lower castes and classes, and women.[3] Dilip Simeon notes that:

the theory of the 'Aryan' racial origins of brahminical civilization, given credence by western orientalist scholars such as Professor Max Mueller . . . gained much popularity among diverse sections of the nationalist intelligentsia, including Vivekananda, Tilak, Justice Ranade, Dayanand Saraswati, Keshab Chandra Sen, Aurobindo Ghose, Bankimchandra and B. C. Pal. The theory could make the Indian elite feel equal to the ruling Englishmen . . . as well as buttress their social superiority over the low-caste sudras. . . . The arrogance of the paramount power was sought to be countered by the assertion of an older tradition of paramountcy with which various strata of the collaborating intelligentsia could identify. (p. 61)

The common-sense assumptions attaching to colour prejudice and racism have slowly come to be conferred upon people assumed to be non-Aryan such as those of Southern India and tribal peoples.[4] British policies, then, actively operated upon existing Indian politics, legitimised existing dominant tendencies and introduced new ones as well.

On the part of the British, the project to differentiate between various colonised people, later to be bolstered by social-Darwinism, is evident in Aryan revivalism. Indians were designated anthropologically superior to African blacks, which crucially affected Indians' own internalisation of racist ideologies. The myth persists that 'prejudice against Indians . . . was more closely related to station and class than it was to race as such' (Moorhouse, 178). It has led to Indian participation in racist structures in East and South Africa, and to a neglect of analyses of racism in their critique of colonialism, which is especially ironical in the context of current intensification of racism against Indians abroad today. As the case of The Tempest will show, this myth played an important role in blocking out identifications of Indians with blacks, persuading them that they occupied an intermediary zone which nevertheless accorded them inferior status (see chapter 6).[5]

Simeon rightly points out that 'nationalism rarely has that pure virginal quality about it in which its ideologues like to indulge themselves. Depending on the social forces and processes which articulate it, it can be defensive or imperialist, tolerant or chauvinist, universalist/humanist or racist' (p. 67). Fanon describes a polarisation, in colonial culture, between those who 'threw themselves in a frenzied fashion into the frantic acquisition of the culture of the occupying power and (took) every opportunity of unfavourably criticising their own national culture' and those who took refuge in 'setting out and substantiating the claims of their indigenous culture in a way which rapidly becomes unproductive' (p. 190). In India, we can locate areas of convergence between the two. This is one of the contexts in which the English literary text became, not a site of conflict, but an accommodative ideal where the humanistic

assumptions of that discipline could include both a Westernised consciousness and a revivalist one.

'A single shelf of good European literature'

Consider the situation in a small rural college in the Midnapur district
of West Bengal, narrated to me by Nirmalaya Samanta, a lecturer there.
English is no longer compulsory for those undergraduates who are not
majoring in the subject, unlike in most other universities. However,
there is an optional English paper; the marks of this paper cannot affect
the division or the position of the student but are mentiond by his/her
degree certificate. The popularity of the course remains unaffected, not
merely because English is necessary for professional and official reasons
but because it immediately confers status: 'the girls who opt for English
will group together and feel that silk parasols are now in order as
opposed to the usual nylon ones. Meanwhile I am left with the problem
of trying to make D. H. Lawrence's "The White Stocking" make sense
to students who live on potato farms and have never seen a stocking,
or a ballroom in their lives' (personal communication).

English was not taught just as a foreign language but was the means
of imposing a culture, a cluster of ideologies, a way of being and seeing,
of which the literary text became the privileged signifier. This centrality
of literature to British education in India has diverse histories, which
recent inquiries are beginning to uncover. Firstly, as Gauri Viswanathan
has shown, given that the British administration's declared policy was
one of non-interference in native religions, English literature became a
means of carrying out its civilising mission and of proclaiming itself as
altruistic and reformist. By the 1820's doubts began to be expressed
about its earlier policy of language teaching and secular education. The
Orientalist Horace Wilson maintained that 'mere language cannot work
any material change' and that only when 'we initiate them into our
literature, particularly at an early age, and get them to adopt feelings
and sentiments from our standard writers, (can) we make an impression
upon them' (Viswanathan, p. 14). The fear that secular education would
nurture native rebelliousness was articulated by missionaries, who
deplored the lack of moral bias in prevailing pedagogy. Since religious
instruction of the sort that was useful in maintaining the status quo in
Britain was not possible on colonial soil, British administrators, 'provoked by missionaries on the one hand and fears of native insubordination on the other, discovered an ally in English literature to support
them in maintaining control of the natives under the guise of a liberal
education' (Viswanathan, pp. 13-17).

In Macaulay's pronouncements, the English literary text occupies the position of an advance guard of the British empire, effecting 'pacific triumphs of reason over barbarism' (Moorhouse, p. 96). He speaks of the propagation of 'that literature before the light of which impious and cruel superstitions are fast taking flight on the banks of the Ganges . . . And, wherever British literature spreads, may it be attended by British virtue and British freedom' (Baldick, p. 71). The superiority of British culture over native ignorance and stupidity is expresssed by the difference between Western and other texts: 'a single shelf of a good European library was worth the whole native literature of India and Arabia' (Macaulay, p. 722). Contradictory claims were made on behalf of English literature: on the one hand, that it was 'imbued with the spirit of Christianity', and, on the other, that it was 'not interwoven to the same extent with the Christian religion as the Hindoo religion is with the Sanskrit language and literature' (Viswanathan, p. 19). Macaulay's Minute reveals that such a double stance allowed English literature to lay simultaneous claim to morality and secularism. The Minute reiterates that the administration 'shall always abstain from giving any public encouragement to those who are engaged in the work of converting natives to Christianity'. But it irks Macaulay that this policy should imply the encouragement of Indian literature, which propogates 'false History, false Astronomy, false medicine . . . (and) false religion' when they could be instructed in a literature that could teach them 'sound Philosophy and true History' (pp. 723-8). And the principles of a 'sound' religion, one might add.

Secondly, English literature also became the prescribed education for the administrators of India. George III had required of his Cadet only that 'he (be) well-grounded in Vulgar Factions, write . . . a good Hand, and (have) gone through the Latin Grammar' (quoted Spivak, 'Rani', 254). The 1853 India Act (also authorised by Macaulay) and the recommendations of the report of the Civil Service of the East India Company of 1855 proclaimed that there would be open competitive examinations for the Indian civil services in which 'English Literature and Language' would constitute a 1,000 marks paper. This resulted in pressure upon English universities to teach these subjects formally. Oxford's first professor of English literature, Walter Raleigh, had earlier taught at the Anglo-Oriental College in Aligarh (see Baldick, chapter three).

The shift in qualifications needed for imperial governance also tied in with the displacement of Classics by English in the home country. Members of the Indian Civil Service affirmed that 'the culture that men got at Oxford and Cambridge was of the greatest importance in dealing with the natives' (Baldick, p. 71); but what culture men got at Oxford and Cambridge was determined also by the British experience in the colonies, where English literature had become the civil counterpart of missionary activity on the one hand and military force on the other – its ideological mission effaced by its supposedly private, individual, universal and non-political nature.

If, as Viswanathan suggests (p. 23), the English literary text 'functioned as the surrogate Englishman in his highest and most perfect state', the *teacher* of English literature became the guru of culture. The implications of 'culture' slide easily from knowledge to decorum and from behaviour to downright submission. One of this tribe published a handbook in 1915, addressed to Indians who might interact socially with the British. It advises them not to chew betel nut, or stroke 'any part of your person', or bite nails or scratch, as such habits are not 'considered polite' in European society, moves on to stress reticence in speech and writing, and European table manners. Then decorum is directly translated as racial and sexual distance: if an Indian should be privileged in being invited to a party: 'remember that a presentation to a lady in a ball-room for the purpose of dancing does not entitle you to claim her acquaintance elsewhere'. Finally, manners and submission to the colonial masters merge: 'Do not be over-sensitive to criticism. Learn to tolerate criticism . . . Englishmen are apt on occasion to be somewhat rough-and-ready in what they say and do but remember that such downright conduct is not necessarily overbearing, and do not convert a hasty word or what is intended only for jest into a deadly insult' (quoted Moorhouse, pp. 176-7).

The fact that many of those schooled in this system did not learn these lessons did not substantially alter the claim that English literature was a universal source of morality and knowledge; even Indian nationalism was attributed to the study of Shakespeare: 'The ideas which were imbibed from the rulers' literature and attitudes were rationalism, civil liberties, and constitutional self-government. No one could be in contact with Englishmen at that time for long or read Shakespeare (prescribed reading in the colleges) without catching the infection of nationalism' (Spear, p. 166). But the ways in which art, and especially literature, functions as an ideological apparatus (in the Althusserian sense) perpetuating dominant power relations involves its organisation and institutionalisation, which include criticism and interpretation. Specific readings of Shakespeare are needed to back the claim that he was an instructor for Indian nationalists; just as others have made possible his becoming a spokesman for right-wing ideologies in Britain (Sinfield, 'Shakespeare and education', p. 135).

'The experiencing type of mind'

A central feature of hegemonic ideologies is their projection of the dominant viewpoint as universally true, transcendentally valid and non-political. In this way, they claim to represent all humanity and fix their 'others' as inferior and finally non-human. Thus 'he' and 'man' are patri-archal representations of all people, and both subsume as well as exclude woman. Thus also white racism implies not only that European culture is superior but that it is the only kind of culture there can be; by exclusion from it the non-European is necessarily non-human, barbaric and animalistic. Knowledge of the East is a specialisation for the European, but knowledge of the West for the Asian or African becomes synonym-ous with education, knowledge, culture *per se*. If we add to this the dominant representation of literature as a repository of some fixed and unchanging human essence, we can begin to approach the significance of the European text in the colonial context, which also resulted in specific kinds of teaching and critical practices.

The primary contradiction engendered in this situation involves the fixing of English literature and the Indian reader into positions that imply a permanent and inherent inability of the latter to comprehend the truths enshrined in the former. At the same time such a comprehen-sion is posited as a *requirement* for knowledge and a *measure* of ability. Macaulay, for example, stresses simultaneously the 'ignorance' of Indians and their ability to be educated: 'there are in this very town natives who are quite competent to discuss political or scientific ques-tions with fluency and precision in the English language' (p. 725, 728-9). The elitist nature and civilising mission of English studies was established through a strategic inclusion as well as exclusion of certain categories of people. T. S. Eliot, I. A. Richards and the Leavises, among others, bemoaned the effects of mass literacy; according to Q. D. Leavis, 'the sudden opening of the fiction market to the general public was a blow to serious reading' (Baldick, p. 207). Indian critics just after indepen-dence also regretted the fact that 'where in the past a few people knew a great deal about Shakespeare today a large number know a little about him' (Muliyil, p. 6). The institutionalisation of English literary studies in Britain involved an inclusion of the uncultured into the 'boudoir' of knowledge, where their inferiority would become apparent and their subservience ensured (see Baldick, chapter two); in India the pattern was repeated but with a more complicated hierarchy; the Europeans, then native informants and then their sucessors were all privileged readers. But both before and after independence, the survival of English literature depended upon its expansion into precisely those people who had been deemed in some ways incapable of appreciating it.

The universality and essential veracity of literature, as well as the special ability to comprehend these, are the two assumptions on which the inclusion/exclusion principle rests: 'Shakespeare appeals to all ages and most temperaments – *particularly to the experiencing type of mind* . . . He is like the universe itself: open to view, *for those who have eyes to see and will use them*' (Menezes, p. 14; emphasis added). This statement, significantly, is from a volume entitled *Shakespeare Came to India*. Although obviously coinciding with the anti-historical thrust of dominant Shakespearian criticism from Coleridge and Samuel Johnson onwards (see Drakakis, pp. 1-25), the universalism of the English text took on a specific dimension in India.

To begin with, it involved a particular appropriation of both individual texts and India. For example, the Orientalist conception of a spiritual, abstracted, soulful India takes on an added meaning in relation to literature, which is dominantly construed to have similar characteristics. It was inserted into Shakespeare criticism in India by Orientalist comparisons between him and Kalidasa which involved an interpretation of both as spokesmen for 'harmony', 'order' and 'regeneration' (see chapter 6). Sri Aurobindo Ghosh even saw Shakespeare as an embodiment of 'creative Ananda of the life-spirit' who created 'a Shakespearian world of his own, and it is in *spite of its realistic elements*, a romantic world in a very true sense of the word, a world of the wonder and free power of life and not of its mere external realities'. Aurobindo, to give him credit, was continually disturbed by 'the defect of Elizabethan work', i.e. the fact that 'the characters are not living beings working out their mutual Karma, but external figures of humanity, jostling each other on a crowded stage' (pp. 132-6). Later readings, however, erased all such discomfort as Shakespeare was elevated to the status of a seer of 'the' human condition.

The stereotype of a pacifist people and the theme of a spiritual India has had a long history; it can be traced to the Vedantic texts, which were fiercely contested; later it was politically useful for the Raj and also for the national movement; it now surfaces in government propaganda to contain the growing violence of a highly stratified society. Colonialist discourse seized upon and reworked such stereotypes of the Orient to legitimise its own patriarchalism.[6] Aurobindo's comments on Shakespeare reveal their interaction with the notion of the universality of literature, and of the English text in particular.

Secondly, as Jasodhara Bagchi has suggested, English literature was a major component in the ideology of nation building that was consolidated under British colonial rule in the nineteenth century. The universal humanism put forward by institutionalised literary studies was useful in the task of hegemonising native elite culture. It offered 'a programme of building a new man who would feel himself to be a citizen of the world while the very face of the world was being constructed in the mirror of the dominant culture of the West' (p. 3). There are apparent contradictions in this reception of the English text. When Milton and Shelley's poetry is mouthed by Indian nationalists, the hierarchy implicit in colonial pedagogy is being strained. On the other hand, such an 'appropriation' rests on the obliteration of cultural difference. Therefore it does not really challenge the ideological premises of English studies but reinforces their claim to universal value, rationality and truth.

An introduction to Tennyson's poems by F. J. Rowe and W. T. Webb, published in 1938, declared that 'the emotions that he appeals to are generally easy to understand and common to all . . . The moral laws which he so strongly upholds are those primary sanctions upon which average English society is founded . . . (Tennyson exercises) a powerful charm . . . over the hearts and minds of all English speaking peoples'. Quoting this, Alan Sinfield notes that the editors were professors of English literature at Presidency College, Calcutta, 'one of the breeding grounds of radical Indian nationalism'. He comments that the word 'all' here 'can be seen both as a justification of cultural imperialism and as wishful thinking' (Alfred Tennyson, p. 2). True, but the radicals of Presidency College would, in all probability, have had no quarrel with that claim. As Bagchi says, this was 'not merely a literature of the masters but it was literature – a harbinger of secular outlook on life and an open sesame to the great treasures of the world'; it 'became the mantra for New India in its fight against obscurantist traditionalism' (p. 4). The duality of the stance must be recognised if we are to locate both a departure from imperialist connotations of the civilising mission of English studies and a continuity that ensures the passage of English studies from the Raj to post-colonial education.[7]

Two other points are crucial. One, this nationalist reading of English literature did not break from the idea of exclusivity of perception or 'the experiencing mind'. At first this mind was naturally either white or wore a white mask; the subaltern reader was inevitably less equipped 'to see'. Thus Geoffrey Kendal, the British actor whose troupe performed Shakespeare for years in every corner of India, received a letter from a theatre group in Kerala, thanking him for bringing them closer to the 'real thing', from which they as Indians were excluded: '. . . to us the news that an English company was coming to Trivandrum . . . was like "dropping manna in the way of starved people" . . . Somehow or other

a bond has linked "Forward Bloc" and "Shakespeareana" together . . .
Let Shakespeare keep India and Britain united' (p. 89).

From universality to Empire is a short step: the editor of a volume
examining Shakespeare in India puts it plainly: 'the England of trade,
commerce, imperialism and the penal code has not endured but the
imperishable Empire of Shakespeare will always be with us. And that
is something to be grateful for' (Narasimhaiah, p. v). The book was
published seventeen years after independence! But the 'experiencing
mind' was not just of the Westernised intellectual, but could include
the upper-class/upper-caste intellectual as well. The ideological effect
of continuing reverence for the canon was to fix the Indian student,
especially one not coming from an English-speaking background, in a
position of disability, exclusion and awe: one of my students in 1980,
who was majoring in chemistry but had to do a compulsory year of
English literature, felt obliged to include 'Jack Austen' on a list of her
'favourite authors'.

Two, the transcendental status of the literary text continued to be
useful in containing the tensions of a society that was not rendered
homogeneous by expelling its colonial masters. In post-independence
discussions of education, conducted from avowed positions of anti-
colonialism, we hear that

Sahitya (literature) in its widest connotation is but the outward expression of
that universal harmony. He who basks in the glorious and radiant sunshine of
true and genuine literature does not recognise such man-made barriers as caste,
class, difference of language and the like . . . . It is such a literature that we now
need for understanding the true meaning of culture and religion . . . (Sadasivayya,
p. 219)

The political implications of valorising a text or an idea that 'transcends'
the 'man-made' are obvious. English studies positioned themselves both
at a 'remove' from the society in which they were conducted and as
the panacea for all social evil. The English literary establishment has
been prey to a nostalgia for the Western homeland, looking down on
regional literatures and isolating itself from other sections of the
academy. Its academic and political conservatism is notorious.[8] And it
has been able to reconcile itself with revivalism of various sorts:
Jasodhara Bagchi has pointed out that in Bengal 'the evocation of the
Hindu Brahminical golden age was conducted within the protective
umbrella of English literary values . . . When the theatre moved out of
the household of the aristocracy into the public commercial stage, Girish
Ghosh . . . (showed) the glory of a Hindu heroism alongside his adaptations . . . of Shakespeare' (pp. 9-10). In 1941, Amarnath Jha, in his
presidential address to the Conference of English teachers asserted that

'the correlation of the Hindu and Western canons is a task that can only be performed by the critic of English literature' (quoted Tharu). Recently, S. Nagarajan suggests that from Edward Thompson's novel *An End of the Hours* (1938), we can establish a 'new context to make the study of English relevant to the traditions of India', i.e. 'the teacher of English as a guru' who will respond to 'This India – of the spirit – (which) knows nothing of the divisions of time' (pp. 13-17). Significantly, for Nagarajan this India is symbolised by a girl who insists on committing sati. In all three instances, the equation of India with Hinduism is significant.

   The ideologies attaching to institutionalised English studies, then, are complex and should not be collapsed into a simplistic notion of cultural imperialism. The strategies adopted in challenging the orthodoxy will have to be responsive to this complexity.

Women and English studies

An overwhelming majority of those who choose to study English litera-ture in India are women and the trend is sharpened by increasing devalu-ation of the subject. Fanon's colonised subject is a male; for women, the split between black skin and white mask is intensified by their gen-dered alienation from white society, which is perhaps encapsulated in their relationship to the Western canonical text. It is somewhat ironical, then, that its understanding and knowledge is supposed to equip them for their roles as better wives and mothers. Alan Sinfield points out that 'whilst Literature is made to operate as a mode of exclusion in respect of class, it disadvantages girls by including them (this seems a paradox, but it only shows Literature's flexibility as a cultural form)' ('Shakespeare and education', p. 136). The alignment of certain disciplines as male and others as female is neither limited to India nor accidental: it needs to be located in relation to the dominant ideologies concerning both women and literature, and their concrete social effects. Women, the literary text, the individual subject and ideology are all interconnected in multiple ways (see Barrett, 'Ideology', pp. 65-85). Separately and in various combinations, each of them comes to be counterposed to the social, to be regarded as transcendent and trans-historical, constituted by some unchanging essence. Literature is a private activity and women are the private life of men; literature is universal and all women are the same; literature is mysteriously produced, women too are irrational; literature is both divinely inspired and a useless activity; women are goddesses or whores; both literature and women are potentially danger-ous, and following Plato, to be excluded from the male republic. These arguments reinforce the patriarchal association of male with rational, and female with instinctual. Despite these analogies women are at the same time disadvantaged as producers of literature because of their exclusion from the privileged spaces supposedly occupied by literature. So the canonical author as well as the academic hierarchy are predominantly male, while the average student of English literature is largely female. In this contradictory coming together of literature, woman and the private, the central philosophical and political premises of patriarchal and idealist thought are laid bare.

The questions of ideology and literature (then naturally) became central to feminist theory and politics which converged with post-Althusserian developments in Marxism and psychoanalysis to seize upon, expose and invert some of these assumptions. The resultant debates opened up questions of subjectivity and the intersection of the individual and the social. However, among some feminists, it led also to a certain reductionism, whereby women were credited with conventionally unrecognised forms of knowing such as intuition and female revolution consequently became largely semiotic, private and pre-social, as in the work of Coward or Kristeva and other French feminists. This marked a slide back into idealist premises and reinforced the patriarchal asscociations of women with some types of knowledge and behaviour.[9]

If neither women nor literature are universal categories, their seemingly global alignment needs to be historicised. Indian women's education under the Raj was crucially involved with their status and schooling earlier in pre-colonial India on the one hand, and the status of women in Britain on the other. Just as Anglicists and Orientalists reinforced the notion of British cultural superiority, and colonial and Indian educationalists concurred in their ideas about the nature of Literature, certain shared assumptions about women and their education made English Literature an ideal choice for their schooling in both otherwise divergent situations. At the same time the Empire re-shaped patriarchal relations in both countries. But such manoeuvres also included the racist domination of British men and women over Indians, and class contradictions within either country as well, so the feminisation of English Studies in India points to complex intersections of patriarchal and colonial histories.

Women's education is crucial to, although it constitutes a later stage in, the imperial project. Diane Barthel's analysis of the case of Ghana is pertinent:

In the first stage, education of males was seen as critical to the political control of the colony and to the ideological goals of the association or assimilation. The educated male elite would serve a key role in the colonial economy, functioning as privileged buffer between the white administrators and the mass of African people. But by educating this male elite in the first stage, the colonists were laying the groundwork for the second stage, when a female elite would be educated to correct the resulting social disequilibrium and, more broadly, to solidify colonial control by transmitting knowledge and appreciation of Western cultural forms to their children. (p. 153)

In India, higher education provided by the British government was initially restricted to potential recruits for the administration, i.e. upper-class men (Liddle and Joshi, p. 20). British efforts at 'educating' Indian women were begun early in the nineteenth century, but were under-mined by social conservatism regarding women's learning and restric-tions on their movements and contact with men; this itself cannot be attributed to 'the Indian way of life', as British accounts tended to suggest. Over many centuries the exclusion of women from learning had evolved (rather unevenly) in conjunction with increasing caste orthodoxies; with the tightening of caste and class barriers, brahmins had 'increased the exclusiveness of education . . . Women were no longer allowed to attend the democratic assemblies, and high-caste women were withdrawn from their previous occupations in education and the arts' (Liddle and Joshi, p. 63). But of course such traditions were contested, not simply imposed.

Indian and British patriarchal attitudes were mutually re-inforcing. On the one hand, Indian oppression of women was constantly used by the British to justify Empire and to become the self-proclaimed liberators of native women; on the other, Indian men had time and again used the idea of protection from foreign males to increase confinement of women. One example of the complicity between British and indigenous patriarchies is the suppression of matriliny in areas such as Malabar in Kerala, where at puberty women married men for three days only and subsequently entered into free *sambandhan* relationships with visiting husbands. In the nineteenth century the brahmins decreed that these husbands could not be dismissed without the permission of the entire clan or village; in 1868 the British legislated that a man provide for his wife and children, whereas till then property was inherited by his sister's children. In 1896 the Madras Marriage Act made the *sambandhan* relation-ship a monogamous marriage (Liddle and Joshi, 99. 28-9).

Kum Kum Sangari has traced some of the complex manoeuvres that accompanied the development of a paternalistic and feudal colonial government between 1770 and 1830. The British selected aspects of India's pre-colonial past as the basis for their own rule. The antiquity and continuity of native customs is stressed by evoking the submissive-ness of the Hindu woman to her husband. The passive Hindu woman is simultaneously a model of feminine behaviour which can be prescribed for the British woman and a signifier of the meekness and governability of the Indian people. But the stereotype of the libidinous Eastern woman also hovers on the margins, and justifies the need to govern her (and by implication also the Indian male). Sangari also links the self-projection of the British state as a benevolent patriarchy to the emergent familial norm in Britain itself ('What makes a text literary').[10] Mies has also shown how the submissiveness of Burmese women to their own men was perceived by the British as essential to smooth colonial government (quoted Rughani, p. 19).

After the 1857 war for Indian independence, when education, language and literature were stepped up as (despite Macaulay) more subtle and more effective methods of control, women's education became a priority for the Raj.[11] A crucial point was the arrival of women missionaries from England in the middle of the century, when as many as thirty per cent of women over twenty were single, and defined as 'redundant' since women were meant to be wives and mothers. These women posed a problem in a way that poorer single women who became domestic servants did not: the latter were seen to 'fulfil both essentials of women's being: they are supported by, and they minister to, men' (Forbes, p. WS 3). So the shipping of women as missionaries to India served a dual purpose: the problem faced by male British educationists was overcome as they began to penetrate the seclusion of Indian women and to educate/civilise them, and 'redundant' (i.e potentially subversive) women were removed from the home country. Forbes reminds us that 'women missionaries of the period were not only the helpmates of the imperialists but were themselves imperialists re-enacting the drama of the coloniser and the colonised within the confines of the zenana'.

Simultaneously with British education, Indian reformist groups also began indigenous schooling, which was radical in that it asserted the cultural independence and progressivism of Indian traditions, but not in its aim to prepare women as better companions and mothers (see Kishwar, 'Arya Samaj'). The idea of equal education is not necessarily based on the premise of equal intelligence and may serve only to reinforce the gender differentiation established elsewhere. In nationalist attitudes to women we may trace similarities with humanist writings on female education during the English Renaissance. Jayawardena points out that for Indian nationalists, 'modernity meant educated women, but educated to uphold the system of the nuclear, patriarchal family'. Sir Thomas More's letter to his children's tutor explained that education prepared men for public employment and women for maternal and wifely service: 'A woman's wit is to be cultivated all the more diligently, so that nature's defect may be redressed by industry' (Warnicke, p. 24).

In any case English language remained central to much indigenous schooling: 'it is ironical that even though the Arya Samaj movement was initiated with the idea of propagating Vedic learning, none of its leaders could escape the stranglehold of English' (Kishwar, 'Arya Samaj', p. WS 17). So both types of education were consonant with patriarchal and colonial premises. However, as in the case of women's learning during the Renaissance, both their methods and the effects generated were complicated, because they also opened out spaces for women's resistance (see chapter 3).

The association of female and irrational, literature and mysterious, has been used to justify the exclusion of women from some types of knowledge and to limit their professional and productive activity. Today it also ties in with the increasing technocratic bias of education. The psychologist Burt categorised literature as a subject that girls are good at (The English Studies Group, p. 253); very early in its history it became a women's subject, 'an additional accomplishment' preparing them for the marriage market (see Baldick, pp. 67-9). In India, education and even a job are increasingly required qualifications for sucessful husband-hunting. Yet both of these must maintain subordinate female status: 'If a girl is highly educated . . . she will be too proud . . . she will have ideas of her own' (Blumberg and Dwaraki, pp. 53-4). English literature, like education at a convent, ensures culture and status, and is also seen to equip women for the perfect female occupation, which is a 'natural' extension of their nurturing and mothering role, besides being 'genteel', not too time-consuming and not too highly paid. At the same time, there is a relative exclusion of women from male strongholds of science, engineering, and management, so that gender hierarchies are reproduced in the job market. In the early debates on women's education, there is much resistance to their studying sciences, but not a single one to literature. Matrimonial advertisements are an index to preferred brides, and they abound with specific requests for convent-educated girls, for teachers and even directly for English literature graduates. The choice of English literature thus has the capacity to instruct women in a 'variety' of roles – the guardian of culture, the decorous home-maker, and the subsidiary earner.[12]

Recently the Government of India proposed to overhaul higher education; despite its rhetoric about the advancement of women, its draft policy document The Challenge of Education carries no separate section or perspective on women's education. Yet subjects like 'morals or values in education' or 'keeping politics off the campus' have high priority sections devoted to them (The Times of India, 22 March 1986). The efforts to maintain patriarchal attitudes towards women's work, education and marriage, and to keep education 'apolitical', are interwoven. To seal off the text (and its claims to 'value') from history or politics is also to legitimise existing gender relations.

The establishment

The vastness of the English studies empire in India needs to be indicated in order to spell out what is at stake. The education system dramatically expanded and grew after the British left in 1947; whereas in 1950-51 there were only twenty-seven universities with 362,000 students, by 1983-84 the figures had swelled to 140 and 3,360,000 respectively (The Times of India, 22 March 1986). The corresponding increase in primary and secondary school education was even more dramatic. This means that today, more than a very small section of the elite has access to higher education, and students may be drawn from lower middle-class, trading, and farming backgrounds. Even though the majority of people are far more alienated from British culture than was the case during the Raj, this expansion has meant a huge increase in the absolute numbers studying English literature. A case in point is Delhi University, every one of whose 140,000 odd students must study English literature for at least one year during their undergraduation. There are over 700 lecturers in the subject.

Sunder Rajan points out that this edifice is not free of neo-colonial control:

To a very large extent English language and literary studies in India function under the aegis of two quasi-governmental foreign agencies, the British Council and the USIS (United States Information Service). These organisations perceive English and American literatures as the cultural products of their respective countries and promote them accordingly. There exists therefore a well-established system of funding, grants, patronage, publications, libraries, centres for advanced studies, seminars and workshops that is administered by these institutions. Not surprisingly, literary criticism in India is defined by the very material conditions created by these institutions. (p. 31)

The result is obvious: dominant Western criticisms, critics, institutions define the critical debates in India. The dependence of Third World intelligentsia upon First World institutions is clearly related to the lack of funds and poor research facilities and working conditions in our countries, and has been discussed elsewhere (Said, Orientalism, pp. 323-5; Altbach, 'Servitude of the Mind'). In relation to English studies the western hegemony is particularly pernicious, given that imperialism is hardly a thing of the past. Macaulay had articulated the common-sense assumptions of any colonial regarding the 'civilisation' of other peoples and therefore the spirit of his statements informs even some post-Raj 'revaluations'.[13] For example, despite 'changes in the Indian scene requiring a re-interpretation of the facts', Percival Spear is quick to censure Indian historians' efforts as too 'compartmental'; he claims for himself the prerogative of writing 'a true history' which will 'fuse' diverse elements into 'an integrated whole', 'a single consistent theme' (p. 13); in his case this is a modernisation theory: 'to portray the transformation of India under the West into a modern nation state' (quoted Spivak, 'Rani of Sirmur', p. 260).[14] Modern-day versions of Macaulay are abundant. He had said that a 'single shelf of good European literature is worth the whole native literature of India and Arabia' (Bhatt and Aggarwal, p. 3); in 1982, a chief 'A' level examiner for the University of London pronounced that 'the fact remains that, with the possible exception of Naipaul, there is nothing in African and Caribbean literature to match in quality those works which are normally found within the substantive body of texts set at Advanced level' (Parker, p. 197).

I have already indicated the centrality of the text to English courses. So it may well be that at least 20,000 students have read Shakespeare in Delhi University annually. These numbers are important in order to underline that no matter how marginalised English literature may seem in the context of today's technocratic expansion and emphasis on more 'useful' disciplines, dominant readings are being deployed on an enormous scale. English department hierarchies may control the careers of many hundreds of people in each university.

The figures also indicate the commercial aspects of English Literature: the role of publishing firms, for example, is important here. Their profits from a single anthology prescribed for compulsory reading are enormous. As Rukun Advani says 'the potential market for English at this level is absolutely vast, the stakes in it running into several crores of rupees . . . One BA Pass anthology prescription means a sale of around 200,000 rupees' (p. 2). He points out that both money and offers of publication may be used by some publishers to secure contracts for printing anthologies from particular universities; thus a vicious circle of mediocre (and conservative) criticism and a rigidity of syllabi is set up.

The emphasis on the text has obvious pedagogical implications. It ensures a reverence for the canon and the passivity of the reader. When texts are studied as discrete and autonomous their contextualisation is precluded; this in turn makes it more difficult to discuss the relativity of their 'truths'. Walter Raleigh, implementing Macaulay's cultural crusade in India, soon found that his task was simply 'to cram a well-worn subject into a given number of well-worn heads' (Baldick, p. 76).

In 1964, an article titled 'Teaching Shakespeare in India' (written by an Englishman as the first article of a book evaluating Shakespeare in India) suggests that 'a number of plays be read, even by the pass student, and read rapidly' (Rollo, p. 3). In 1986, says Sunder Rajan, such a policy of 'saturation' continued to be recommended (p. 30). It would be worth considering the ways in which such teaching practice interacted with hegemonic learning traditions prevalent earlier in India. The brahminical methodology of derivative scholarship, based on established texts and conducted through a high emphasis on retention, duplication and inviolate sanctity of the received canon (see Altbach, 'In search of Saraswati') was a fruitful ground on which to implant a teaching of the western text that placed the student in an uncritical passivity. While English education (and the universalism of the English literary text) sought to expand learning beyond the narrow circle permitted by brahminical learning, perhaps it can be suggested that in other ways the two interacted to ensure the passivity of the learners and the status of the received text.

Today, a token shuffling of texts takes place within a very narrow spectrum – *The Duchess of Malfi* may go and *Macbeth* may come in, but the canon of greats remains undisturbed. Englishness is broadly the qualifying criterion, and the exceptions are those that this orthodoxy would permit – mainly American writers (Hemingway, Miller) and V. S. Naipaul, who is the only non-white author included in the English honours BA course in Delhi. Of course women writers, outside of Austen or George Eliot or Emily Brontë do not figure at all, and feminism is still officially frowned upon.

From her own experiences on a syllabus revision programme, Sunder Rajan realised that rather than any notions of excellence or suitability, 'immense and complex network of forces' determine (which usually means block) course revisions. Translations are by and large ruled out, and the 'saturation' of students with English is recommended. She concludes that 'teachers of undergraduate colleges (for whose students the courses are intended) have little more than recommendatory powers in the selection of texts. A massive hierarchical edifice consisting of the university post-graduate English department, a committee of courses made up of senior teachers, the Faculty of Arts, and the Academic Council exists to authorize a syllabus revision' (p. 30).

Of course there have been shifts in what English literature popularly signifies, and serious inroads into its prestige. At one time Shakespeare's plays monopolised university, school and elite urban theatre. Kendal's company, *Shakespeariana*, gave 879 performances between June 1953 and December 1956; the audience included royalty, schoolchildren, urban middle classes and semi-urban masses. The company wound up as they found 'that English was no longer the language it used to be in India. At one time English plays meant everything; unless you could quote Shakespeare you would not get a job' (Kendal, p. 161). Today, students with the highest marks in school would rather opt (among the non-science subjects) for economics, commerce or history. These subjects ensure wider career options, and are now more useful while taking civil service examinations. Obviously the requirements for ruling India have changed since the Raj! The alignment of women with literature thereby becomes more pronounced. Education policy in India seems to be going the way of Thatcher's Britain, with impending cuts, tighter controls, retrenchment and the ideology of functionalism which is used to hit out at subjects such as literature. In the context of neo-colonialism, it perpetuates the theory of development according to imperialism, which is that Third World countries should 'produce' rather than 'think'. The politics of English departments ironically reinforces that division, all the while asserting the ivory-tower superiority of literature.

But the centrality of English literature to language teaching has ensured it a wider readership and academic circulation than it would otherwise have. During the transfer of power during Independence, the Indian bourgeoisie 'found the continued use of a European language advantageous for social and political control. They could maintain their own privileged position through their monopoly over the colonial language' (Whittey, p. 6). English was not just a 'a window on the world' but remained a central signifier of social difference although the difference itself shifted from one of race to that of class, and is tied in both with the current 'brain drain' and an internal cultural imperialism.[15] Because English Literature is well-entrenched in general education, it continues to be posited as a measure of learning: during recent debates on the pass-course syllabus, for example, it was argued that if a student could not comprehend Shakespeare, s/he did not deserve to graduate! The status of English studies and its satellite activities is therefore deeply contradictory – at once declining and stable, marginalised yet still central.[16]

Seizing the book

There are passionately held differences as to the ways in which the post-colonial subject can deal with the historical burden of the alien tongue. The Kenyan writer Ngugi Wa Thiong'o points out that since language is 'a carrier of culture', education in a foreign language ensured that 'learning, for a colonial child, became a cerebral activity and not an emotionally felt experience' (*Decolonizing the Mind*, pp. 13, 17). The resultant schisms have also been indicated by Paulo Friere, who noted that colonised intellectuals were condemned to a 'duality . . . in their innermost being' for they are simultaneously 'themselves, and the oppressor, whose consciousness they have internalised' (pp. 32-3). Athough we need to resist a simplification of 'the third world intellectual' into a person undifferentiated by geographical, historical or sexual positioning (see chapter 6), it would not be wrong to suggest that s/he lives with this Othello-like split consciousness, the wedge being the alien language, which has kept her/him 'whoring after English Gods'; in Victor Anant's words, we are all 'Macaulay's bastards' (quoted Parthasarathy, p. 67). Thiong'o concludes that 'a black African writer publishing in a European language is colluding with the covert imperialism that still operates; the European language is that of his own country's bourgeoisie and of international politics and commerce; it is not the language of the people' (*New Socialist*, no 44, p. 33).

But David Dabydeen from Guyana quotes James Baldwin to the contrary: 'I will write in any language that will bear the weight of my experience'. He argues that black African English is not the white man's English, and that two or three centuries of use have made the language indigenous to the African people (see *New Socialist*, no. 44, p. 33). The relationship of Africans, Afro-Americans and Indians to the English language is not identical, and so there is no universally 'correct' attitude to the coloniser's language. In India, it would be hard to deny the elitist connotations of English, and yet to see it just as a foreign language would be to ignore the history of the last two centuries. The language question is extremely complicated in a multilingual, multinational, multiethnic state and intersects with the issue of regional chauvinism; for example, in many regions, English is prefered to Hindi because of resentment against the political and cultural domination of the Hindi-speaking belt.

All these issues are tied up with the question of an alternative pedagogy of English literature. It seems to me that creative writing in English should be distinguished from teaching English literature. Do cultural differences imply that the teaching of any foreign literature cannot break from the reverence for an alien culture? What is an alien culture? In a recent seminar, Ruth Vanita pointed out that alienation applies not just to the English literary text: it is difficult to teach Raja Rao's *Kanthapura* in Delhi, because students there are ignorant and dismissive of South Indian culture. The question is not limited to what language is used, for the ideologies dominant in English studies intersect with orthodoxies in the study of other literatures; the notion of the inviolate, transcendental text which should be kept free of contextual contamination may be found in departments of Hindi, Bengali or other literatures as well. It is clear that alternative pedagogy will have to question not only the criterion of Englishness that dominates our curricula, but also the boundaries between literatures and other disciplines: we need to teach not only different literatures but all literatures differently.

It may be argued that to re-interpret the Western text in a way that makes it 'more meaningful' is simply to entrench it further into our education, and that we need to throw out the book instead of appropriating it. The debate is complicated, and many of our positions may be only strategic. We may need to distinguish between specific situations – for example, between a politically committed theatre and alternative academic practice in India. In the first case, it is arguable that urban theatre in English is limited to elite circles, and has not absorbed the dynamic influences of indigenous traditions, which have of late fruitfully lent themselves to alternative theatre practices. But given the enormity of English studies within academic institutions, a radical intervention is far more urgent and imperative. This again can take various forms: for example, one could locate the possible subversion latent in the ways that Indian students do not comprehend English literature. Or in the ways in which the teacher and the class room experience is increasingly becoming redundant as students prefer to rely on locally produced 'key'-books, which offer summaries, translations, and simplified (often mutilated) condensations of Western criticism all in the space of a few pages.[17]

But to imagine that the text is being quietly subverted in these ways, even as we know its institutionalised deployment to be hegemonic is somewhat naive, for jobs, education and many hours of classroom contact are still at stake. One script of a school-leaving examination that I saw contained the following remarks on Oliver Twist: 'Fagin was a sweet old lady . . . One night before Oliver was born, his mother died'. The student failed, and if s/he had obliquely resisted what s/he was supposed to learn, the result was hardly revolutionary. As teachers who are not about to resign our jobs en masse, we have to look for other alternatives rather than romanticising subaltern incomprehension.

The appropriation of literature itself can take different forms; texts can be deliberately re-written to suit contexts different from their original ones, as in the African and Caribbean appropriations of The Tempest (see chapter 6). Alternatively, they may be adopted by an 'alien' culture or people as expressive of their own reality, as Theodorakis used Neruda's 'Canto General' as a statement of resistance against dictatorship in Greece. Or else, appropriation may involve re-interpretation – a simultaneous examination of their meaning in more than one culture, and than one history.

in this sense that I approach Renaissance drama, which constitutes the privileged core of the canon of master texts of English literature. In terms of language it is a body of literature far removed from Indian students, and therefore may be seen as the most alien of imposed texts. While we may continue to question this presence, in the absence of any immediate likelihood of it being removed from existing curricula, we can explore the possibility of identifying ways in which the texts can interact with the students' own reality. Women, who have been seen to be at the centre of the dominant deployment of literature, will also be my focus. I need to emphasise that 'interact' here does not mean expanding the universal applicability of the text. The colonial and post-colonial reader has been forced to cope with alienation by suppressing it, since it is taken to be the very index of his/her inferiority. Thus Othello's colour, which is simultaneously a point of identification for such a reader and a point of alienation from dominant readings that erase Othello's blackness in favour of his 'universal' passion, jealousy, is suppressed in the Indian classroom. Masculine jealousy and female passivity become 'natural' human conditions (see chapter 2). Again, dominant criticism works to efface the subaltern woman's history and experience in order to 'persuade' her to adopt a white male positioning. For example, an Indian woman who is made to see Cleopatra as the stereotype of the Oriental seductress 'turns herself into an object', to adopt a phrase from John Berger (p. 47). When Cleopatra herself transforms into Antony's Roman wife, we are told to understand it as a process of romantic sublimation rather than an act of tragic compromise, a pathetic attempt to erase the contradictions of her existence (see chapter 5). Or the violence against women in Jacobean drama is 'explained' to women who themselves experience daily violence as an indication of spiritual chaos; the transgressive woman here becomes a reflection and indication of degenerate society. The female reader, potentially if not actually rebellious, is silenced along with the literary creation.

Appropriation here does not question only institutionalised readings but the text as well, which may be seen to contribute to the marginalisation of Othello, or Cleopatra, or the disorderly woman. In order to focus on this – to recover these marginalised voices or see why they cannot be recovered – a series of barricades erected around the literary text must be negotiated, and these include the way in which the reader's encounter with the book is lifted from the historical, geographical and gendered spaces in which it occurs. This is only one strategy possible in some specific classroom situations; it will, I hope, problematise both dominant readings and feminist reductionism in Western discussions of female oppression and resistance in Renaissance drama by drawing on racial difference in the texts, and in the readerships of the texts.

Notes

1 I am indebted to Rajeswari Sunder Rajan's 'After Orientalism', Gauri Viswanathan's 'The beginnings of English literary studies in British India', chapter three of Chris Baldick's *The Social Mission*, and the papers presented at a seminar, 'The study of English literature in India: ideology and practice', held at Miranda House, University of Delhi, in April 1988. All of these have marked out a crucial area of inquiry. I was pleased to find that Thomas Cartelli's, 'Prospero in Africa', acknowledges that it was 'the product of a deepening involvement in the study of postcolonial literature and its clarifying impact on our understanding of western cultural practices' (p. 99).

2 Marilyn Butler was delivering the V. Krishna Memorial lecture at Miranda House, University of Delhi, on 11 December 1987; this was almost identical to her article, 'Revising the canon' (*TLS*, 4-10 December 1987) which was earlier presented as a lecture at Cambridge.

3 Movements that challenged brahminical domination and caste traditions also revolted against educational orthodoxy by using languages other than Sanskrit, such as Prakriti, Pali and Shauraseni. Buddha taught in Magadhi, and 'Jaina teaching was first preserved in an oral tradition' (Thapar, p. 63); thus the authority of Sanskrit and dominant educational traditions was undermined.

4 Romila Thapar (pp. 28-50) and Liddle and Joshi (pp. 51-70) both suggest that Aryan-speaking peoples had suppressed the indigeneous Dravidian and tribal peoples of the subcontinent, who had been relegated as racially inferior, and whose own traditions, including that of matrilinear organisation had been enclosed gradually within a patriarchal and highly stratified society. This view has been generally accepted so far, but I have been informed by Nayanjot Lahiri that recent archeological work is challenging the notion of a conquest in the strict sense. So without attributing patriarchal and racist notions to a Aryan conquest, I am here confining myself to the ideological results of a conflict with racial, sexual and regional underpinnings.

5 'It was under the influence of Darwin that a Fellow of the London Anthropological Society argued in 1864 that the Chinese and Indians were superior to the Africans, being more notable for docility, intelligence and industry (Moorhouse, p. 175).

6 In E. M. Forster's *A Passage to India*, for example, the spirituality and emotionality of Indians is directly interwoven with their immaturity, irrationality and incapacity to deal with practical matters. Their government with the less likeable but rational English then becomes a regrettable necessity. Incidentally, this book is widely taught in India and examination questions are concentrated around the representations of 'the Hindus as soul, the Muslims as heart and the British as head' while the political meaning of these remains unexamined.

7 In the transition from the Raj to Indian self-government, despite a strong and determined opposition to the British, radicalism was kept in check both by British strategy and the leadership of the nationalist movement. On the one hand

> If the British had been unyielding and had not gradually introduced parliamentary institutions into India during the last forty years of British rule, the nationalist movement must have organised itself in a revolutionary form; it must have become a nationalist junta, like Kuomintang in China, or more probably in contemporary conditions, a communist party. (Strachey, quoted Lawrence, 'Just plain commonsense', p. 67)

On the other hand, the leadership of the nationalist movement itself consolidated its bourgeois character by deflecting radical challenges. The idea of a non-violent struggle was a brilliant strategy on the part of Gandhi, not the least because it also guarded against more militant and revolutionary alternatives. No doubt there were conflicting elements even here, since Gandhian politics simultaneously mobilised large sections of the people, including women, into action. Even so, the continuity of certain hegemonic attitudes was insured: for example, women were drawn out of the home, but under a patriarchal leadership and on *nationalist* not feminist platforms. For a fuller discussion of this see Kumari Jaywardena's *Feminism and Nationalism*.

8 Not only are English departments the most resistant to syllabi changes, or democratic functioning, but they have largely isolated themselves from teachers' politics. A recent all-India teacher's strike is a case in point. An overwhelming majority of Delhi University's English department teachers (i.e. those not employed by the colleges and involved only in post-graduate teaching) refused to join. They stressed their loyalty to 'department decisions', rather than to those of the Delhi University Teachers' Association or the all-India organisation. Even when 230,000 teachers in universities and colleges all over India were on strike against the government's impending policies whereby teachers recruitment, promotion and evaluation would be bureaucratically monitored and their service conditions would worsen, they did not stop teaching. Arguments stressing the difference between teachers and industrial workers, the morality of teaching as a noble profession above pecuniary interests and a teacher's moral obligation to students to teach no matter what the conditions of teaching, were made in justification. One also heard these through the government propaganda machinery. If one had any doubts about the politics bred by institutionalised English studies, they were set at rest during this period. On the other hand, especially among younger college teachers, a questioning of the critical practice taught by this orthodoxy has led not only to greater inter-disciplinary research and commitment to alternative pedagogy, but also to a more active participation in teachers' politics.

9 See Alison Jaggar, p. 373; Rosalind Coward, p. 22; Ann Rosalind Jones, 'Julia Kristeva', p. 60; Michele Barrett, 'Ideology', p. 75; Stuart Hall, 'Recent developments', p. 162.

10 I am referring to Sangari's paper as it was delivered at the Miranda House seminar on English in India (see note 1 above). Pratibha Parmar points out that even today discussions of the hardships of Asian women can provide 'further fodder for the liberal racist' and can all too easily reinforce ideas of Asian men being more sexist than white men' (p. 252). The case of sati is especially relevant in this connection; it has been dicussed elsewhere (see Mani; Spivak, 'Rani'; Liddle and Joshi); we only need to recall that it provided a major moral justification for continued British rule. The British consulted brahmins while formulating legislations on sati, thus giving official sanction to the right of this high-caste group to represent the diverse and enormously varied customs and traditions of the Indian people. As Liddle and Joshi point out, 'It is significant that sati was a practice of the higher castes, with whom the British had made alliances, whereas matriliny was a form of family structure which both British and patriarchal high castes found immoral' (p. 30). Hence British 'non-interference' as well as their 'reforms' intensified and calcified existing patriarchal tendencies. Such manouvres extended to women's economic life as well.

11 I am indebted to Geraldine Forbes's article for facts about women's education cited in these paragraphs.

12 The following matrimonial advertisement is typical: 'French diplomat (Indian origin) visiting India this December . . . draws monthly 3,500 dollars seeks marriage with bride . . . god fearing, pretty, fair, slim, Tamil-speaking BA (literature)' (*The Times of India*, Bombay, 9 November, 1986).

13 I use the notion of 'common-sense' here and subsequently drawing on the discussion in Errol Lawrence's essay 'Just plain common-sense'. Following Gramsci, he defines common-sense as contradictory, not as

constituting a unified body of knowledge. It does not have a theory underlying or 'hidden beneath it', but is perhaps best seen as a 'storehouse of knowledge' which has been gathered together, historically, through struggle ... in common-sense terms, historically and culturally specific images of femininity and masculinity are presented as 'natural' attributes of females and males. Whilst we should not forget that these definitions are contested, we must also remember that they are embodied within the dominant institutional order and are inscribed within the social relations of everyday life. This 'massive presence' has the effect on the one hand of disciplining the subordinate classes in practice and on the other hand of giving these common-sense ideologies their 'taken-for-granted' character. (pp. 49-50)

14 Not surprisingly, Spear finds those Indians who supported English education as 'for-ward-looking' (p. 126). Similarly, Geoffrey Moorhouse's glossy India Britannica is anxious to distance itself from the conventional imperialist stance but also to emphasise what Empire 'did for India'. Moorhouse also smugly comments that Roy's praise of the British empire has 'a ring of truth' (pp. 85-6).

15 Today English is spoken by roughly seventy one million people in India, i.e. more than the number in Britain (McCrum et al., p. 322). It is a crucial link language in a multilingual country with fifteen recognised languages and over 300 dialects. It has aquired the status of 'being a passport to all the important government posts controlling the economy' and ensures a new export of labour to the west: according to a recent news-paper report, one in three students of the Indian Institute of Technology finds employ-ment in the United States of America 'because all our qualified professionals speak English' (The Times of India, 22 March 1986).

16 There has also been a downward filtration of 'high culture' over time. Shakespeariana was patronised by the local ruler, whose order that they sit down and 'tell sad stories of the death of kings' speaks of the cultural schism of the upper classes in India. But it is important to remember that the players survived because of their popular performances in little halls and stages in small towns dotted across the land (see Pym, The Wandering Company). In many ways, subtle, oblique, and hard to document, this influence is still visible – in the casual phrase thrown in in a Hindi or Tamil film and in the general equation of 'highbrow' with English literature. I was recently told a joke about a famous villain of the Hindi screen: he asks his henchmen to administer 'Hamlet poison' to the hero. 'What is that, boss?', they ask him. 'It is a poison that will convert his "to be" to "not to be"' replies the boss. Although 'only a joke', this captures the survival of the text in unexpected places: someone also told me that a traffic hoarding at a particularly dangerous spot on a mountain road on the way to a famous shrine in the Himalayas reads 'When shall we three meet again, / In thunder, lightning or in rain?'.

17 Sunder Rajan invokes Homi Bhabha's analysis of the ambivalence of subaltern response to colonial authority, where mimicry and camouflage also mark subversion ('Signs taken for wonders'). She suggests that we should see the responses of Indian students, who, 'confronted by the double authority of the book itself and the English teacher ... go back to the colourfully translated Hindi version of the text and memorize the "proper" answers from the same source, thus making both teacher and text redundant', as an appropriation along the lines of Anund Meseh in Bhabha's article.

Sexuality and racial difference

Men's power

In the context of its female Indian readers, the violence repeatedly committed on the female body in Renaissance (and especially Jacobean) tragedy takes on an urgent contemporaneity that challenges not only the self-enclosed and self-referential readings of traditional criticism but also a simplistic First World feminism which is in danger, as Spivak points out, of becoming complicit with imperialism ('Imperialism and sexual difference', pp. 225-6). It is true that the similarity between violence in the plays and that which is directed against women in India, is startling and, I shall suggest, an important factor in assessing how these plays can be received. Even the most sober and conservative estimates of the latter would have to acknowledge the following: wives are murdered for dowry (in Delhi alone, the reported figure is two such deaths daily) rapes and sexual exploitation of 'poor and *dalit* (lower-caste) women, and of nurses, office-workers, domestic servants, by landlords, employers and policemen, (are) part of their daily lives' (Kishwar and Vanita, p. 255) and are daily escalating; age-old and high-tech methods coexist as female infanticide continues and intrauterine chromosomal examination (amniocentesis) is used to abort female foetuses on an unprecedented scale (see Miller); the practice of widow immolation, sati, is vigorously defended in its sporadic revival, 169 years after being officially abolished and in the countryside, women are still harassed and even killed on the grounds that they are witches. These are but a few examples of a situation where the average woman is constantly vulnerable to patriarchal and class violence and the ideologies attaching to it. While recounting such facts we need always to bear in mind the long history of Western accounts of the pitiable condition of non-European women, a history which inevitably went on to suggest the barbarity and primitivism of such societies and the superiority of Western civilisation. As Indian feminists have stressed, however, the increasing oppression against women must be analysed in the context of modern Indian society and its contemporary contradictions, not as an unfortunate remnant of a feudal past.[1]

It is in this context too, that we need to see how institutionalised readings of Renaissance tragedy work. In this body of drama, female transgression, both real and imagined, is repeatedly and ruthlessly oppressed by the family, state, church and judiciary: Desdemona (Othello), the Duchess of Malfi, Vittoria (The White Devil), Bianca (Women Beware Women), Annabella ('Tis Pity She's a Whore) and Beatrice-Joanna (The Changeling) all break the rules of female conduct and are punished. Early modern Europe witnessed the mass-scale burning and torture of women as witches, and Renaissance drama makes it clear that 'witch' is a category flexible enough to cover any sort of female deviance and rebellion.

The much-vaunted theory of the spiritual chaos of Jacobean drama implicitly connected female disobedience with a degenerate social order, and thus contributed to silencing any notions of disobedience which actual women readers may harbour. In the Indian classroom, it commits another violence – that of imposing universalised models of human relationships upon subaltern readers; paradoxically, the points of intersection with our lives are carefully excluded. For example, as undergraduates at Miranda House, Delhi (the name is not insignificant – see chapter 6) who were 'dissatisfied' with Desdemona's silence in the face of her husband's brutality, we were told that we did not 'understand' her because we had never been 'in love'. Othello thus became a sort of universal text of love, and love implied female passivity. It can be argued that in many ways we were 'prepared' for such readings by the popular Western romantic novels which flood the Indian market, and which are consumed by English-speaking urban schoolgirls in vast quantities. In these novels, as the English Studies Group point out, 'The subordination of the woman to the narrative-ideological syntax of home and children is strikingly visible in the progressive extinction of her powers of articulate speech'. They cite an instance from Barbara Cartland's Lord Ravenscar's Revenge: ' "That is ... what I ... felt", Romara said, "but I never ... thought, I never ... dreamt, that you would ... feel ... the ... same". "You seemed in so many ways to be like my mother", Lord Ravenscar said' (p. 261). 'High' and 'low' literature thus together reinforce common-sense assumptions about a woman in love.

Many college students in India occupy a very uneasy space where romantic love, 'free choice' and sexual passion can exist as ideals (nurtured also by popular cinema, where they become reconciled to common-sense notions of female obedience), but where the probable reality of their own marriages is entirely different. Desdemona's defiance of her father plays on and encourages such an ideal, but she then betrays it by her submissiveness. Discussions with my own students later located such a betrayal as the source of our uneasiness. By being murdered,

Desdemona comes uncomfortably close to the battered wives that now crowd the Indian (especially urban) scene. A recent Indian feminist interpretation of several Shakespearean plays as spectacles of wife-murder can be seen as a response (though unacknowledged as such) to the similarities; it also implicitly addressses the discomfiture of readers told to accept rather than question Desdemona's silencing and locates this within the daily experience of Indian women (see Vanita, 'Men's power, pp. 32-9).

Such a view is both compelling and disturbing. But reading the play as a black woman immediately problematises the notion of men's power and therefore also any comparisons we may make. I found it difficult to accept that 'Othello's words could easily be interchanged with Claudio's' or that 'universal harmony' is at stake here (Vanita, p. 35). Western feminist interpretations have also claimed that 'the play's central theme is love – and especially marital love, its central conflict is between men and women' (Neely, p. 212). If Othello is treated as a prototype of universal man and his blackness is not even hinted at, we return to the paradigms of preferred readings: 'Othello, like most men, is a combination of the forces of love and hate, which are isolated in impossibly pure states in Desdemona and Iago' (Kernan, p. 80). If we probe deeper into how male violence is constructed in the plays, however, our critique of the silencing of women in literature and in the classroom can include an exposure of other sorts of violence and silences. A text like Othello can then be seen to have a more complex resonance in the Indian situation, and indeed in the Western classroom as well.

Christopher Norris has pointed out that, despite variations, Othello criticism from Johnson to Leavis can be seen as part of 'a certain dominant cultural formation in the history of Shakespeare studies. It is an effort of ideological containment, an attempt to harness the unruly energies of the text to a stable order of significance' (p. 66). I suggest that this stable order, could only be invoked by the simultaneous exclusion of both gender and race; therefore, firstly, as a recent feminist essay points out, both 'Othello critics' (who sentimentalise Othello) and 'Iago critics' (who emphasise Iago's realism and 'honesty') 'badly misunderstand and misrepresent the women in the play' (Neely, p. 212), and secondly, as Ruth Cowhig indicates, the question of race is 'largely ignored by critical commentaries' (p. 8).[2] In 1693, Thomas Rymer interpreted the play as 'a caution to all Maidens of Quality, how, without their parents' consent they run away with Blackamoors...' (p. 89). This combined a patriarchal view of female waywardness and the necessity of obedience, a racist warning against the rampant sexuality of black men, and a class consciousness which prioritises the submission of women 'of Quality'. Nearly 300 years later, Leslie Fiedler, among the first in recent times to acknowledge the connections between the racial and sexual themes, argues that Othello moves from being a stranger whose colour establishes his difference ('cultural' rather than ethnic) to becoming, towards the end of the play, 'colourless: a provincial gentleman-warrior, a downright English soldier fallen among foreigners; which means that he no longer functions archetypally even as a stranger, much less a black' (p. 160). For this downfall of the inwardly white Othello, Desdemona the 'white witch' and Iago the true black are jointly held responsible. Emilia is 'first and last an untamed shrew' and generally, the women 'by their lives and functions . . . seem rather to sustain Iago's view of women' (p. 141).

It is a measure of the problem I want to highlight that although Carole Neely criticises Fiedler's misogyny, she both ignores his racism (which is less crude than Rymer's or Ridley's but there nevertheless) and makes no attempt to analyse the impact of Othello's blackness on the sexual relations in the play.[3] To address sexual difference at the expense of the racial is to produce what Newton and Rosenfelt have called 'a feminist version of "the" human condition' (p. xvii) which is especially invalid for women in the 'third world', who are at the juncture of both sorts of oppression. Although the question of race has been admirably discussed recently (see Cowhig and Orkin's essays), it is often ignored or underplayed even by those concerned with alternative and political criticism, and has not been fully inserted into discussions of gender difference.[4]

In a brief article, Ben Okri points out that 'to reduce the colour is to diminish the force of the sex. Working together they can be quite unbearable' (p. 563). Even though no simple mapping of racial difference on to the sexual is possible precisely because Othello's colour and gender make him occupy contradictory positions in relation to power, I shall suggest that firstly, Othello's blackness is central to any understanding of male or female sexuality or power structures in the play; secondly, the filtering of sexuality and race through each other's prism profoundly affects each of them, thus indicating more clearly what Lentricchia has called the 'multiplicity of histories' of both authority and resistance; and thirdly, such interweaving does not dissolve the tensions between different forms of oppression but acknowledges and addresses . them, as well as placing the schisms and discontinuities of identity (which recent criticism has seen as foregrounded in Renaissance drama; see Dollimore, Radical Tragedy, and Belsey, The Subject of Tragedy) within the neglected context of racial difference.

Historicising racism

It had been a major problem for critics of the play to reconcile Othello's blackness with his central position in the play. Therefore either his colour was ignored, or much critical effort was expended in trying to prove that Shakespeare did not intend him to be black at all (see Cowhig, p. 16). Both views are premised upon racist notions of black inferiority. The notion that 'all men are the same' includes the apparently conflicting one that 'blacks are inferior, and hardly men at all'. Ridley's efforts to prove Othello's non-negroid racial origins are notoriously and crudely racist: 'There are more colours than one in Africa, and that a man is black in colour is no reason why he should, even to European eyes, look sub-human' (p. li). Then we also hear that 'for Shakespeare, "black" does not describe an ethnic distinction . . . . "fair" has a primarily moral significance'; that there was no racism in Elizabethan England, that the kind of horror that contemporary audiences might feel at a black/white mating is therefore no part of the play; that since 'miscegenation had not yet been invented' we are to read the blackness of Othello as primarily symbolic' and finally, 'it is no real surprise, therefore, to discover that Othello was not ethnically "black at all" in the sources from which Cinthio drew his story' (Fiedler, pp. 143-5). It is no real surprise either to discover that Fiedler's moral categories quickly slide back to ethnic ones. How colours come to be invested with moral connotations is precisely the history of racism.

Evidence of such a history during Elizabethan times has been accumulating, and here I will only amplify aspects that crucially link it with the question of gender. G. K. Hunter identifies a 'powerful and ancient tradition associating black-faced men with wickedness . . . (which) came right up to Shakespeare's own day' (p. 35). Part of this tradition derived from a Bible-centred conception of the world in which humanity was graded according to its geographical distance from the Holy Land – hence black people were devilish because they existed outside both the physical and the conceptual realm of Christianity. Blacks became identified with the descendants of Ham, and their colour a direct consequence of sexual excess. The devil and his associates, even in Reginald Scott's fairly rationalist *The Discovery of Witchcraft*, were inextricably linked with blackness: 'a damned soul may and doth take the shape of a blackamoore' (Hunter, p. 34).

Hunter also includes a general cultural hostility to strangers as a factor influencing racial prejudice, but erroneously locates this to 'a response to the basic antinomy of day and night' which to him explains the presence of racism 'all over the world (even in darkest Africa) from the earliest to the latest times'. This dangerously universalises and naturalises white racism, whose various histories indicate interlinking situations of oppression rather than a trans-historical colour consciousness. Eldred Jones's pioneering study *Othello's Countrymen* established that Shakespeare did not depend on literary sources for his portraits of black people and that there was a growing black presence in England with evidence of its widening contact with white inhabitants. Hakluyt's *Principal Navigations* bears witness to the beginnings of slave trade: between 1562 and 1568, Hawkins brought 'blackamoors to England' and sold hundreds of black slaves to Spain; so there were 'several hundreds of black people living in the households of the aristocracy and the landed gentry' (Cowhig, p. 5).

Thus Hunter's arguments that Elizabethans had 'no continuous contact' with black people and 'no sense of economic threat from them' (p. 32) are historically disproved. But the crucial point is that the black presence was both perceived and constructed as a threat by the state. Royal proclamations and state papers nervously point to the 'great numbers of negroes and blackamoors in the country, of which kind of people there are already too manye'. Queen Elizabeth's correspondence with the Privy Council, seeking to deport eighty-nine black people, is significant. A warrant issued on 18 July 1596 contrasts black or 'those kinde of people' with her white subjects or 'Christian people' in a passage startlingly illustrative of the Orientalist split between a superior European culture, constituting 'us', and the inferior non-European peoples and cultures, constituting 'them'. This split, as Said has argued, is a crucial component in establishing the hegemony of the former (*Orientalism*, p. 7). But Elizabeth's communique also crucially puts forward the argument that blacks will create unemployment, 'want of service', for her white people. Here again she evokes the myth of a rampant black sexuality and their 'populous' numbers, seeking to limit and control black presence in the imperial country (quoted Cowhig, p. 6).[5]

Its echoes in today's immigration and deportation laws are not accidental but are ensured by a continuous reworking of past prejudices in later relations of dominance. Cedric Robinson speaks of the ways in which the ideologies of earlier feudal relations were both preserved and transformed in the new mercantile and colonial situation. He says that the identification of black with evil had not only been directed against strangers but had also sought to preserve the superiority of the upper classes, since the European nobility projected itself as drawn from different ethnic and cultural groups than the common people. Thus travelling merchants were regarded as foreigners. According to Robinson, racism was not simply a result of capitalism. Rather, capitalism itself was profoundly shaped by ideas of racial differentiation. Therefore, although the ideal of a unified greater Britain was encouraged, the 'tendency of European civilisation through capitalism ... was not to homogenise but to differentiate – to exaggerate regional, subcultural, dialectical differences into "racial" ones' (Robinson, p. 27).

A similar tendency is traceable in the case of women; increasing restrictions upon their activities, inheritance and public participation accompanied the widening separation of the centres of production and consumption, even as the dominant ideology posited the notion of woman as a more equal companion of man (see chapter 3). Women, and indeed other marginalised peoples, were excluded from the projected ideals of self-fulfilment and self-fashioning, of personal achievement and mobility; sexual difference became a central preoccupation of religious and secular authority. Irreconcilable contradictions with respect to women as well as 'those kinde of people' are opened up by such exclusions; in both cases, medieval differentiations were not simply adopted, but modified and altered in the new circumstances.

Therefore the definition of 'black' supplied by a pre-sixteenth century version of the Oxford English Dictionary as 'deeply stained with dirt ... having dark or deadly purposes, malignant' was useful beyond medieval religious and cultural chauvinism. Even this chauvinism has been attributed by Robinson to the failure of the project of a greater or unified Europe during the eleventh and twelfth centuries and to its transference 'from one of terrestrial social order to that of a spiritual kingdom, Christiandom' (p. 10). Both Hunter (p. 3) and Said (Orientalism, p. 63) note that the new knowledge about foreign peoples generated by Renaissance expeditions was filtered through and shaped by existing ideologies and prejudices. But 'a traditional religious outlook' which Hunter uses to explain why increasing factual information 'lay fallow' was itself adapted and pressed into colonial service. Winthrop D. Jordan says that the linkage between black and devil 'represented a projection onto the African of the bourgeoisie's own anxieties about their role as entrepreneurs in the burgeoning capitalist developments that threatened to disrupt the social order' (quoted Lawrence, pp. 61-2). It is true that racist ideologies are not solely constructed for the purposes of rationalising the economic aspects of colonial plunder, but this rationalisation is certainly a crucial component of them (see Lawrence, 'Just plain common-sense', p. 57).

Hence common-sense attitudes towards black people in Othello (which will be identified shortly) indicate both the older tradition of hatred towards blacks and a newer expediency, a more complex ideology of racism. The attitudes of modern audiences/readers may not be identical with those of Shakespeare's original audiences; moreover, the play's readership is not a unified category and Indians among them have experienced a different history of racism. Even so, contemporary colour prejudices are interlinked; they draw upon and rework this earlier history.

There is a historical dependency between patriarchalism and racism. In Europe, the increased emphasis on heterogeneity of peoples and groupings that Robinson mentions occurs alongside the escalation of patriarchal discourses on the separateness of female identity from masculine. As I have said, in the Indian subcontinent, the consolidation of power involved racial, sexual, and caste exclusions. In the colonies, racism specifically 'called out the basic sexist tendencies' in the colonised countries and cultures, 'calcified existing ones and introduced others' (see Ogundipe-Leslie). Helen Carr points out that 'colonialist, racist and sexist discourse have continually reinforced, naturalized and legitimized each other during the process of European colonization' (p. 46). Although the *specificity* of racism and patriarchy should not be blurred by this analogy, the connections are important. Both women and racial 'others' are posited as biological and natural inferiors and similar characteristics are attributed to them:

. . . in the language of colonialism, non-Europeans occupy the same symbolic space as women. Both are seen as part of nature, not culture, and with the same ambivalence: either they are ripe for government, passive, child-like, unsophisticated, needing leadership and guidance, described always in terms of lack – no initiative, no intellectual powers, no perseverance; or on the other hand, they are outside society, dangerous, treacherous, emotional, inconstant, wild, threatening, fickle, sexually aberrant, irrational, near animal, lascivious, disruptive, evil, unpredictable. (Carr, p. 50)

Thus the operations of patriarchalism seek to extend the control and authority of man as father over women, and white man as father over black men and women. Both black people and women are in need of guidance, yet both threaten to elude and disrupt it.

'Ravenous tigers' and 'inhuman dogs'

Cowhig points out that 'only as we recognise the familiarity of the figure of the black man as villain in Elizabethan drama can we appreciate what must have been the startling impact on Shakespeare's audience of a black hero' (pp. 4–5). Shakespeare made significant departures from his source material, from other representations of blacks on the Renaissance stage, and from his own earlier portraits of Moors (as both Hunter and Cowhig have shown). The tradition of the black villain-hero in Elizabethan drama resulted in a series of negative portrayals of black men, such as Muly Mahomet in Thomas Peele's *The Battle of Alcazar* or Eleazor in *Lust's Dominion*, written by Dekker and others. In Shakespeare's *Love's Labour Lost*, 'Black is the badge of hell / The hue of dungeons and the school of night' (IV.iii.250-1). In Cinthio's version of the Othello story, his 'blackness already displeases' Desdemona, and Othello carefully plots how to murder her without being caught. Hunter points out that Shakespeare changes many features of Cinthio's tale, but not the colour of the hero. A brief look at Shakespeare's earlier fullest treatment of race in *Titus Andronicus* reveals the extent to which *Othello* departs from the usual linkage of black men with deviant white women.

In *Titus Andronicus* the 'siren' queen, Tamora (II.i.23) and the 'inhuman dog, unhallowed slave', Aaron (V.iii.14) are not only lovers, not only accomplices in unleashing a tale of 'murders, rapes and massacres, / Acts of black night, abominable deeds, / Complots of mischief, treason, villainies' (V.i.63-5) but are almost interchangeable: each is separately referred to as a 'ravenous tiger' (V.iii.95 and V.iii.5). The recurrent horrors of the play are actually the result of a savage tussle for 'Roman empery', which has recently been consolidated by a victory over the 'barbarous Goths' (I.i.22, 28) but they are projected onto the 'others' of Roman imperial patriarchy.

Roman nobility claims to be both masculine and 'civilised'; Titus is its grand patriarch, deriving his status from his twenty-five sons, twenty-one of whom have been 'slain manfully in arms' (I.i.196), from the beauty and virtue of his daughter, 'gracious Lavinia', who is 'Rome's rich ornament' (I.i.52) and from his own military exploits. If Rome has become a 'wilderness of tigers' because of its rulers' disregard for the people, and because of their brutal traditions and scramble for power – Tamora points out: 'was never Scythia half so barbarous' (I.i.131) – what better scapegoats than a black man and a disorderly woman?

The play does not really acknowledge them as scapegoats, however, for blackness and deviant womanhood emerge as pathologically evil. Significantly, there has been no debate about the colour or ethnic origins of Aaron the Moor, no effort to prove that Shakespeare had not seen Moors, or that racial hatred and miscegenation had not been invented in Elizabethan times for, unlike Othello, Aaron is more easily reconciled to the stereotype of black wickedness, lust, and malignity. His unmitigated evil is repeatedly linked to his physical features, both by himself and by others. Thus he refers to:

> My fleece of woolly hair that now uncurls
> Even as an adder when she doth unroll
> To do some fatal execution. (II.iii.34-6)

Or again,

> Let fools do good, and fair men call for grace:
> Aaron will have his soul black like his face. (III.i.205-6)

Tamora, Aaron's lover, is white, but she is a Goth and therefore barbarous. She and Lavinia between them split the patriarchal stereotype of woman, for if Lavinia is civilised, 'gracious' (I.i.52), 'gentle' (II.v.16), passive, virtuous, chaste and obedient, Tamora is 'barbarous', 'most insatiate and luxurious woman' (V.i.88) and a 'siren' (II.i.23). Lavinia is enclosed by Roman patriarchy: king, father, brothers, husband, nephew; Tamora challenges it: militarily (by waging a war against Rome), sexually (by marrying and manipulating its ruler and maintaining a lover), and racially (because she and her lover are both 'barbarous'). Appropriately she becomes the agent of Lavinia's destruction, along with the 'irreligious Moor, / Chief architect and plotter of these woes' (V.iii.121-2). Tamora's sons are wicked because of their mother: 'O, do not learn her wrath – she taught it thee . . . Even at her teat thou had'st her tyranny' (II.iii.143-5). But Tamora is no simple image of maternal destructiveness. She combines the attributes of the warrior woman – masculine prowess, military skill – and of the Amazon – usurping of male authority, sexual promiscuity (see Shepherd, *Amazons*). She is both the epitome of stereotypical female duplicity and the converse of stereotypical female subservience.

Both Tamora and Aaron become embodiments of pure evil; the supposedly uncontrollable sexuality of women and blacks motivates their liaison. Aaron's blackness makes here honour

> . . . of his body's hue,
> Spotted, detested and abominable.
> Why are you sequest'red from all your train,
> Dismounted from your snow-white goodly steed,
> And wand'red hither to an obscure plot,
> Accompanied but with a barbarous Moor,
> If foul desire had not conducted you? (II.iii.73-9)

Their child is accordingly a 'devil', 'as loathsome as a toad / Amongst the fair-fac'd breeders of our clime' (IV.ii.67-8). At the end of the play, evil is exposed and purged through the literal expulsion of Aaron and Tamora. He is to be walled up and starved, while she must be thrown 'to beasts and birds of prey' (V.iii.198). Lavinia, the compliant woman is, by contrast, to be embraced in the bosom of the civilised world and 'closed in our household's monument' (V.iii.194). But passive as she is, her rape has made her too impure to live.

Thus evil is officially located outside Roman patriarchy. But we are reminded that Rome itself is 'a wilderness of tigers' (III.i.54); that Tamora's reign of terror is unleashed after she becomes 'incorporate in Rome, / A Roman now adopted happily' (I.i.462-3); that Titus himself 'threw the people's suffrages/ On him that doth tyrannize o'er me' (IV.iii.19-20); that Tamora at one level merely revenged Titus for what he did to her son. Moreover, Aaron occasionally strains his stereotype. Whereas both Tamora and Titus are responsible for their children's deaths, the black man, stereotypically denied human emotions, barters his own life to ensure his son's safety. What is more important, it is while defending his child that Aaron 'momentarily becomes a representative of his race, protesting against prejudice' (Cowhig, p. 3). He claims to be better than his white adversaries: 'ye sanguine, shallow hearted boys! / Ye white lim'd walls! Ye alehouse painted signs' and asserts that 'coal black is better than another hue' (IV.ii.97-9). Thus even in this play the apparently secure stereotypes of black barbarity and female deviance are, although marginally, opened out. In Othello, I shall suggest, common-sense ideas about blacks are evoked but more clearly questioned, disclosed as misrepresentation. And, crucially, this disclosure is closely interwoven with the disturbance to patriarchal authority.

Racism / patriarchalism

I will locate a movement which is precisely the opposite of the one seen by Fiedler and will trace Othello's passage from an honorary white to a total outsider, a movement that depends on the impact of both racial and sexual difference.[6] In other words, Othello moves from being a colonised subject existing on the terms of white Venetian society and trying to internalise its ideology, towards being marginalised, outcast and alienated from it in every way, until he occupies his 'true' position as its other. His precarious entry into the white world is ruptured by his relation with Desdemona, which was intended to secure it in the first place, and which only catalyses the contradictions in Othello's self-conception. So instead of the unified subject of humanist thought, we have a near schizophrenic hero whose last speech graphically portrays the split – he becomes simultaneously the Christian and the Infidel, the Venetian and the Turk, the keeper of the State and its opponent. At the same time, Desdemona passes from being his ally who would guarantee his white status to becoming his sexual and racial 'other'. As will be discussed later, she too is a split, inconsistent subject and occupies not one but various positions in the play, not only as Othello's 'other' but also that of the Venetian patriarchy.

The 'central conflict' of the play then, if we must locate one, is neither between white and black alone, nor merely between men and women – it is rather between the racism of a white patriarchy and the threat posed to it by both a black man and a white woman. But these two are not simply aligned against white patriarchy, since their own relation cannot be abstracted from sexual or racial tension. Othello is not merely a black man who is jealous, but a man whose jealousy and blackness are inseparable. Similarly, Desdemona's initial boldness and later submission are not discordant in the context of her positions as a white woman and a white *woman*. There is thus a tripartite and extremely complex relationship between black man, white woman and the state.

In the first 125 lines of the play, racist images of Othello's blackness abound – he is 'thick lips', 'old black ram', 'a Barbary horse', 'devil' and 'a lascivious Moor'. It is significant that, unlike Aaron's case, these images are evoked almost exclusively in the context of his contact with a white woman, which transforms the latent racism of Venetian society into Brabantio's virulent anger and Iago's disgust. From honoured guest to that of an inhuman Othello becomes 'such a thing as thou' (I.ii.71) whose liaison is 'against all rules of nature' (I.iii.101) (see Cowhig, p. 8). Brabantio's conviction that Othello has used magic to win her at once dislodges Othello to the status of a barbaric outsider, an animal whom he claims his daughter was afraid to look upon. Here Othello is associated with an activity with overwhelmingly female connotations i.e. witchcraft. Cleopatra too, it may be recalled, is accused of magically enchanting Antony. But Cleopatra's feminine wiles are specifically linked to her being an Egyptian and we are reminded that sorcery is repeatedly constructed as being an uncivilised and un-Christian activity as well; in themselves Othello and Cleopatra cannot be sexually attractive.

Constructing the other

Othello is a Moor, but there is no real clarity as to his precise origins despite references to his being sold in slavery and to his unChristian past. Debates over whether Othello was black, brown or mulatto anxiously tried to recover the possibility of his whiteness from this ambiguity which, on the contrary, alerts us to the very construction of the 'other' in Orientalist and colonial discourses. While we must recognise that each non-white race or group has an individual identity, a uniformity is conferred upon them by their common differentiation from white civilisation. Robinson notes that 'prior to the eleventh or twelfth centuries the use of the collective sense of the term barbarian was primarily a function of exclusion rather than a reflection of any significant consolidation among these peoples' (p. 10). Thus, to consider Othello as a black man is not to gloss over the textual confusion but to concur with Fanon that colonial discourse itself erases differentiation between its various subjects and treats all outsiders as black; while locating its racism therefore, we need to stress the common exclusion of its 'others', whose political colour rather than precise shade of non-whiteness is what matters.

The conversion of the outsider to the service of dominant culture is a crucial feature of the European encounter with other peoples. Hence the alien must also be incorporated (Said, *Orientalism*, p. 71). Othello is valuable as a Christian warrior, or the exotic colonial subject in the service of the state. In the Senate scene, the Venetian patriarchy displays an amazing capacity to variously construct, co-opt and exclude its 'others'. Brabantio is certain that the Senate will back his opposition to Othello's marriage, and if it appears strange (or remarkably liberal) that they don't, we need only to recall their concern with the Turkish threat. Othello the warrior is strategically included as one of 'us' as opposed to the Turkish 'they': 'You must therefore be content to slubber the gloss of your new fortunes with this more stubborn and boisterous expedition' (I.iii.227-8).

Iago's famous 'motiveless malignity' (as Coleridge called it) according to Greenblatt still 'remains opaque' (*Renaissance Self-Fashioning*, p. 236). This is partly because many of Iago's statements are often regarded as irrational, and as evidence of his almost mythic, hardly human wickedness. The following passage is often cited as an example of such illogical behaviour:

> . . . Now I do love her too;
> Not out of absolute lust, though peradventure
> I stand accountant for as great a sin
> But partly led to diet my revenge,
> For that I do suspect the lustful Moor
> Hath leap'd into my seat; the thought whereof
> Doth like a poisonous mineral gnaw my inwards;
> And nothing can, nor shall content my soul
> Till I am even'd with him, wife for wife . . . (II.i.285-93)

In what sense does Iago love Desdemona? Does he really suspect Emilia with Othello? Rather than confusion of motive, the passage illustrates the way in which sexual desire is expressive of a power struggle, here in a specifically racist context. Iago 'loves' Desdemona in the same way as Ferdinand loves his sister, the Duchess of Malfi. In the latter case, erotic desire, brotherly possessiveness and male authoritarianism blend as expressions of aristocratic bonding, and of protection of state and family power. Similarly Iago's 'love' speaks of a racial and patriarchal bonding whereby he becomes the 'protector' of all white women from black men. More specifically, as a white woman, Desdemona belongs to him rather than to Othello. Such possessiveness over all white women is also reflected in the fear (rationalised as 'suspicion') of losing his wife to Othello.

As Cowhig indicates, Iago's disgust at Desdemona's choice reveals an almost phobic racist horror:

Not to affect many proposed matches,
Of her own clime, complexion and degree
Whereto we see in all things nature tends –
Foh! one may smell in such a will most rank,
Foul disproportion, *thoughts unnatural*. (III.iii.233-7; emphasis added)

This interchange between Iago and Othello allows us to see that the 'naturalness' which dominant ideologies invoke to legitimise themselves, and which is central to common-sense thinking generally, is a flexible category. For Othello, seeking to efface his own blackness through Desdemona's love, a patriarchal view of female constancy as 'natural' is necessary. Therefore for him Desdemona's supposed dishonesty becomes 'nature erring from itself' (III.iii.231). But Iago reinterprets erring nature to define Desdemona as a white woman, whose love for and constancy to Othello is 'unnatural'. So he yokes together stereotypical notions of both 'black' as repulsive and 'female' as ever-capable of unnatural transgressions.

As Lawrence correctly points out, whereas the rapes of black women by white men were seen as a sort of favour to the black race, the mating of white women with black men was regarded as fatal. Whereas the first extended the power of the white man over all women, the latter eroded his own territory, and allowed for the possibility of its 'invasion'. In the Indian context, British (and other colonial) men indulged in widespread sexual liaisons with (including rapes of) Indian women as a matter of course. But the horrors of British women taking on Indian lovers are obsessively foregrounded in literature as diverse as Forster's *A Passage to India*, Paul Scott's *The Raj Quartet* and Jhabvala's *Heat and Dust*; they persist as a feature of contemporary racism: 'in Britain today, the question is never: would you allow your son to marry a black girl? It is always: would you allow your daughter to marry a black man?' (Lawrence, 'Just plain common-sense', p. 72). Such a nexus of the fears evoked by black and active female sexuality is responsible for engendering the extreme horrors of *Titus Andronicus*, where it results in racial pollution. From Elizabeth I's communiqué deporting blacks, referred to earlier, to today's British immigration laws, the 'preservation' of the white race is seen to be at stake. Fanon offered a psychoanalytical explanation for this fear, pointing out that racist phobia always reduces the black man to his sexual potential: 'the father revolts because in his opinion the Negro will introduce his daughter into a sexual universe for which the father does not have the key, the weapons, or the attributes' (p. 165).

So what is especially threatening for white patriarchy is the possibility of the complicity of white women; their desire for black lovers is feared, forbidden, but always imminent. The spectre of a combined black and female insubordination 'threatens to undermine white manhood and the Empire at a stroke' (Lawrence, p. 64). The effort then becomes to project the white woman's desire as provoked by the animalistic lust of the black man, a notion which is traceable as far back as the fifteenth century in Europe and much earlier in India. The myth of the black rapist is even more useful, for it perpetuates black animalism while obliterating female agency, and thus simultaneously 'erases' the two most problematic areas for patriarchal racism – the humanity of the alien race and the active sexuality of women.

Even if she is passive, however, the white woman's contact with the alien male pollutes her. In chapter 6, the black man's supposed rapacity will be further discussed in the context of The Tempest. But in Othello the problem arises precisely because Othello is not a rapist and Desdemona is not an unwilling victim of his sexual assault. Their desire cannot be contained within the myth of the black rapist. In spite of this, Iago's racism and his misogyny together make him confident that the 'relation between an erring barbarian and a super-subtle Venetian' can be easily disrupted (I.iii.356).

'Haply for I am black'

Othello is described in terms of the characteristics popularly attributed to blacks during the sixteenth century: sexual potency, courage, pride, guilelessness, credulity, easily aroused passions; these become central and persistent features of later colonial stereotyping as well, as I remarked in the first chapter. At the beginning of the play he is seemingly well entrenched in and accepted by Venetian society – an honorary white, whose hyperbolic speech is an attempt to speak better than any the language of his adoptive civilisation (see Serpieri, p. 142). The vulnerability of his entry prompts him to reiterate his intrinsic merits, his lineage and his achievements; he appears confident that these will match

Brabantio's racism:

> My services which I have done the signiory
> Shall out-tongue his complaints . . . (I.ii.18-19)

Othello needs to believe that 'my parts, my title and my perfect soul / Shall manifest me rightly' (I.ii.31-2). He is to discover that the dominant ideology encouraged by his adoptive society, especially the notion of the power and indestructible essence of the individual, is doubly illusory when your skin is black.

But if Othello is not archetypal man, neither is he simply *any* black man. The drama of racial difference is played out on spaces already occupied by divisions of class. He is involved in the process of social mobility and self-fashioning as are others around him, but on somewhat different terms. Brecht rightly pointed out that

he doesn't only possess Desdemona, he also possesses a post as general, which he has not inherited as a feudal general would, but won by outstanding achievements, and presumably snatched from someone else; he must defend it or it will be snatched from him. He lives in a world of fighting for property and position, and his relationship with the woman he loves develops as a property relationship. (quoted Heinemann, p. 217)

Iago is jealous of Cassio's preferment, and also of Othello, who is more successful in their common pursuit of status. Iago gains considerable wealth from duping Roderigo: 'I have wasted myself out of my means. The jewels you have had from me to deliver to Desdemona would half have corrupted a votarist' (IV.ii.186-88).

However, class differences cannot be sealed off from others, as Stuart Hall has pointed out in the context of contemporary Britain: 'Race', he says, 'is the modality in which class relations are experienced' (quoted Gilroy, p. 276). Applied to *Othello*, this illuminates the profound invasion, intensification and alteration of class or gender relations by race. Iago's jealousy of Cassio's advancement does not become deflected into hatred for Othello, as is sometimes supposed. Rather, each breeds the other, for Othello is the racial inferior who is socially superior, the outsider who has become the means of Iago's own preferment. Greenblatt has persuasively and correctly argued that Iago's ability to improvise and control events and the lives of others should be located as an effect of colonial ideology which seeks to 'sustain indefinitely indirect enslavement' by moulding the psyche of the oppressed (Greenblatt, *Renaissance Self-Fashioning*, p. 229). But we need to add that such an ideology is not just generally imbibed but shaped and spurred by Iago's specific experience of racial hatred.

Desdemona is both her father's 'jewel' (I.iii.195) and her husband's 'purchase' (II.iii.9). As the guarantee of her husband's upward mobility, she is similar to Bianca (*Women Beware Women*). But unlike the latter, Desdemona is also the gate to white humanity. Slowly his conception of his own worth comes to centre in the fact that she chose him over all the 'curl'd darlings' of Venice. Her desire for him – 'for she had eyes, and chose me' (III.iii.193) – replaces his heritage or exploits as proof and measure of his worth. It thus becomes the primary signifier of his identity; that is why 'my life upon her faith' (I.iii. 294) and 'when I love thee not, / Chaos is come again' (III.iii.92-3). That is why if she loves him not, 'Farewell! Othello's occupation's gone' (III.iii.361). Frantz Fanon's description of the encounter between the black man and white woman, although somewhat reductive of female sexuality, illuminates this aspect of Othello's desire:

Out of the blackest part of my soul, across the zebra striping of my mind, surges this desire to be suddenly white ... who but a white woman can do this for me? By loving me she proves that I am worthy of white love. I am loved like a white man.
    I am a white man ... I marry white culture, white beauty, white whiteness.
    When my restless hands caress those white breasts, they grasp white civilization and dignity and make them mine. (p. 63)[7]

At the same time, we must remember that Othello actually emphasises his difference in order to bridge it and win Desdemona. His 'magic' consists of invoking his exotic otherness, his cultural and religious differences as well as his heroic exploits, which involve strange peoples and territories. He oscillates between asserting his non-European glamour and denying his blackness, emphasising through speech and social position his assimilation into white culture. He is thus hopelessly split; as Homi Bhabha writes in relation to Fanon's split subject: 'black skins, white masks is not ... a neat division; it is a doubling, dissembling image of being in at least two places at once which makes it impossible for the devalued ... to accept the colonizer's invitation to identity' ('Introduction', p. xvi).

Desdemona's disobedience

The erosion of Desdemona's power and assertiveness has already been presented as central to evaluations of the play. Fiedler characteristically calls it the power of the 'white witch'; Tennenhouse desribes it as 'the power to speak the language of the law, which in turn gives her the power to give her own body in marriage' (*Power on Display*, p. 125). Greenblatt, by contrast, locates it in her very submission to desire which

arouses sexual tension in Othello (*Renaissance Self-Fashioning*, p. 250).
I suggest that Desdemona's disobedience and later submission are both
related to the shifting positions she occupies in relation to Othello, and
to the contradictions that they impose upon her. Cowhig insightfully
locates Desdemona's love in the context of a white woman's fantasies
for the exotic male:

> . . . is she not more attracted to the exotic myth of 'otherness' than to the real
> man? Given the enormous popularity of travel books among white women (the
> Earl of Shaftesbury in 1710 was to lament the fact that 'a thousand Desdemonas
> were so obsessed with stories of African men that they would readily abandon
> husbands, families and country itself to 'follow the fortunes of a hero of the
> black tribe'), can we not say that Desdemona was an early travel book 'fanatic'?
> (p. 13)

If we are not to subscribe to the usual myths about female propensity
for 'romance', however, the susceptibility of Desdemona and her sisters
(for example, later figures such as Hardy's Tess) to the proverbial outsider must be viewed in the additional context of the confinement of
the woman and the increasing restriction of her mobility and freedom.
If Iago's 'love' for Desdemona and Ferdinand's for the Duchess are
emblematic of the desire to 'protect' race, property and power through
the enclosure of the woman, Desdemona's fascination conversely indicates her desire to break the claustrophobic patriarchal confine. Travel,
adventure, and freedom being male domains, she first wishes 'that
heaven had made her such a man' and then begins to love Othello 'for
the dangers I had pass'd' (I.iii.163, 167). Projected on to the outsider
are all the fantasies of freedom and love, both of which are unable to
be even visualised from within her world. It is true that Desdemona
only invokes the right to owe duty to her husband and not her own
autonomy. But in so doing she defies patriarchal control over her
desires. Desdemona's eroticism is particularly disturbing in its explicit
and frank avowal of the 'downright violence' of her passion and her
claim to 'the rites for why I love him' (I.iii.248, 252; see also Greenblatt,
Renaissance Self-Fashioning, p. 250).

Tennenhouse underlines the connections between sexual relations
and the political body of Elizabethan and Jacobean England: 'Desdemona poses a specifically Jacobean assault on monarchy when she
assumes authority over her body and persuades the senate to assert the
priority of a contractual relationship over and against the will of the
patriarch' (*Power on Display*, p. 127). The early modern state was not only
increasingly misogynist but made explicit the usefulness of patriarchalism for tightening its authoritarian controls. State legislation
strengthened the household as an instrument of social control, and laws

against every category of potentially deviant people – the poor, vagrants, prostitutes, witches and even alternative religious orders – attempted to sweep the population within the boundaries of the household and strengthen the authority of the father (Hill, *Society and Puritanism*; Stone, *The Family*, Kelly, *Women, History, Theory*). The consolidation of the state involved a consolidation of the family as its primary unit: 'the word "father" is an epitome of the whole gospel' (Thomas, p. 319). Gordon Schochet has pointed out that social hierarchies were explained in terms of natural or divinely sanctioned status and political authority, understood in terms of the patriarchal theory of obligation. The parent-child relationship served the precise function of making governance intelligible and 'all that had to be done was to expand the experienced and comprehensible and therefore acceptable category of relationships subsumed under the parent-child rubric to include that between ruler and subject' (p. 439). Hence James I argued that 'By the Law of Nature the King becomes a naturall Father to all his Lieges at his Coronation' (p. 55).

Tennenhouse is therefore right in concluding that 'if Jacobean drama proves one thing . . . it is that sexual relations are always political' and that Desdemona's desire is politically subversive. At the same time, I am uncomfortable with his intention to '*dissolve* the sexual theme into those (thematics) which . . . determined the components of Jacobean drama and the nature of their relationship: Kingship versus kinship; natural versus metaphysical bodies of power; the signs and symbols of state versus the exercise of state power' (*Power on Display*, pp. 123-4). For if sexual relations are political only in the way that the non-sexual is, their very specificity is denied. As Gerda Lerner put it, 'all analogies – class, group, caste – approximate the position of women but fail to define it adequately. Women are a category unto themselves; an adequate analysis of their position in society demands new conceptual tools' (quoted Kelly, p. 6). The sexual theme can be contextualised but not dissolved, and the analogy of the wife-husband or child-father relation to that of subject and king cannot explain the entirety of Renaissance gender relations. Active female sexuality is disruptive of patriarchal control, not just because it is an emblem for, or analogous to, other sorts of rebellion, but because it directly threatens the power base of patriarchy which is dependent upon its regulation and control.

I will emphasise again that Desdemona's desire is especially transgressive because its object is black, which Tennenhouse ignores and Greenblatt underplays. If Desdemona is the most explicitly erotic and sensual of Shakespeare's heroines, it is precisely because her choice is seen as 'unnatural', not only by Iago and Brabantio (and even, naggingly, by Othello himself), but also, most probably, by the audience. Her expressions of love do not unambiguously confirm their suspicions about female response to black men because they also shatter the assumption that black men need to force their attentions on white women.

In the senate scene, while Desdemona is surprisingly bold and explicit for a modest maiden facing the Venetian state, Othello finds it necessary to deny 'the palate of my appetite'. I would agree with Cowhig that 'these speeches relate directly to Othello's colour. Desdemona has made it clear that his "sooty bosom" is no obstacle to desire; while Othello must defend himself against the unspoken accusations, of the audience as well as of the senators, because of the association of sexual lust with blackness' (p. 10). At the end of the scene, Othello is exonerated from the sexual slur and accordingly pronounced an honorary white: 'your son in law is far more fair than black' (I.iii.290).

Consider also the meeting of the lovers at Cyprus after the storm. Othello would happily die in order to arrest the perfection of their meeting for 'not another comfort like to this/ Succeeds in unknown fate' (II.i.190-1; emphasis added). Desdemona's reply, on the contrary, optimistically looks forward: 'our loves and comforts should increase / Even as our days do grow'. For Neely, this is evidence of her greater realism, and more generally, of greater female maturity in sexual relationships. I prefer to see it, at least partly, as an indication of her greater confidence, which Othello, as a black man, cannot share. His words betray an insecurity which has already been catalysed by Braban-tio's reaction; his present 'wonder' and 'joy' are partially compounded of disbelief at actually possessing her just as his desire to revel in the moment betrays uncertainty about the future.

Desdemona's power, then, is the confidence of both race and class – of an upper class Venetian beauty, secure in the attentions of men around her and in the advantages of her position. She shares something here with the confidence of Beatrice-Joanna in Middleton's The Changeling (see chapter 4). Desdemona's persistence on Cassio's behalf, for exam-ple, reflects an upbringing where women are taught that their power lies in their ability to cajole and chide men into favouring them. Her initial confidence in her own persuasiveness and her methods, coquet-tishly insistent, owe something to the illusion of female power in the ethic of courtly love. This slowly gives way to the more sobering reality of the power of the husband over the wife, a power that Othello asserts despite his blackness, or is it because of it? Away from the world in which she has grown up, Desdemona becomes less assured and confi-dent. Her transformation from a woman who confronts both her father and the Venetian Senate to the wife who submits to her husband's insults is not a result of truly feminine love but a manifestation of the contradictions imposed upon her by a racist, patriarchal and bourgeois society.

It is important, of course, to guard against reading dramatic characters as real, three dimensional people. But, as Alan Sinfield says, Desdemona seems even more discontinuous than Othello because she is 'less a developing consciousness than a series of positions that women are conventionally supposed to occupy . . . (She) makes sense not as a continuous subjectivity . . . but in terms of the stories about "woman" that were and are told in patriarchal ideology' ('*Othello*', pp. 20-2). Female inconsistency (which I deal with at length in chapter 4) is a complex amalgam of being 'scripted by men' (the phrase is Sinfield's), not only literally, in the plays, but generally, in patriarchal society.

Desdemona's obedience

Othello needs to encourage Desdemona's sexual freedom up to the point that it ensures his own mobility but also subsequently to curb it. He is proud of her speech in the beginning of the play, for it confers a power and a legitimacy on him. Later he smothers her voice, for she must speak and move on his behalf only and not when it is suspected that he is not the object of her passion – 'O curse of marriage, / That we can call these delicate creatures ours, / And not their appetites' (III.iii.272-4). This is not a general male dilemma however: if we take into account the importance of Desdemona for Othello's entire existence in white society, then the power of the misogynist idea of the changeability, duplicity and frailty of women to rouse and disturb Othello and his vulnerability to Iago's tales of female inconstancy become clearer. He has begun to feel the limits of self-fashioning for a black man in a white world.

At each point that women's frailty is impressed upon Othello, it is in conjunction with his own blackness. Brabantio is the first to plant the possibility of Desdemona's duplicity in Othello's mind ('She has deceiv'd her father and may thee', I.iii.293) which is picked up by Iago later;

> She did deceive her father, marrying you;
> And when she seem'd to shake and fear your looks,
> She lov'd them most. (III.iii.210-12)

The interweaving of misogyny and racism in Iago's later speeches cannot be missed. Women, in his opinion, are capable of the most unnatural acts, such as loving black men, and the greatest fickleness, such as ceasing to love them. By asking Othello to acknowledge this he both questions

Othello's humanity and appeals to his manhood: 'Are you a man? Have ✕
you a soul or sense?' (III.iii.378); 'Would you would bear your fortune
like a man'; 'Good sir, be a man'; 'Marry, patience; / Or I shall say you ✕
are all in all in spleen / And nothing of a man' (IV.i.61, 65, 87-9). The
more he questions Othello's humanity, the more he appeals to his masculine power over women. Promising to kill Cassio, he begs Othello to ✕
'let her live', although Othello has up to that time never hinted at killing
Desdemona. Just as Othello's white identity was dependent upon
Desdemona's love, his destruction of her involves a belief in women's
frailty which helps him 'rationalise' her supposed infidelity. Desdemona
begins to embody the common patriarchal dichotomy of the white
devil. For Othello, this is the only way to yoke together the otherwise
contradictory experiences of being black and a man. Therefore
Desdemona's schisms are deepened as Othello's are, even though one
seeks to heal itself at the expense of the other.

Greenblatt accounts for Othello's vulnerability to Iago's narrative by
referring to the guilt that Christian orthodoxy imposes upon all forms
of passion or sexual pleasure and specifically excluding racial difference:
'Nothing *conflicts* openly with Christian orthodoxy, but the erotic inten-
sity that informs every word is experienced in tension with it. *The tension is less a manifestation of some atavistic "blackness" specific to Othello than a
manifestation of the colonial power of Christian doctrine over sexuality*' (pp. 241-2;
emphasis added). Why should Christianity, an adoptive religion for
Othello, inform his psyche more fundamentally than the blackness
which pervades every aspect of his history and identity? On the contrary,
sexual guilt (possibly including that conferred by Christianity) is rooted
in and intensified by a colour consciousness. Thus Othello begins to
subscribe to what we may see as a Christian patriarchal view of woman
as deceiver and sinful, but because of, not over and above, his blackness.

Evident in the imagery of black and white is Othello's internalisation
of his own inferiority as well as the wickedness of women. As his position
as honorary white erodes, Desdemona becomes the honorary black;
her duplicity makes her 'a subtle whore, / A closet-lock-and-key of
villainous secrets' (IV.i.21-3) as well as 'begrim'd and black / As my own
face' (III.iii.391-2). In the speech at Desdemona's bedside, the whiteness
of her skin makes it both necessary and difficult to kill her – necessary
because her beauty makes it possible that 'she'll betray more men'
(V.ii.6) and therefore Othello must act on behalf of all men (including,
ironically, Brabantio), thus 'transcending' his colour to become, in his
view, a sort of everyman; difficult because it is still the signifier of all
that is desirable to Othello, and all that he cannot have, reminding him
that he cannot be everyman. Desdemona, or rather, what she represents

and what she is made to represent by Iago, thus makes Othello alternate
between two definitions of his own identity – he is a man in relation to
her femininity and black in relation to her whiteness. The contradictions
should be kept in mind when we view his necrophiliac fantasy to 'kill
thee,/ And love thee after' (V.i.17-8).

Alongside the sexual tension the play charts Othello's increasing racial
isolation. As his precarious integration into white society vanishes he
becomes more obviously the alien (critics have often noted the upsurge
of his non-European past, his pagan history), and more alone and isolated; it becomes even more obvious that he is also the only black
around. Compare the confident Othello of the senate scene to the lonely
figure of the last scene, desperately recalling his services to the state,
and unlike Hamlet or Antony, delivering his own eulogy. As already
noted, his last words graphically capture the split of his identity into
Christian and infidel – he becomes the 'circumcised dog' that he once
killed. The Turk's crime was that he 'beat a Venetian and traduc'd the
state' (V.ii.357). Thus even a last picture of the time when he could act
on behalf of white society, as one of 'us' cannot be simply evoked but
is slashed by his position as outsider. The flimsily put together zebra-
striping of his mind disintegrates into its constituent polarity of black
and white.

Lonely figure, yes, but he is also the murderer of his wife. An opposition of male to female, as feminist critics have pointed out, is most
clearly articulated by Emilia:

> They are all but stomachs, and we all but food;
> They eat us hungerly, and when they are full,
> They belch us. (III.iv.105-7)

But to prioritise this, to set up an uncomplicated opposition between
the world of men and the world of women, the former being 'political,
loveless and undomesticated' (Neely, p. 215), would contribute to the
rupture posited in patriarchal thought between private and public, political and domestic. The world of men is itself deeply divided, as indeed
is the world of women. Moreover, racist innuendoes inform even the
most casual moments of the play:

> If she be black, and thereto have a wit,
> She'll find a white that shall her blackness hit. (II.i.132-3)

Who is 'the patriarchy' or 'the authority' in the play – Iago, Othello,
Brabantio, the Senate? If it is all of them, what do we make of the tensions
between them? If Othello the patriarch triumphs, what of Othello the
black man who disintegrates? *Othello* should neither be read as a patri-

archal, authoritarian and racist spectacle, nor as a show of fer
black superiority. Iago has often been seen as related to the Vice figu.
in a morality play. Unlike the morality Vice however, he does not simply
challenge accepted morality but is also the spokesperson for racist and
patriarchal platitudes. His position as a sort of mediator between audience and action and his oft-commented upon role as producer of the
play within the play are crucial. He undoubtedly articulates many of the
viewers' common sense attitudes, and hence even while his plot offends
them, it seeks their complicity. As Peter Stallybrass says, Iago's narrative
is believed by others 'not because Iago is superhumanly ingenious but,
to the contrary, because his is the voice of "common sense", the ceaseless
repetition of the always-already "known", the culturally "given"' ('Patriarchal Territories', p. 139). Jean E. Howard has made the same point in
relation to Don John in *Much Ado about Nothing*, who, like Iago, is often
seen to be constructing the plot and manipulating the characters of the
play. His trick of substituting Margaret for Hero at the bedroom window
'silently assumes and further circulates the idea that women are universally prone to deception and impersonation . . . Don John lies about
Hero, but his lie works because it easily passes in Messina as a truthful
reading of women' (Howard, 'Renaissance antitheatricality', pp. 174-5).

Therefore, not merely Iago's, or Brabantio's, but the audience's
assumed responses are under scrutiny. At one level, the stereotypical
is upheld, for Desdemona is duplicitous and Othello is barbarous. But
the play is open to a radical and alternative reading precisely because it
unravels and problematises these stereotypes by laying bare the process
of their construction. We then get a view of duplicity and barbarity as
ideological constructs rather than natural aspects of women or black
people.

Ben Okri became painfully aware of Othello's colour during a production in London's Barbican:

> It was the first time I had seen it performed on stage. I was the only black person
> in the audience. The seats beside me were occupied by three white girls. They
> noisily crackled their packets of sweets and giggled a lot. I wanted to tell them
> to be quiet. But I suspected that if I spoke faces would turn towards me. After
> a while I couldn't bear it any longer. When I spoke what I feared happened.
> Faces turned, eyes lit up in recognition. My skin glowed. I felt myself illuminated,
> unable to hide.
>
> I used to agree with C. L. R. James that *Othello* is not a play about race . . . If it
> did not begin as a play also about race, then its history has made it one. (pp. 562-3)

This history has been varied: Martin Orkin has recently shown how
'in South Africa, silence about the prevailing racist tendencies in *Othello*
actually supports racist doctrine and practice' ('Othello and the plain

face of racism', p. 166). Orkin places the continuing prescription, for South African students, of the Arden edition of the play, with Ridley's notoriously racist introduction, in the context of the apartheid state (*Shakespeare Against Apartheid*, p. 107). Surely the fact that it is also the standard text in India, as is Kermode's edition of *The Tempest* (see chapter 6) cannot be viewed as an accident. Nor is it inconsequential that African students are the butt of racist jokes in Delhi. In India, the assumption often is that we are outside racist structures, even while our own brands of colour prejudice, which are complexly intertwined with caste, regional and class differences, and which have been deepened by the colonial encounter, not only flourish but are being intensified. Many of the common-sense notions that have been identified in white racism would be closely echoed in the instance of an inter-caste marriage in India. Finally, the patriarchalism of Indian society does not stand outside its own history of colour consciousness.[8] Instead of allowing it to become a means of confirmation of these attitudes, *Othello* must be seized as a point from which we may examine and dismantle the racism and the sexism which both our own hegemonic ideologies and years of colonial education have persuaded us to adopt.

Notes

1 Kishwar and Vanita's *In Search of Answers* includes many accounts of contemporary violence against women in India. See also Mies, *Patriarchy and Accumulation* for an analysis of how older customs are given a modern revival and intersect with 'modern' practices. For a report on persecution of women as witches in Bihar see *Hindustan Times*, 11 October 1987. Recently, an eighteen year old Rajput girl was burnt on her husband's pyre in Deorala, Rajasthan, while thousands of people watched. Later many more collected for a festival at the site and money poured in to build a temple there. Fierce protests by women's organisations were countered by revivalist processions, meetings and publications. Hindu revivalists have been contending that abolition of sati amounts to a violation of an individual's rights and therefore also of a woman's freedom. Under the guise of sophisticated sociological analysis, there has also been the argument that sati is being opposed today only by a westernised section of the Indian intelligentsia who do not understand India, her customs or their spirit. Kishwar and Vanita's article, 'The burning of Roop Kanwar', shows how sati is not just a simple revival of an ancient practice, but ties in with dominant political and economic interests. It also discusses how, despite its promulgation of new anti-sati legislation, the Indian government has failed to, and is not interested in, dealing with the issue.

2 I am indebted to Cowhig's essay; despite the fact than she concentrates on the neglect of race in *Othello* criticism, whenever she does mention gender relations she relates them to racial politics. I am also indebted to Errol Lawrence's analysis of common-sense racist assumptions, which, along with Fanon, illuminates several aspects of the play.

3 Both views, then – of Othello as an archetypal man and as a black man – are premised upon racist notions of black inferiority. We might assume that crudity such as Ridley's is somewhat passé, but its assumptions are traceable in more sophisticated accounts. Fiedler, for example, ends up asserting Othello's essential, moral whiteness and Iago's

status as the true black. Ridley's arguments, although in other respects very different, similarly oscillate between rescuing Othello from the status of a black (he may be African but is he altogether negroid?), arguing for his inherent inferiority (he is somewhat deficient in reason and intellect though a warm, loving, instinctual creature), and thoroughly ignoring Desdemona (he evaluates her worth by the dignity with which she faces men who have seen her publicly struck).

4 Karen Newman's article, "'And wash the Ethiop white'" and Martin Orkin's book, *Shakespeare Against Apartheid* both make significant departures (in different directions) from previous criticism of the play. I saw them at a very late stage in the production of this project, so I am unable to comment on them fully. Newman's article is unique in beginning to interrelate racial and sexual difference, and Orkin brings together the contexts of production and reception – so both together discuss many of my own concerns here. I differ from Orkin's assessment of the Venetian Senate: 'no evidence emerges in the detail of the language to suggest that they share a hidden racist disapprobation of Othello (p. 65). I also think that to say that 'Othello, Desdemona and Cassio seek only love and honor in the play' (p. 88) is to gloss over the ways in which they are themselves 'flawed' by the racial structures; we need to guard against viewing any of them as simple oppositions to a racist Iago.

Even otherwise radical critics have not purged their language of the racist moral connotations commonly attached to colour: Greenblatt, for example, speaks of the 'dark essence of Iago's whole enterprise' or the 'unfathomable darkness of human motives' (*Renaissance Self-Fashioning*, pp. 233, 251). It should be noted tht such 'slips' coexist with an explicit devaluation of race as a theoretical parameter, which I will discuss shortly. Eagleton's discussion of the play (*William Shakespeare*) takes almost no account of Othello's colour.

5 Elizabeth's communiqué (quoted by Cowhig, p. 6) reads:

An open warrant to the Lord maiour of London and to all Vice-Admyralls, Maiours and other publicke officers whatsoever to whom yt may appertaine. Whereas Casper van Senden, a merchant of Lubeck, did by his labor and travell procure 89 of her Majesty's subjects that were detayned prisoners in Spaine and Portugall to be released, and brought them hither into this realme at his owne cost and charges, for the which his expenses and declaration of his honest minde towards those prisoners he would desireth to have lycense to take up so much blackamoores here in this realme and to transport them into Spaine and Portugall. Her Majesty in regard to the charitable affection the suppliant hath showed being a stranger, to worke the delivery of our countrymen that were there in great great misery and thraldom and to bring them home to their native country, and that the same could not be done without great expense, and also considering the reasonableness of his requestes to transport so many blackamoores from hence, doth thincke yt a very good exchange and that those kinde of people may well be spared in this realme, being so populous and numbers of hable persons the subjects of the land and Christian people that perishe for want of service, whereby through their labor they might be mayntained. They are therefore in their Lordship's name required to aide and assist him to take up suche blackamoores as he shall finde within this realme with the consent of their masters, who we doubt not, considering her Majesty's good pleasure to have those kinde of people sent out of her lande and the good deserving of the stranger towardes her Majesty's subjectes, and that they shall doe charitably and like Christians rather to be served by their owne countrymen then with those kinde of people, will yielde those in their possession to him.

6 I use the term 'honorary black' following Alison Heisch's phrase 'honorary male' in relation to Elizabeth I. Heisch, in her essay, 'Queen Elizabeth I and the persistence of patriarchy', argues that Elizabeth strengthened patriarchal rule by emphasising her masculine attributes; I am suggesting that Othello stresses his usefulness to white society,

his adoption of its rules of conduct, his achievements, which make him acceptable in order to efface the negative connotations of blackness, in the same way that Elizabeth needed to claim that she had a heart and stomach of a king even though she had the body of a woman.

7 I use this comment with some reservations; it needs to be carefully and selectively used for the idea that black men's inferiority has resulted in all of them lusting after any white woman has been used to perpetuate the myth of the black rapist. In the section on *The Tempest* I will return to the limitations of Fanon's approach.

8 Some of the things I have been speaking of surface in the history of the Hindu epic *Ramayana*. This tells the story of the heir apparent to the throne of Ayodhya, Rama, who was exiled to the forest for fourteen years by his father on the direction of the latter's fourth wife. There, Rama's wife Sita was abducted by a demon king, Ravana. The battle which followed resulted in Rama's victory and his sunsequent return to his kingdom. The development of the story over the centuries bears testimony to the grafting on of various episodes emphasising chastity, wifely devotion and obedience, demonising of female propensity for evil as well as idealisation of the stereotype of a passive wife on to an originally simple story. Uma Chakravarti has suggested that these additions were made to the *Ramayana* in accordance with increasing Aryan taboos on women and alongside the socio-economic development of feudal society, and later tied in with medieval consolidation, so that the depiction of Sita represents the codification of the stereotype of a passive Hindu woman (pp. 68-75).

But it still remains to be analysed how this process also reveals a deepening racial differentiation. The original geographical parameters of the story in North India subsequently expanded till Ravana's kingdom became popularly located in the South, and became identified with what is today Sri Lanka. Ravana's people are *rakshasas*; the term originally signified a lower caste and today is taken to mean 'demon'. Rama's originally dark colour has faded to a near-white representation on the stage and cinema, whereas Ravana becomes ever darker. In the story's current serialisation on the national television network, Ravana's court is depicted through South Indian dance and music forms. We need to locate how racial differentiation crept in and how it is connected to the theme of the passive wife, as well as to the depiction of the wicked woman. While Sita, the 'white' wife is chaste and obedient, the 'alien' woman is sexually licentious: Ravana's sister Swarupnakha propositions Rama's brother Lakshmana. Not only does he chop off her nose and ears, but this incident is the provocation for Ravana's abduction of Sita. Thus the wicked step-mother, the promiscuous alien woman and the non-Aryan male collectively constitute the evil forces of the story.

3

The 'infinite variety' of patriarchal discourse

Fragmentation, mobility and women

The theme of racial difference in *Othello* allows us to locate the heterogeneity of patriarchal power and the oppositions to it. But what of other texts of the period in which such a theme either is, or has been generally construed to be, missing? Renaissance and Jacobean tragedy repeatedly poses a real difficulty for dominant Anglo-American critical traditions with their emphasis on what Dollimore, following Fekete, has discussed as a preoccupation with a unified metaphysical and experiential truth, order and stability (*Radical Tragedy*, chapter 3). If L. C. Knights finds that *Antony and Cleopatra* 'embodies different and apparently irreconcilable evaluations of the central experience' (quoted Brown, *Antony and Cleopatra*, p. 172), Clifford Leech feels compelled to confer unity on a text that is resistant to it: '. . . in The Duchess (of Malfi) we are pulled successively in different directions and on the completion of our reading are likely to feel we have the task of constructing a whole of which Webster has given us the separate parts (Clifford Leech, quoted Brown, *Duchess*, p. xlviii). Throughout the history of English studies, texts have not only been interpreted, evaluated and re-written to satisfy this demand for unity, but, as Tony Davies points out, even mutilated if they are seen to be defective (pp. 8-9).

Recent materialist criticism of the Renaissance has been increasingly occupied with 'forces of heterogeneity, contradiction, fragmentation and difference' in society (Montrose, 'Renaissance literary studies', p. 5), with identifying the diversity as well as consolidation of power. The very characteristics of Jacobean drama that liberal criticism read as symptomatic of decadence, chaos or lack of moral cohesion can and have been interpreted as a radical resistance to idealist ideologies, working then, as now, to employ the idea of stability in their favour. I shall suggest that this refusal of Renaissance drama to comply with the drive towards moral and poetic closure is closely related to its foregrounding of disorderly, or at least problematic, women. We certainly get a patriarchal view of disobedient women in these plays. But, first, this view is rather heterogeneously composed, by which I mean it is not presented as having that seamless and inviolate quality which hegemonic ideologies seek to acquire. Instead, we can see the various sources from which it is derived, the purposes which it serves and the strategies which it employs. All of these are not consistent, and in their internal conflicts their politics are revealed. Secondly, patriarchal attitudes are also contested by the women themselves, and the resultant conflict problematises their hegemonic stature. Both of these disturbances affect the structure of the plays. In this chapter I want to examine the construction of disorderly women, and in the next two chapters I will consider the female subject and the form of the dramas.

Especially when viewed from the perspective of a society which has not gone through the same process of consolidation as Western Europe, these texts foreground the efforts at consolidation of patriarchal authority but do not participate in a closure that ratifies the same. I have already indicated that the critical emphasis on a single artistic truth and valid reading worked to exclude the socially marginalised reader. Not only is s/he admitted by the polyphonic foregrounding of disorderly women but her experience may be seen as useful for contemporary feminist evaluations.

The need, in sixteenth century England, to absorb massive social and geographic mobility and political as well as economic upheavals was manifested in the effort to emphasise, almost desperately, that the world could not turn upside down, that it was too solid to melt into air. There is a multifaceted dialectic between movement and change on the one hand, and fixity and stability on the other. Although all change is not necessarily progressive, during this period it becomes particularly threatening for the dominant order which had to face the vast and wide-ranging changes affecting the society of early modern Europe. In the face of unprecedented social mobility, religious and political crisis, there was a 'polarisation and hardening of doctrine' (Sinfield, Literature in Protestant England, p. 8), a reiteration of orthodoxy in the form of providentialist belief, monarchic absolutism and misogyny.[1]

The dominant ideology of the age sought to represent society and nature as stable and static. A conception of the world as a fixed and unchanging hierarchy was the ideological map of the world according to a particular power elite and not, as E. M. W. Tillyard's influential book, The Elizabethan World Picture claimed, an uncontested and firm belief in 'the collective mind of the people' (see Dollimore, 'Shakespeare, cultural materialism', pp. 5-7). Montrose quotes the officially prepared homily 'Exhortation, Concerning Good Order and Obedience to Rulers and Magistrates' (1559):

Almightye God hath created and appoynted all things, in heaven, earth and
waters, in a mooste excellente and perfecte order ... Everye degre of people
in theyr vocation, callying, and office hath appointed to them, theyr duety and
ordre. Some are in hyghe degree, some in lowe, some kynges and prynces,
some inferiors and subjectes, priestes, and laymenne, Masters and Servauntes,
Fathers and chyldren, husbandes and wives, riche and poore, and everyone
have nede of other: So that in all thynges is to be lauded and praysed the goodly
order of god, wythoute the whiche, no house, no citie, no commonwealth can
continue and indure or laste. For where there is no ryghte ordre, there reigneth
all abuse, carnal libertie, enormitie, synne, and Babylonicall confusyon. ('The
purpose of playing', pp. 53-4).

Not only does the picture presented here attempt to erase all contradictions between the sexes, classes and other social groupings, as well as
those within them, and thus patently falsify the actual state of affairs,
but it also implicitly acknowledges the spectre of disorder and the challenge to social hierarchy – 'a collapse of most of the props of the medieval
world picture' (Stone, p. 654).

   It is in this context that the foregrounding of the woman question at
this time needs to be placed – not just in literature, but in religious tracts
and sermons, in state policies, in the non-fictional writings of both men
and women, in educational theories, conduct books and pronouncements on the family. The political and ideological necessity to redefine
the nature and status of women becomes obvious in the face of unprecedented changes that included gender relations. These changes span
the economic and social status of women, their demography and spatial
placement within society, and also the ideologies of their containment
and scope for resistance.

   Assessments of women in the drama have fluctuated in accordance
with differences about the status of real life women in the early modern
period: Juliet Dusinberre's now much refuted view, in *Shakespeare and
the Nature of Women*, that there was an emergent feminism in Renaissance
society, and consequently in the plays, has been challenged by Lisa
Jardine's contention, in *Still Harping on Daughters*, that the decline in
women's actual status was accompanied by the punishment of assertive
femininity on the stage which served as a warning against transgressive
women. Both views suppose a mimetic relationship between history
and literature; rather more sophisticated is Belsey's argument that the
drama moves towards a bourgeois-liberal split between private and public, woman and man. Feminist criticism needs to contextualise the frag-
mentary and ruptured identities of the disorderly Jacobean heroines
more fully in terms of recent documentations of the heterogeneity and
complexity of Renaissance society; the literary representations of

women emerge as both constructed by and radically disruptive of an authority which was historically simultaneously being consolidated and in crisis.[2]

Both the fear and the possibility of female mobility increased in the transition from feudalism to capitalism. Increasing urbanisation made new spaces available to women hitherto confined to feudal estates: shops, theatres, streets, each others' homes. This, at least theoretically, opened up the possibility of new movement for women and undermined effective male supervision over their smallest actions. Bianca's sexual transgression is mapped out in terms of her literal movement away from the symbol of privacy, the home:

> She was but one day abroad, but ever since
> She's grown so cutted, there's no speaking to her.
>   (*Women Beware Women*, III.i.3-4)

Yellowhammer in Middleton's *A Chaste Maid in Cheapside* calls city women 'the daughters of the freedom' (I.i.115); although this freedom is not realised, the possibiliy of mobility becomes an aspect of female disobedience in the drama. Moll Cutpurse's rejection of stereotypical femininity is expressed also by her quick movements, her restlessness: 'I cannot stay' she repeats (*The Roaring Girl*, II.i.165, 184). Based on the real life Mary Frith, Moll dresses like a man, refuses to marry and appropriates the normally male role of keeper of social peace. Both literally and ideologically she 'strays so (far) from her kind' (I.ii.211). The Duchess of Malfi conceives of her own transgression in terms of a pioneer movement 'into a wilderness, / Where I shall find nor path nor friendly clew / To be my guide' (I.ii.278-80). (Interestingly, in Hindi a morally loose woman is *chalu* – literally, 'one who walks'.)

The women as well as their adversaries, then, although from very different perspectives, emphasise physical and conceptual female mobility. The repeated comparisons in the literature of the period of woman with gold, jewels, money and other easily transferable property express, among other things, a notion of the unstable nature of wealth and women. (In the Indian context, a comparable idea is conveyed by the reference to girls as *paraya dhan*, or alien wealth.) But mobility and transference contain the possibility of escape. For Leantio, in *Women Beware Women*, Bianca is 'a most unvalued'st purchase' and 'a most match-less jewel' (I.i.12, 162). But he has spirited her away from her parents, she is the 'best piece of theft' (I.i.43) and, like other property, may be stolen away again. Therefore she must now be 'cas'd up from all men's eyes' (I.i.170) and taught

> To keep close as a wife that loves her husband;

> To go after the rate of my ability,
> Not the licentious swinge of her own will. . . . (I.i.90-2)

Thus Monticelso defines whores as 'treasuries by extortion fill'd / And emptied by curs'd riot' and compares Vittoria to a 'guilty counterfeited coin' (The White Devil, III.ii.94-5, 99). Here we see how the mobility of a cash-oriented society as compared with a land-based one reinforces the instability of patriarchal gender relations; images comparing women to property evoke the potential loss of both. The medieval notion of female changeability and duplicity is thus reworked in terms of the political implications of movement.

This is not to discount the authoritarian consolidation of the state and the family and the increasing confinement, exclusion and oppression of women. The plays themselves often proceed towards their literal enclosure, which is now something which cannot be taken for granted but must be repeated, often violently. Middleton's Yellowhammer is not alone in his intention to

> lock this baggage up
> As carefully as my gold. She shall see
> As little sun, if a close room or so,
> Can keep her from the light on't.
>
> (A Chaste Maid in Cheapside, III.i.40-3)

The Duchess of Malfi, Beatrice in The Changeling, Bianca in Women Beware Women, Penthea in The Broken Heart and Annabella in 'Tis Pity She's a Whore are variously confined, locked up, and closed: the attempt to control female deviance becomes spatially explicit.

Economically the productivity of Renaissance women was lessened as they were eased out of traditional occupations such as brewing, spinning, weaving, and midwifery, and from skilled, retail and provision trades (see Clark, The Working Life). Joan Kelly suggests that since patriarchy derives its historic forms from the current mode of production, the separation of home and workplace during this period intensifies women's oppression. The family becomes increasingly restricted to two essential roles – as the unit for individual consumption, and as the means of biological reproduction and regulation of sexuality – and women begin to be economically, spatially and ideologically restricted to its domain. Although Protestantism to some extent resisted medieval forms of misogyny, its redefinition of woman was consistent with the strengthening of patriarchy within the family as well as the parallel and related tightening of monarchic control and state authority. The supposedly 'democratic implications' of Protestant thought were certainly limited for, firstly (as Tawney has shown), it accepted the main institutions of commercial civilisation and provided a creed for the classes who were to dominate the future, and secondly, women were clearly excluded from the individualist ideals of personal fulfilment and were increasingly defined by their relationships to men instead of being invited – even theoretically – to participate in any self-fashioning. Witch mania reached its height in the 1650s and an overwhelming majority of those brought to trial were social deviants.[3]

Therefore, on the one hand, feminist historiography effectively removed Renaissance women from 'a footing of perfect equality with men' where earlier historians had placed them (Kelly, p. 3); on the other, evidence and expressions of their resistances and of the instability of the status-quo have also increasingly been brought to light. Although I see no paradox here – surely repression is likely to intensify precisely when authority is challenged – many feminist critics have found it difficult to reconcile the two. Thus literature ranging from pamphlets to plays has often been regarded as either unconnected to actual female rebellion, or seeking to contain the same: Woodbridge dismisses sections of her own vast and valuable documentation of the literature generated by the Elizabethan and Jacobean debates concerning the nature and status of women as 'a formal controversy' or 'intellectual calisthenics' (p. 44); similar arguments have been advanced concerning the four-century long *querelle des femmes* (see Kelly, chapter four); and Jardine suggests that the assertive dramatic heroine is no indication of a proto-feminist impulse in the drama or society of the period (*Still Harping* and '*The Duchess of Malfi*').

Elsewhere I have argued that against a background of great social upheavals and woman-oriented discontents (if not actual feminist actions) it is hard to read the writings of the *querelle* either as a purely academic exercise or as an intellectual conspiracy to contain female assertiveness.[4] Firstly, although the debate was formally isolated from political action, there is evidence of active female resistance – ranging from the Beguines of late medieval cities (who were celibate lay women living in female communities and supporting themselves by their collective work) to women within the radical English sects who actively tried to liberate themselves from male clerical and familial authority, although they did not theorise their rebellion (Kelly, p. 68); and from women who 'turn up rebuking priests and pastors, being central actors in grain and bread riots in town and country, and participating in tax revolts and other rural disturbances' (Davis, 'Women on top', p. 176) to the significant percentage of women in seventeenth century English enclosure riots. In Calvinist Edinburgh, in 1637, the resistance to Charles I's imposition of the Book of Common Prayer was opened by a crowd of 'rascally serving women' as was the tax revolt at Montpellier in 1645. In England, proletarian women become increasingly vocal and specific in voicing their demands to Parliament (Shepherd, *Amazons*, pp. 31, 51). The *querelle* remained unaware of activists and vice versa but *their coexistence is not coincidental*; the former was an answer to the ideological justification of the oppression of women which was resisted in a different way by the latter.[5]

Secondly, we need to pay attention to the powerful ideological contradictions in the dominant discourses about women. For example, what emerges in the writings of the humanists is a kind of quasi-egalitarianism in which there is a sense of equality between the sexes that derives from increasing emphasis on individualism; but gender-roles are still sharply defined. These are now expressed both in terms of rules governing conduct and statements about the essentially different nature of men and women, which had been the hallmark of medieval thought and orthodox Christianity. The humanists stress civic virtue and social roles, but end up with even stricter control over female activity than traditional Christian culture. Women are permitted education via a variety of arguments – sometimes because their minds are conceded to be equal to those of men, as in Henry Cornelius Agrippa's *A Treatise of the Nobilitie and Excellencye of Woman Kynde* (1542), and at other times to rectify nature's defects, as with Thomas More; but both kinds of logic work to exclude them from public life, as in *Utopia*. More seems to be generally in favour of a typically patriarchal household, and yet is it completely typical? He writes to his daughter and favourite pupil Margaret:

May God . . . grant you happily and safely a little one like to his mother in everything except sex. Yet let it by all means be a girl, if only she will make up for the inferiority of her sex by her zeal to imitate her mother's virtue and learning. Such a girl I would prefer to three boys. (Kaufman, 'Juan Luis Vives', p. 892)

Similarly, Juan Luis Vives takes a radical view on female education in *The Instruction of a Christian Woman* but in the same essay goes on to proscribe the role of teacher for the female sex (see Kaufman, 'Vives', p. 892). Despite their social prescriptions, the very contradictions of humanist arguments allow a space for female learning, which rapidly strains the limits prescribed for it: Joan Kelly has aptly characterised early feminist theorists as 'daughters in revolt against fathers who schooled some of them for a society they forbade all women to enter' (p. 69).

Then too, the rationalist attack on custom and tradition gave contemporary feminists powerful arguments to resist the roles imposed upon women (see Smith, 'Feminism in Seventeenth-Century England' and *Reason's Disciples*). For example, in the debates over cross-dressing *Hic Mulier* or the mannish woman, neatly demonstrates that change is a part of nature and that every custom and social value is both relative and transitory:

It is a fashion or custome with us to mourne in Blacke: yet the Agian and Romane Ladies ever mourned in white . . . for you to cut the hayre of your upper lips, familiar heere in England, every where else almost thought unmanly . . . I might instance in a thousand things that onely custome and not Reason hath approved. To conclude *custome is an Idiot, and whosoever dependeth wholly upon him, without the discourse of Reason, will* . . . *become a slave indeed to contempt and censure*. (*Haec-Vir*, 1620, emphasis added)

Many humanists were using similar arguments – William Heale's *An Apologie for Women* for example, considers law as man-made and therefore changeable, not as natural or divine. It argues that it is lack of education that has 'disabled (women) of mental courage for revenge'. Heale also reverts to the patriarchal stereotype of women as 'the patterne of innocencie, the Queene of loue, the picture of beauty, the Mistresse of delight' (pp. 2-13; see also his chapter four). Such oscillation between remnants of earlier thinking on the woman question and newer arguments reflects the problematic inconsistencies in the forgrounding of women in Tudor and Stuart social thought. But *Hic Mulier* uses the attack on custom to assert female equality: 'We are as free-born as men, have as free election, and as free spirits, we are compunded of like parts, and may with like liberty make benefit of our creations'.

My point is that Protestant and humanist doctrines were more inconsistent than traditional misogyny because on the one hand they invoked logic and rationalism to question many existing orthodoxies, and on the other hand sought to legitimise women's subordinate position (which women's defences of the period clearly related to custom) without the full authority of the crude but powerful 'natural' arguments of medieval misogynists. By stressing that women are equal to men and still not the same, by advocating mutual affection in marriage and frowning on passion, by advancing 'holy matrimony' as an ideal and yet tightening parental control, by excluding women from the new emphasis on self-fulfilment (which itself was apparently paradoxical in view of state authoritarianism), the dominant ideologies tried to redefine women's status in the changing circumstances; but actually they opened up irreconcilable contradictions that could only be uneasily yoked together and could also be seized upon by women writers. So Christine de Pisan had earlier begun to counter misogynist arguments by asking women to 'notice how these same philosophers contradict each other' (p. 7).

Moreover, women's defences and other writings of the *querelle* went beyond utilising rationalist elements of male discourses – they began to confront and challenge masculine learning. Of course these writings are themselves riddled with contradictions. Woodbridge says that they are not feminist in the twentieth-century meanings of the term. Surely any such expectations would be ahistorical. Christine de Pisan had warned women against male arguments and logic:

> Remember, dear Ladies, how these men call you frail, unserious, easily influenced but yet try hard, using all kinds of strange and deceptive tricks, to catch you, just as one lays traps for wild animals. Flee, flee, my ladies, and avoid their company – under these smiles are hidden deadly and painful poisons. (pp. 256-7)

In England, at least some women writers picked up this tone of passionate opposition to male institutions and ideas: 'We are contrary to men because they are contrary to all that which is good . . . Their unreasonable minds which know not what reason is make them nothing better than brute beasts' (Jane Anger, *Protection of Women*, 1589). We can hardly dismiss such protest as academic.

White devils: the politics of changeability

Not only is patriarchal thinking on women itself contradictory, but it seeks to confer upon them a duplicitous and changeable identity, as Christine's remarks above indicate. In Renaissance drama, such views are frequently mouthed. The splitting of feminine identity in patriarchal stereotypes is adequately summed up by Brachiano in *The White Devil*: 'Woman to man / Is either a god or a wolf' (IV.ii.88-9). Such an oscillation between pit and pedestal is common in European feudal society which treated women as a curious mixture of 'saints in the Church, angels in the streets, devils in the kitchen and apes in bed' (Rowbotham, p. 20). Sublimation and malediction had been ingeniously reconciled in St Paul's view that 'the purity of the body and its garments means the impurity of the soul' (Russell, p. 43). Women's beauty was the instrument of temptation, hiding 'the loathsomeness under . . . within she is full of phlegm, stinking, putrid, excremental stuff' (Chrysostom, quoted Brustein, p. 37). Hence the common theme of the white devil, the 'cunning devils' whose real nature lurks within the exterior of 'fair-fac'd saints' (*The Changeling*, V.iii.108-9).

Although such a splitting appears universal in patriarchal thought, the stereotype is neither simple nor stable but is culled from a vast variety of historically specific inputs. For example, there is no precise counterpart to Eve in Hinduism, and initially no formal malediction of woman as in Christian thought. The feminine principle was neither subordinate nor weak or inferior but appeared as *Shakti* or energy, force and power. However, with the consolidation of feudal relations, *Shakti* worship gradually dwindled into a secret practice and survives today largely as black magic (see Chattopadhyay). The power of the goddess figure is now split – into the figure of the benevolent married goddess and that of the malevolent single goddess: 'The blood thirsty goddess . . . never appears in a matrimonial context, but rather alone, and surrounded by the paraphernalia of killing . . . But as the consort of any of the gods the goddess seems to undergo a kind of transformation into what is almost (an) antithesis . . .' (Babb, p. 141). Thus despite totally different contexts Hinduism began to posit a dichotomy of female purity and malignity analogous (but never identical) to that in Christian thought, and a comparable demonisation of active femininity as witchcraft.[6]

The notion of female duplicity and changeability is premised upon such a dichotomy. It reflects the attempt to contain the possibility of female change within a patriarchal stasis – by offering a notion of the eternal changeability of woman, a theory of female instability is employed in support of universal and unchanging female nature and a uniform but not unified identity is conferred upon all women. The stasis of the oppressed is crucial to any system of power: in pre-Copernican thought the stillness of the earth guarantees the movement of the sun, in the Elizabethan world picture the fixity of each link ensures the stability of the chain, in colonial discourses the racial other is immobilised and the stillness of women is posited as crucial for social, familial, cosmic harmony: 'Thy firmness makes my circle just / And makes me end where I began' (Donne, 'Valediction Forbidding Mourning').

Patriarchal thought incorporates the possibility of female movement in order to control it, investing women's stability with moral values. Thus the wandering woman is evil, and it is no accident that witches are mobile, riding through the air on broomsticks. The good woman is still. But every woman is a devil within, so all women's capacity for movement must be anticipated and curtailed. The attempt is to fix them in relation to men, and also to construct their duplicity as eternal. Such an effort becomes particularly imperative in the context of Renaissance politics and its obsession with change. The theme of female duplicity runs through the drama: Iago, Bosola, the Cardinal, Flamineo, Monticelso, Alsemero, DeFlores, Antony, Othello are all preoccupied with the changeability of women. However, its repetition should not lead us to suppose the stability or uniformity of the stereotype, which actually enriches itself from a variety of sources and adapts itself to changing conditions.

The language of patriarchy

The figure of Cleopatra is the most celebrated stereotype of the goddess and whore and has accommodated and been shaped by centuries of myth-making and fantasy surrounding the historical figure. In Shakespeare's representation of her, we can identify several different strands of contemporary meaning which intertwine with connotations attaching to her from earlier stories. My purpose in unravelling these is to suggest that Shakespeare does not simply indicate a stereotype but depicts it as constructed by various male perspectives in the play. Later, in chapter 5, I shall suggest that such a construction is then challenged and dismantled; here we can see how Renaissance politics and stagecraft shape Cleopatra's representation.

Firstly, like Monticelso's characterisation of whores (see pp. 87-8 below) or Iago's view of Desdemona or the pronouncements of Flamineo, Bosola, Ferdinand, DeFlores and Alsemero (see chapter 4), the construction of Cleopatra draws upon the medieval notion of the sexual appetite of women as rampant and potentially criminal: as the primordial sexual being she is also maledicted as 'immoral', the 'false soul' (IV.xii.25) and 'a boggler' (III.xiii.110). Ellen Terry, one of the first actresses to play Cleopatra, believed that through her, Shakespeare had 'told the truth about the wanton' (quoted Brown, *Antony and Cleopatra*, p. 54). Therefore she is simultaneously Isis and goddess as well as gypsy and 'triple-turned whore' (IV.xii.13).

Secondly, Cleopatra's social status places her in a contradictory position. Status, wealth, class are refracted in their operation through the prism of gender, and do not work in the same way as for men. For example, in Middleton's *The Changeling*, Beatrice-Joanna thinks that she can buy DeFlores; her wealth gives her the illusion of power. But DeFlores, although literally her servant, is a man, and as such is beyond the reach of her class power. Soon he has *her* kneeling at *his* feet:

> Beatrice. Stay, hear me once for all; I make thee master
> Of all the wealth I have in gold and jewels;
> Let me go poor unto my bed with honour,
> And I am rich in all things.
> DeFlores.   Let this silence thee:
> The wealth of all Valencia shall not buy
> My pleasure from me;
> Can you weep Fate from its determin'd purpose?
> So soon may you weep me. (III.iv.155-62)

Beatrice cannot simultaneously be a woman and have power over a man. Throughout the drama, women find the need to 'appropriate masculine virtue' (see Belsey, The Subject of Tragedy, pp. 183-4). Since femininity and power are increasingly incompatible, to be a woman in authority of any sort is necessarily to occupy an uneasy space.

As the 'precious queen' Cleopatra is deified into the goddess Isis, recalling the attempts to depict Elizabeth I as the Virgin Queen, which fixed her visually as a goddess and served to fill the iconographic vacuum created by the exit of Catholicism. Elizabeth needed, however, to reinforce her power by negating her femininity; she could only secure her status as ruler by 'transcending' the limitations of her sex, i.e. by repudiating it: 'I know I have the body of a weak and feeble woman, but I have the heart and stomach of a king, and of a king of England too' (Heisch, 'Queen Elizabeth I and the Persistence of Patriarchy', p. 55). Cleopatra similarly asserts:

> A charge we bear i'th' war,
> And as president of my kingdom, will
> Appear there for a man. (III.vii.16-18)

Despite this, both Elizabeth and Cleopatra evoke specifically Renaissance fears of female government; John Knox's First Blast of the Trumpet against the Monstrous Regiment of Women (1558) was directly addressed to Mary Tudor, but other queens – Mary, Queen of Scots, Margaret of Parma, Catherine de Medici, and Mary of Lorraine – contributed to the spectre of female government which it attacks. Ironically, such fears were heightened even as actual female authority in several spheres was dismantled. Evidence is available that women constituted a substantial part of medieval armies and often occupied leading positions within them (Hacker, pp. 643-71; Kelly, p. 86). Moreover, during the early Middle Ages, the queen had reigned as a royal partner, but as the state consolidated into a centralised authority, her political power dwindled into a ceremonious role, a token and a symbol of glamour. This was also emphasised by the prescriptions for female behaviour in medieval conduct books and in books such as Castiglione's The Courtier (1561). By 1656 Margaret Cavendish testified that 'all heroic actions, public employments, powerful governments and eloquent pleadings are denied our sex in this age' (Kelly, p. 86).

The distinction made between warrior women and Amazons by Shepherd is useful here: like Elizabeth, Cleopatra enters the realm of androgyny, but unlike Elizabeth, who remained within the confines of female chastity, Cleopatra is more properly the Amazon who brings together patriarchal (and particularly Renaissance) fears of female government as well as sexual activity. Since women as lovers function as the private lives of men, their trespass into the public world of politics implies a dual identity, a changeability which also contributes to Cleopatra's construction as an inconstant and shifting being.

Thirdly, the idea of Cleopatra's dichotomous identity is elaborated in the images of her play-acting, dressing up, putting on disguises, planning and stage-managing her encounters with both Antony and Caesar. She is the supreme *actress* – theatrical, unruly and anarchic, whose 'infinite variety' also derives from the roles she plays. Not only does she play the queen with theatrical grandeur and self-consciousness, she also assumes various other identities and becomes in turn masculine, or ultra-feminine, the jealous lover, the angry mistress, the penitent woman, and finally the Roman wife. Twice she makes specific references to disguise – once when she recalls wearing Caesar's armour (II.v.22-3) and again when she conjures up the image of a boy-actor impersonating her in Rome (V.ii.213-20). She is as unpredictable as the theatre, and controls her audience at least partially by surprising them, as she does her lover by her changeability. But this last is misogynist Enobarbus's concept, and he conjures up the image of her seated in the barge to imply a scene meticulously executed to flaunt her beauty, power and glamour to Antony. The negative implications of this link with play-acting are derived from the precarious social position of popular theatre and the threat it posed to the status quo during this period (see Weimann, p. 172; Montrose, 'The purpose of playing', pp. 51-74; Dollimore, 'Shakespeare, cultural materialism, p.4). Hence the fears inspired by the duplicitous heroine are explicitly analogous to those generated by the theatre itself.

Fourthly, Cleopatra's play acting specifically reverses gender roles; she not only wears Caesar's military attire but 'put my tires and mantles' on Antony (II.v.22). Although cross-dressing is evident in translations of classical drama, of Greek romances and medieval stories, and in texts such as *Metamorphoses, Decameron, Orlando Furioso, Arcadia, The Faerie Queene,* and much stage comedy, its emergence as 'a central Renaissance trope' (see Staton, pp. 79-89), one which was repeatedly interwoven with the themes of female rebellion in the drama and in the pamphlets on cross-dressing – *Haec-Vir, Hic-Mulier* and *Mulde-Sacke* – can hardly be attributed to stage convention alone. As Jardine points out, dress emerges as a crucial signifier of sexual and social identity in the prescription and enforcement of elaborate and precise codes of dressing during the reign of both Elizabeth and James (*Still Harping*, pp. 141-2, 150). From indicting women's extravagant and lustful natures, satire against cross-dressing became specifically directed against their appropriation of male prerogatives. Monticelso identifies 'Impudent bawds / That go in men's apparell' as among 'the notorious offenders / Lurking about the City' (*The White Devil*, IV.i.56-7; 33-4). The female transvestite is seen to transgress into male territory and becomes a hermaphrodite, a monster who threatens sexual (and by implication all social) distinctions.[7]

Hence the fear that Cleopatra has the power to unman men echoes throughout the play, making explicit the threat posed by the monstrous woman to male power and authority. It is visually expressed by the images of cross-dressing. More generally this ties in with the usurping of male positions by any disorderly woman: Philo in the opening lines talks of Antony, 'the triple pillar of the world transform'd / Into a strumpet's fool' (I.i.12-13). In the next scene Antony sees his great love as a bondage: 'These strong Egyptian fetters I must break / Or lose myself in dotage' (I.ii.113-14). Caesar too refers to the relationship as a reversal of gender roles:

> . . . he fishes, drinks and wastes
> The lamps of the night in revel; is not more manlike
> Than Cleopatra, nor the queen of Ptolemy
> More womanly than he. (I.iv.4-7)

This reversal is seen to compromise the masculinity of Antony's soldiers as well: Canidius comments, 'So our leader's led / And we are women's men' (III.vii.69-70) and Enobarbus warns Antony 'Transform us not to women' (IV.ii.36). The fears posed by disguise, theatre, female government and sexuality thus flow into one another.

Finally, Cleopatra is the non-European, the outsider, the white man's ultimate 'other'. In *Othello*, as we have already seen, colonialist, racist and sexist discourses are mutually dependent. Cleopatra embodies all the overlapping stereotypes of femininity and non-Europeans common in the language of colonialism. She is dangerous and snake-like, 'the old serpent of the Nile' (I.iv.25), the 'serpent of Egypt' (II.vii.26). On the one hand, she has a mysterious power over Antony, on the other he constantly reminds her that he found her 'As a morsel cold upon / Dead Caesar's trencher', a 'fragment / Of Cneius Pompey's' (III.xiii.116-18). The white man's love confers worth upon her, and she is made whole only by Antony's attentions. The recurrent food imagery reinforces her primitive appeal: she makes men hungry, she does not cloy their appetite (II.ii.240-2); she is Antony's 'Egyptian dish' (II.vi.122), she is 'salt Cleopatra' (II.i.21). She is the supreme actress, artifice herself, and simultaneously primitive and uncultivated.

The identification of Cleopatra with Egypt points to more than her status as its queen. In colonialist discourse, the conquered land is often explicitly endowed with feminine characteristics in contrast to the masculine attributes of the coloniser (see Hulme, pp. 17-32). All Egyptians, represented and symbolised by their queen, are associated with feminine and primitive attributes – they are irrational, sensuous, lazy and superstitious. Therefore Cleopatra's identification with a place conveys her power as ruler and also specifically identifies her as alien territory. The tensions between Rome as masculine and imperial and Egypt as its threatening 'other' will be elaborated in the next chapter. The images that cluster around Cleopatra are specifically Orientalist in nature: her waywardness, emotionality, unreliability and exotic appeal are derived from the stereotypes that Said identifies as recurrent in that discourse (*Orientalism*, p. 207).

In another context, Carr has described the metamorphosis of the opposition of virgin / whore into that of good wife / witch (p. 51). Cleopatra participates in both sets of dichotomies; she is 'whore' as well as 'witch' (IV.xii.13, 47). Witches are both the projections of exaggerated patriarchal fears (Stallybrass, '*Macbeth*', pp. 189-209; Garrett, 'Women and witches') and also a colonial fantasy whereby the non-Christian outsider is connected to devilry. The episode with the soothsayer paves the way for a connection of all Egyptians and particularly Cleopatra with magic: she is an 'enchantress', a 'great fairy' (IV.viii.12) but of an alien variety – a 'gypsy' (I.i.10; IV.xii.28). So Pompey's desire, that 'witchcraft join with beauty, lust with both' to charm Antony into inaction (II.ii.22) clearly unites both patriarchal and racial implications of witchcraft. So Cleopatra emerges as the composite deviant, a 'most monster-like' (IV.xii.6) 'other' of the Roman patriarchal 'self'.

The representation of a duplicitous woman on the Renaissance stage is not just derived from a transhistorical stereotype but betrays the 'infinite variety' of sources from which it is constructed.

Consolidation – the politics of violence

Of course this variety also reveals a consolidation: diverse authorities seal their pact over the female body and their unified action is violent and ruthless. Here I will discuss the ways in which violence against women reveals both a point of synthesis and a point of crisis in authorities hostile to women. The drama, I will suggest, focuses on both these aspects, so that, again, violence against disorderly women appears as a social and contested strategy, and is not authorised as the final statement erasing the disruption offered by these women.

Early modern Europe and contemporary India can loosely be called transitional societies in that in both we can locate a tension between different forms of social relations. I do not want to force the comparison, which is necessarily qualified – not only by the vast differences between European and Indian feudalism and capitalism and by the fact that in Europe feudalism preceded capitalism whereas in contemporary India both are concurrent and are also subject to the intervening colonial and imperialist histories; but also by the enormous range of cultural, geographical and historical differences. Above all, I want firmly to distance myself from modernisation theories whereby the historical processes of Europe are replicated in the development of the rest of the world.

The analogies are here employed to approach the apparent contradictions between patriarchal consolidation and female discontents by emphasising that violence against women intensifies for at least three reasons: firstly, to sharpen the expropriation of their productive and reproductive labour; secondly, to enforce anew the changing ideologies of their subjection; and thirdly, to 'address' the instability of these periods when both oppression and the challenges to it intensify. Violence against women is a part of all patriarchal societies but I suggest that it escalates during such obviously transitional phases.

At such times violence seems 'irrational' and 'excessive', beyond what appears 'necessary' for patriarchal control, or even inconsistent with the economic processes of capitalism. Women in Jacobean tragedy are not simply killed, but tortured – often elaborately over a period of time – by a combination of familial, judicial and religious authorities. Many end up by begging for death as merciful release: 'Yes', says Vittoria, 'I shall welcome death / As Princes do some great Ambassadors' (The White Devil, V.vi.217-18); The Duchess of Malfi knows that 'It is some mercy, when men kill with speed' (IV.i.109) and Lavinia weeps: ''Tis present death I beg' (Titus Andonicus, II.iii.173). By making women demand their punishment, are the playwrights seeking to incorporate violence committed on the female body into her own guilt and thus blur the edge of the sexual confrontation? I will return to this later. For the moment I want to suggest, through a comparison with the confessions of witches (contextualised, as they must be, against their trials, tortures, burnings and hangings) that the ideological effect of the spectacle of female punishment cannot have such a simple effect, because it is a staged representation and its crucial elements must be decoded. Like the punishment of the stage heroine, the witch trials are not simple exterminations, but elaborate and sometimes apparently inefficient and wasteful procedures. The paradox here between what patriarchal ideology needs and what it actually enforces can be juxtaposed to violence against women in India and the ideologies attaching to it, which have ensured that today there are only 935 females to 1,000 males – the most negative sex ratio in the world (Kishwar and Vanita, p. 7; see also Liddle and Joshi, pp. 29, 52, 77 n12). Surely men do not want the extinction of the female of the species. Surely capitalism should ensure cheap labour by increasing female participation in economic activity, instead of easing them out of formal production, as in the Renaissance. In India, too, they are being displaced from traditional occupations (see Mies, pp. 126-7).

Two points here are crucial – one, that crude 'economism' ignores the ideological thrust of oppression, which cannot be directly and in a linear fashion reconciled to profit; and second, that ideology, even when it appears to contradict economic relations, is inextricably, although not reductively, connected to these relations. It is worth stressing that the procedures outlined below are far more complex that this brief account can fully acknowledge, and that ideologies are not a matter of crude intentionality or conspiracy but are gathered together slowly, heterogeneously and even contradictorily.

Initial mercantile and capitalist processes find it more profitable to dislocate women's economic activity while the ideology of their subjection is overhauled so that later, women will either 'willingly' confine themselves to unpaid work, or even when they are economically independent will obey patriarchal rules, or will be brought back into production at lower wages and in non decision-making jobs. But in the intermittent years their literal confinement and forced exit from visible production is necessary. Middleton's Isabella laments women's internalisation of patriarchal ideologies:

> Oh the heart-breakings
> Of miserable maids, where love's enforc'd!
> The best condition is but bad enough:
> When women have their choices, commonly
> They do but buy their thraldoms, and bring great portions,
> To men, to keep 'em in subjection,
> As if a fearful prisoner should bribe
> The keeper to be good to him, yet lies in still,
> And glad of a good usage, a good look
> Sometimes, by'r Lady. No misery surmounts a woman's.
> Men buy their slaves, but women buy their masters . . .
>   (Women Beware Women, I.ii.166-76)

This is painfully evident in contemporary India, where among recent victims of dowry murders are lecturers, doctors, civil servants, graduates – women who were economically independent but ideologically confined.

Webster's The Duchess of Malfi provides a useful point of entry into the relationship between the economic and the ideological in women's oppression. Lisa Jardine's incisive analysis shows how it demonstrates the ways in which 'female sexuality regularly represents women's uncontrollable interference with inheritance' (Jardine, *Still Harping*, p. 92). But Jardine is unable to reconcile the apparent disproportion between the 'actual' threat the Duchess poses to the patriarchal family and the 'punishment' meted out to her. On the one hand Jardine herself documents how during the early modern period 'female kin had come to be seen as destructive of estate conservation' and great landowners, under direct threat from wealthy status-seeking burghers, tinkered with wills to ensure their estates; at the heart of every such tinkering 'one is almost certain to find a woman'. On the other hand she sees no 'actual' threat to the patriarchal order from the Duchess's marriage since property rights of women had in fact been severely curtailed during this period; she complains that the Duchess 'acts out on stage her inheritance power which in real life was no power at all for the individual woman' ('*The Duchess of Malfi*', pp. 206-16).

But what is 'actual' in social relations? Surely the paranoid and violent attempts to control female independence, property rights, movement and sexual autonomy indicate that the fears generated by the possibility of female transgression are *real* and *actual*, even where such subversion is only potential. Let us consider, as an example, the transformation of courtly love from an adulterous sexual relationship to the asexual Petrarchan ideal that it later becomes. Joan Kelly has argued that even in its initial sexually permissive stage courtly love was never simply an expression of women's sexual freedom but rather of the social relation of vassalage which was an integral part of feudalism. On the one hand it reinforced the practice of political marriage; on the other, it was a sort of 'concession' to women since, given their property rights at that point, land consolidation required female support. But, most importantly, adultery could be tolerated because of the relative indifference to illegitimacy that accompanied primogeniture, where younger children posed no threat to patriarchal lineage (Kelly, pp. 22-30). Therefore, co-existent with the apparent idealisation of woman in courtly love was her devaluation, her subservience to the concerns of property.

This is clear from Malory's *Le Morte D'Arthur*: King Arthur seems to have been aware of the 'longe love' between Sir Launcelot and Queen Guinevere but takes a stand only when the lovers are finally discovered together. He is deeply moved, but his tears are neither for the loss of his honour nor because of his Queen's infidelity but for the now imminent break-up of the Round Table, which is the real basis for his power as king:

Ihesu mercy, sayd the kynge, he is a merueyllous knyghte of prowesse. Allas, me sore repenteth, sayd the kynge, that ever Sir Launcelot shold be ageynst me.

Now I am sure the felauship of the Round Table is broken foreuer . . . And moche more I am soryer for my good knyghtes losse than for the losse of my fayre quene, for quenes I myghte have ynowe, but such a felaushyp of good knyghtes shalle never be togyders in no company. (pp. 562-5; emphasis added)

The subsequent transformation of courtly love into a chaste ideal is a counter-indication that adultery had begun to threaten patriarchal institutions. Against a background of peasant disorders and riots, the fleecing of an entire national economy by a parasitic court through monopolies, tax-farming and enclosures, and a more fundamental transformation of society taking place throughout Europe, the reinforcement of social stratification, including female inferiority, was imperative. This was true both for the old feudal state which had no police force and no standing army and therefore not the modern state's instruments of control, and for the newly centralising mercantile-capitalist one which had yet to consolidate its power and develop adequate means of enforcing it (see Schochet). Therefore, even as the family structure and state controls tighten and there is a gradual deepening of women's subjection from the sixteenth to the eighteenth centuries, the fears of female transgression increase and are foregrounded obsessively. Tennenhouse is surely right in connecting the fears of deviant sexuality to the new mobility of social relations, where adultery has serious implications for the classes in power: 'On the one hand, Jacobean tragedy makes it possible to enter the aristocratic body, as Othello, Malfi's husband, Vittoria Corombona, and countless others do. On the other hand such transgression produces disease, filth, and obscenity which must be purged in order to produce a pure community of aristocratic blood' ('The politics of misogyny', p. 10). But the point also is that women who are the targets of violence in Jacobean drama threaten the class and race limits of patriarchal societies *through their wayward sexuality.* The Duchess, Desdemona, Vittoria, Bianca and Beatrice-Joanna are all punished, whereas Shakespearean comic heroines, who are seemingly independent and who appropriate masculine dress, movement and speech are finally reconciled to the patriarchy, as Andreson-Thom points out (pp. 259-76). The crucial difference between them also is that the former are unchaste by patriarchal definition, whereas the latter are not. Thus sexual and social transgression in the case of women are inextricably connected.

I will return to this later and also to the Duchess's story; here let me briefly refer to the violence against widows in India. One does not have to be a feminist to conclude, as did a popular newsmagazine conducting a survey of widows' status soon after an incident of sati in 1987, that the sexual harassment, social ostracism and torturous existence of widows is attendant upon property fears:

rural or urban, the common thread that unites these widows in a chain of misery is the forcible deprivation of property and economic independence. Even though the law – the Hindu Succession Act – confers equal property and inheritance rights on women, widows are rarely given their fair share. In rural India, patwaris and tehsildars (customary local administrators) usually help the contenders for property left to a widow and transfer it to other names. (*India Today*, 15 November 1987, p. 143)

At the same time, many layers of prejudices enfold the property fears and are expressed as taboos against any expression of a widow's sexuality which is seen to have drastic implications for the health of society in general – hence a Rajasthani proverb warns that kohl in a widow's eyes predicts destruction for the community. Frank Wadsworth suggests that widow remarriage was not technically forbidden in sixteenth century England (p. 398). Yet we can easily see from the drama of the period that it evokes disapproval and even paranoia which is not dissimilar to the situation I have been discussing in India: the Cardinal in Middleton's *More Dissemblers Besides Women* pronounces:

> Once to marry
> Is honourable in woman and her ignorance
> Stands for a virtue, coming new and fresh
> But second marriage shows desire in flesh,
> Thence lust, and heat and common custom grows. (III.i.76-80)

The violence provoked by a widow's sexuality in *The Duchess of Malfi* would have a specific resonance in the Indian situation where, whether or not widows are in any position to actually threaten or challenge male control of property, the potential threat they pose to patriarchal economic and sexual structures receives a very real punishment. Often, the brutality is disguised in popular representations of widowhood, and the punishment is sublimated in order to reinforce normative prescriptions against widow remarriage. Hence, one of the biggest money-spinners of the Hindi screen, *Sholay*, allowed its hero to fall in love with a widow. But their affair never transgressed the boundaries of physical chastity and the problem was finally resolved by the hero's death. To teach *The Duchess* to a class fresh from weeping over *Sholay* is an exercise that cannot be performed within the boundaries of traditional English studies. But the play can be made to disturb precisely those assumptions that the film underlines, as the next chapter will substantiate.

So violence against women serves an ideological purpose and is more directly connected to the process of capital accumulation than is usually acknowledged. For example, the persecution of witches served at once to demonise every category of deviant woman and to establish male hegemony over certain female-dominated professions, such as mid-wifery and natural medicine, as well as to enrich the persecuting authorities. As Mies says:

The capital accumulated in the process of the witch-hunt by the old ruling classes, as well as by the new rising bourgeois class is nowhere mentioned in the estimates and calculations of the economic historians of that epoch. The blood-money of the witch-hunt was used for the private enrichment of bankrupt princes, of lawyers, doctors, judges and professors, but also for such public affairs as financing wars, building up a bureaucracy, infrastructural measures, and finally the new absolute state. This blood money fed the original process of capital accumulation, perhaps not to the same extent as the plunder and robbery of the colonies, but certainly to a much greater extent than is known today. (p. 87)

If Cornelius Loos called the witch-trials 'a new alchemy which made gold out of human blood', dowry in India can be seen as 'a source of wealth which is accumulated not by means of the man's own work or by investing his own capital but by *extraction, blackmail and direct violence*' (Mies, pp. 87, 162). It is most prevalent and exorbitant in the big cities and among upper and middle classes: bureaucrats, doctors, engineers, businessmen, traders and capitalist farmers. It is vital for the growth of the consumer industry, and provides an outlet for 'black money' as well as capital investment for a host of small entrepreneurs. Moreover it maintains existing class relations, since its ideology filters downwards even to those who cannot afford it and incur huge debts to pay it. This maintains the hold of the money-lender over their lives and legitimises the devaluation of female children. Hence, dowry is actually increasing in India, both in terms of what is demanded and in terms of its spread – it has begun to permeate all communities, religions and classes, even where it was previously unknown (see Krishnakumari and Geetha).

While it is true that economic determinism can never fully explain the subordination of women, it is also a fact that women have been excluded as a category from economic analysis – even fundamental data regarding their exploitation is not fully available. For example, in the case of European Renaissance and contemporary Indian women, the dominant effort has been to make their labour invisible. Ashoka Mitra writes:

In the last thirty years after independence, Indian women have increasingly become an expendable commodity, expendable both in the demographic and in the economic sense. Demographically woman is more and more reduced to her reproductive functions, and when these are fulfilled she is expendable. Economically she is relentlessly pushed out of the productive sphere and reduced to a unit of consumption which is then undesired.[8]

Stressing the interplay of economic and ideological 'motives' allows us to see that violence attaching to both witch hunts and dowry murders is neither purely a remnant of feudal ideology or social relations nor indicative of universal misogyny but is also part of the emergence of 'modern' society. Violence escalates precisely in response to the crisis in the structures of female oppression: the crisis itself is not to be measured by any simple or obvious collapse of patriarchy, but also by its demonisation of its 'others'.

Moreover, the persecuted woman is not even necessarily actually transgressive. One of the myths whereby oppression is maintained is that although the deviant will be punished, the 'normal' person will be looked after. Feudalism promises parental attention to the hard working serf, capitalism a rosy future to the industrious worker and patriarchy a romantic idyll to the obedient woman. A recent study of Indian women claims that 'the formally subordinate role of Indian women to Indian men is spelled out in sacred literature, in law, and in practice. Yet there is no doubt that the woman who accepts this role and plays it to perfection, the ideal Indian wife and mother, is revered and loved (Blumberg and Dwaraki, p. 3). In *The Duchess of Malfi* this same myth is in operation and is exposed. The Duchess is the much 'loved' and 'protected' sister, as long as she conforms. Even she tries to seek refuge in this belief, pointing out that she is not really breaking any custom, that she is technically within the rights patriarchally accorded her:

> Why might not I marry?
> I have not gone about, in this, to create
> Any new world, or custom. (III.ii.110-12)

In India today it is precisely the most obedient woman who is subject to the most violent fate: the acquiescent daughter who has 'bought her master' in a dowried marriage and not created any 'new world' is not less vulnerable than her defiant sister. That monstrous women are also made so by the punishment accorded them and not only by their actual deviancy is clear both in Jacobean tragedy and contemporary India.

'Religion: oh, how it is comeddled with policy'

If the Venetian Senate in *Othello* demonstrated its skill at variously constructing its 'others', Jacobean drama also reveals the alliances between varied structures within what we only loosely term patriarchy. An aspect of transitional societies is that, since their apparatuses of control are more fluid, their coming together and hence the contingency of the law becomes more obvious.

Webster's *The White Devil* (along with *The Duchess of Malfi*) is widely taught in India. As Dollimore has suggested, more than any other play of the period, it reveals the dependence of individual identity upon social interaction (*Radical Tragedy*, p. 231). We witness the combined operation of state and church and judiciary against the deviant woman. Although culturally and historically so different, some recent Indian events lay bare the political thrust of Vittoria's punishment.

Vittoria's marital situation would be familiar to Indian readers: that of a young girl unhappily married to an older husband whose cousin Monticelso later complains that Camillo had 'receiv'd in dowry with you not one julio' (III.ii.239). The play exposes the double standard whereby the adulterous woman remains a 'whore' even for her lover while Brachiano's wife is advised to be patient since a husband's faithlessness is only 'a slight wrong' and must suppress her 'killing griefs which dare not speak' (II.i.240, 277). Like the Indian wife who lies even from the death-bed where her husband has sent her in order to fulfil her wifely duty of protecting him, Isabella has internalised the ideology of her own oppression.

On the other hand, although it is identical with Brachiano's, Vittoria's transgression is not seen as a private wrong against her husband but becomes a public crime that outrages the entire state and church. Monticelso pronounces Vittoria a 'whore' in a passionate outburst during her trial which makes it clear that the unchaste woman is a moral rather than legal category, and since female morality is not a private matter, she is a public criminal:

> Shall I expound whore to you? Sure I shall;
> I'll give their perfect character. They are first
> Sweetmeats which rot the eater: in the man's nostril
> Poison'd perfumes. They are coz'ning alchemy,
> Shipwracks in calmest weather! What are whores?
> Cold Russian winters, that appear so barren,
> As if that nature had forgot the spring.
> They are the true material fire of hell,
> Worse than those tributes i'th' Low countries paid,
> Extractions upon meat, drink, garments, sleep;
> Ay even on man's perdition, his sin.
> They are those brittle evidences of law
> Which forfeit all a wretched man's estate
> For leaving out one syllable. What are whores?
> They are those flattering bells have all one tune,
> At weddings, and at funerals: your rich whores
> Are only treasuries by extortion fill'd,
> And emptied by curs'd riot. They are worse,

>   Worse than dead bodies, which are begg'd at gallows
>   And wrought upon by surgeons, to teach man
>   Wherein he is imperfect. What's a whore?
>   She's like the guilty counterfeited coin
>   Which whosoe'er first stamps it brings in trouble
>   All that receive it –. (III.ii.78-101)

Monticelso's language draws upon medieval misogynists' arguments of woman's fallen nature, Christian doctrines regarding sensual pleasure and Hell, but also upon the more recent fears of counterfeit money, riot and downward mobility, and the imagery of medical science. Similar assumptions have been incorporated in the conceptual apparatus of modern law.

As recently as 1950, Otto Pollack's influential *The Criminality of Women* assumed that women are more deceitful than men because of biological factors (they are capable of feigning arousal / orgasm), a combination of social and biological factors (they are socialised into concealing menstruation) and purely social factors (as child rearers they have to conceal sexual information from children). Pollack therefore regarded a woman's deviant behaviour as based on her sexuality and claimed that female emancipation would serve to increase female criminality. The medieval view of woman as temptress is reworked by modern law: in 1960, Reiss investigated 1,500 cases of juvenile sexual crime which had been presided over by the same judge. It was found that while he 'refused to treat any form of sexual behaviour on the part of boys as warranting more than probationary status', girls were regarded as 'the cause of sexual deviation in boys in all cases of coitus involving an adoloscent couple and refused to hear the complaints of the girl and her family; the girl was regarded as a prostitute'. In 1973, Vedder and Sommerville cautioned that 'while studying delinquent girls let us keep in mind: when you train a man you train an individual, when you train a girl you train a family'. Citing the others, Drakopoulou comes to the conclusion that, even today, 'rather than involving transgressions of the legal code, female delinquency involves transgressions of the moral code' (pp. 4-20).

In patriarchal criminology therefore, female crime is sexual and female sexuality is itself potentially criminal. The implication should not be that all patriarchal laws are the same, but that they certainly modify, alter and codify previous bias. For example, the emphasis Vedder and Sommerville place on the female link with the family is Protestant in temper but retains the older Catholic bias against female sexuality. Sometime during the first two centuries AD in India, Manu compiled a legal code which formalised the low status of women, laying down that a woman must be governed by men all her life – her father in childhood, then her husband and finally her son. Significantly, it regarded women and the lower castes as equally contemptible, with slavery inborn in them (Liddle and Joshi, p. 65). The codification of modern Indian law was completed by Lord Macaulay (of the Minute on Indian Education fame) in 1861; according to Spear, 'it introduced English procedures and the assumptions behind them into all Indian courts' (p. 127). With an unintended irony K. M. Panniker comments: 'It is the genius of this man, narrow in his Europeanism, self-satisfied in his sense of English greatness, that gives life to modern India as we know it. He was India's new Manu, the spirit of modern law incarnate' (Moorhouse, p. 256). The prejudices of both Manus and echoes of Monticelso are evident in current Indian legal practice. In the infamous Mathura rape case, a fifteen-year-old landless labourer was raped by two policemen in the Chandrapur police station where she had gone to inquire after her illegally detained brother. The prosecution went on for eight years: the accused were acquitted by the lower court, convicted by the High Court and finally, freed by the Supreme Court. The assumptions of the last judgement are not far from Monticelso's: it was assessed that Mathura was not a virgin at the time of her rape and therefore assumed that she had 'willingly submitted' to the drunken policemen; although the doctor's report testified to her being beaten black and blue, the judges declared that 'the alleged intercourse was a peaceful affair' and that 'her cries of alarm are of course concoction on her part'. Since she was not a virgin, the conclusion was that 'she was of loose moral character' (Forum Against Rape, leaflet, 23 February 1980). Like Vittoria, Mathura's crime was her sexuality.

In *The White Devil*, Monticelso is applauded by Francisco as a 'worthy member of the state' (IV.i.68). The Indian state is hardly in the relatively nascent stage of Renaissance authority, but in aspects of its functioning, the relationship between religion, law and civil authority is revealed as starkly contingent and fluid. The recent Shah Bano case indicates a 'comeddling' of religion and policy, with woman at the centre of the alliance. In 1985, the Supreme court of India granted alimony to 73-year-old Shah Bano, whose husband had divorced her ten years earlier. Muslims are governed by the highly patriarchal Islamic personal law, the *Shariat*, rather than the civil code that otherwise applies. Among other blatant differentials, under *Shariat* law women cannot receive alimony. Feminists, including Muslim women, hailed the Supreme Court judgement as a step towards their demand for a uniform civil code in India. Islamic fundamentalists bitterly opposed this, under the banner of religious freedom. (Interestingly, Hindu revivalists have recently defended

widow immolation on the grounds of personal freedom of choice).
Under pressure, Shah Bano withdrew her claim. The Indian state bowed
to 'unprecedented Islamic resurgence' or rather to a quick survey of
the future elections, and withdrew its support of the judgement. Instead
it placed before parliament a special bill on the rights of Muslim women,
which violates the principle of the Indian constitution not to discrimin-
ate among citizens on the grounds of religion, race, sex, caste and place
of birth (Times of India, 25 February, 1986). Thus a government whose
declared aim is to usher in the computer age in India made its pact with
what appears to be medieval misogyny. The point of course is that the
woman repeatedly becomes a site for the shifting alliances of power.

From this perspective, the punishment of Vittoria stands out clearly
as a misogynist coalition between religion and policy. To read The White
Devil as typical of the 'Jacobean pessimism' suggested by institutionalised
criticism with its emphasis on the 'hectic portraits of vice and depravity'
(Ornstein, p. 3), marked by a 'sense of defeat . . . of the futility of man's
achievement . . . a spiritual uncertainty' (Ellis-Fermor, p. 152) is to efface
the politics of the text and of the readers' own existence.

F. L. Lucas's introduction to the text invites us to view the play as a
real moral problem: 'How were we to be made to care what became
of these beings who felt no shame and knew no pity and kept no faith?
How was Milton in like case to make us care for the Devil himself?' (p.
37). If the play was to show only the punishment of Vittoria, and not
her own sharp dismantling of its political purpose, we might enter into
such a problem. Instead, as I shall later demonstrate, she sharply underlines the point made by a contemporary pamphlet, The Lawes Resolution
of Women's Rights, written by one 'T.E.' in 1632:

Women onely women . . . have nothing to do in constituting Lawes, or in hearing
them interpreted at lectures, leets or charges, and yet they stand strictly tyed to
mens establishments; little or nothing excused by ignorance, me thinkes it were
pitty and impiety any longer to hold from them such customes, Lawes, and
Statutes, as are in maner, proper, or principally belonging to them.

There is clearly a difference between the placement of Shah Bano and
Vittoria in their respective trials. Of course, both women are inconsistent
subjects: Shah Bano retracts her petition under pressure; Vittoria defies
the patriarchal court but submits to a lover who calls her 'a stately and
advanced whore' (IV.ii.73). But although she is divided subject, who
can only see her own assertiveness in terms of impersonating men,
Vittoria is insistently present in the play. Shah Bano, on the other hand,
disappears from the controversy she sparks – she becomes the object
of protection in various legal, political and feminist discourses but her
own subjectivity is effaced as she ceases to speak (see Pathak and Sunder

Rajan). Vittoria, confused as she is, refuses to be represented by others; her contradictions are an indication of her placement in society (see Belsey, *The Subject of Tragedy*) and also of her resistance.

Notes

1 Dusinberre, *Shakespeare and the Nature of Women*; Belsey, *The Subject of Tragedy*. The title of Christopher Hill's book, *The World Turned Upside Down*, picks up not only the representations of a topsy-turvy world which, as Natalie Davis suggests, actually serve to legitimise the normative hierarchy, but also refers to the widespread threats to the status quo which the book documents. Marx and Engels's *Manifesto of the Communist Party* refers to the slow dissolution of feudal economy as a period in which 'all that is solid melts into air' (p. 35). For discussions of the changes affecting early modern Europe see Aston, *Crisis in Europe*; Stone, *The Family, Sex and Marriage*; Lever, *The Tragedy of State*; Hill, *Society and Puritanism*; Hobsbawm, 'The Crisis of the seventeenth century'. Kelly, *Women, History, Theory* focuses especially on their implications for women. For ideological aspects of the change see Dollimore, *Radical Tragedy*; Montrose, 'The purpose of playing'; Sinfield, *Literature in Protestant England* and Tawney, *Religion and the Rise of Capitalism*.

2 Dollimore's *Radical Tragedy* discusses discontinuous identity in Renaissance drama in the context of the decentring of man during the period and as foregrounding the social construction of the self; Catherine Belsey's *The Subject of Tragedy* places women's discontinuities in the context of the contradictory construction of the liberal humanist subject and its denial of unified subjectivity to women. I am indebted to both analyses, although I differ from Belsey's reading of texts such as *The Duchess* as 'a perfect fable of emergent liberalism' (p. 197).

3 Keith Thomas has said that Protestantism's stress on a direct relation with God had 'democratic implications' in political matters which proved ' a powerful solvent of the established order, and whose impact was also felt by the family' (p. 320). For documentation of the anti-woman implications of Protestantism see Stone, *The Family*; Kanner, *The Women of England*; Kelly, *Women, History, Theory*.

4 See my 'Disorderly Women in Jacobean Tragedy', chapter two.

5 Both Jardine and Woodbridge advance the unhelpful argument that we cannot identify emergent feminism in sixteenth-century texts because what they and real life women during that time were demanding would be 'trivial' by twentieth-century standards. Surely feminism, materialism, or any other ideology is not static or uniform – there are at least as many differences between varieties of contemporary feminisms as between Renaissance and modern women's demands. Surely too demands correspond to reality and to set a single transhistorical yardstick for feminism is to lapse into idealistic premises; secondly, writings of the *querelle* are occasionally far clearer than some modern day feminists for the former begin to emphasise that gender relations are socially constructed and changeable rather than natural, whereas the latter revert to transcendental and universalist definitions of masculinity and femininity.

6 I suggest that materialist thought is conducive to feminist premises since both emphasise the social construction of identity and relationships and the potential for change. Hence early Indian materialism, *Vedanta*, and Chinese *Taoism* are proto-feminist; conversely, idealism, by splitting mind and matter, is the perfect ground for fostering transcendental binary oppositions of male and female. It also seeks to contain changeability by positing static binary oppositions such as that of goddess and whore (see also Eva Figes, *Patriarchal Attitudes* and chapter one of my 'Disorderly Women').

7 The issue of cross-dressing has generated much recent discussion – see Montrose, 'The purpose of playing'; Greenblatt, *Renaissance Self-Fashioning*; Jardine, *Still Harping*; Travitsky,

'The lady doth protest'; Rose, 'Women in men's clothing'; Clark, 'Hic Mulier'; Dollimore, 'Subjectivity, sexuality and transgression'.

8 Ashoka Mitra, 'The status of women', *Frontier*, 18 June, 1977. Mies writes that in India, women are not merely displaced from economic sectors but 'reintegrated into capitalist development in a whole range of informal, non-organised, non-protected production relations, ranging from part-time work, though contractual work, to houseworking, to unpaid neighbourhood work' (pp. 126-7). As in Europe, they are not really reduced to consumers, they do not really become unproductive, but the ideology of their inferior status is made viable by their apparent invisibility.

4

Women's division of experience

Credulity

'The greatest fault that remains in us women is that we are too credulous', wrote Jane Anger in her passionate protest against women's inferior status written in 1589 (p. 35). The point remains central to feminism today: as Catherine Belsey asks, 'why, since all women experience the effects of patriarchal practices, are not all women feminist?' ('Constructing the subject', p. 45). The functioning of dominant ideologies hinges on their internalisation by the oppressed subject. Patriarchal discourses, which I have identified as heterogenous, are not necessarily experienced as such by women, although they confer a dichotomy upon the latter which is not always stable; on the contrary, as we saw in the case of the Elizabethan world picture, they seek to efface contradictions and appear as 'natural' and 'obvious', as 'plain common-sense'. In the texts we have been looking at, women internalise the values conferred upon them, as did that early feminist Christine de Pisan. She was at first overwhelmed by the force of male disdain of women:

And I finally decided that God had made a vile creature when He made woman . . . a great unhappiness and sadness welled up in my heart, for I detested myself and the entire feminine sex, as though we were monstrosities in nature . . . Alas, God, why did You not let me be born in the world as a man . . . and in my folly I considered myself most unfortunate because God had made me inhabit a female body in this world' (p. 5).

In Renaissance drama, women repeatedly express similar desires to be either men or to possess what Vittoria calls 'masculine virtue' (*The White Devil*, III.ii.135). Beatrice cannot express her solidarity with Hero, for womanhood robs her of the power to act – 'O God, that I were a man' (*Much Ado About Nothing*, IV.i.304); Isabella in *The White Devil* echoes her: 'O that I were a man, or that I had power / To execute my apprehended wishes' (II.i.242-3). Conversely, to assert this power is to deny femininity, and Cleopatra declares 'I have nothing / Of woman in me' (*Antony and Cleopatra*, V.ii.236-7). Desdemona wishes that 'heaven had made her . . . a man' (*Othello*, I.iii.163); Beatrice-Joanna reiterates this, for to be a man is 'the soul of freedom' (*The Changeling*, II.ii.109). In the comedies, such wishes take physical shape as women step out of both gender-roles and costumes; Moll Cutpurse (in *The Roaring Girl*) adopts both male clothing and a single status permanently. As Belsey comments: 'predictably, these creatures who speak with voices which are not their own are unfixed, inconstant, unable to personate masculine virtue through to the end' (*The Subject of Tragedy*, p. 183). Their very attempts to transgress their limitations rob them of a unified subjectivity and express their self-negation, so typical in the psyche of the colonised: with their female skins and male masks, they approximate the splitting of colonial subject whom Fanon describes as oscillating between black skin and white mask.

The point, however, is to assess the ideological effect of this split as represented in the drama. Recent Renaissance criticism has pointed out that while on the one hand contradictions are the very means by which power achieves its aims, on the other these also set in motion the process which undermines it (see for example, Goldberg, *James I*; Brown '"This thing of darkness"'). Homi Bhabha has analysed the complexity of the terrain on which colonial authority and the colonised subject interact; he has suggested that the effectiveness of colonialist discourse is undermined not only by its internal fissures but by its (mis)appropriation by its native recipient (see 'Signs taken for wonders'). In the case of patriarchal authority, an analogous process may be traced. The similarity is neither accidental nor fanciful, given the historical parallels and overlaps between patriarchal and colonial authority.

Patriarchal discourse invites women to inhabit spaces split by a series of oppositions (for example, between man and woman, goddess and whore, public and private). But as we saw earlier, such a discourse itself is heterogenously composed, unevenly imposed and subject to conflicts with the lived reality of the oppressed subject. As in the case of the colonial subject, the divisions involve a constant shifting, a torturous but dynamic movement between two positions which it is impossible to occupy at the same time. To the extent that women have internalised patriarchal ideology, they live the divisions and contradictions imposed upon them and also the myth of their duplicity. As long as this ideology is not in crisis, the inherent opposition between women's lived experience and taught roles is kept in check. But when there is an ideological crisis, the various contradictions imposed on women serve to destabilise the supposed fixity of patriarchal notions. No longer reconciled within a fixed and static whole, these contradictions result in change, alienation, and finally resistance. What needs to be examined is whether women live the myth of duplicity exactly on the terms of the oppressors or whether it is altered, used against the intentions of the patriarchy.

It is important to remember, however, that we are speaking of female protagonists of male authors, not of living women. Neither are they psychologically 'whole' or real entities with the subjectivities we may assign to real women, nor are they even the products of a self-consciously feminist imagination. Time and again feminist critics have asked whether we are not simply investing the plays with our own concerns, expecting the male authors to rise above the limitations of their sex and time, in reading an emergent feminism in the plays. The answer will be discussed over the next two chapters. As I have previously mentioned, women characters are scripted both by a male author and by men within the plays. But, as Alan Sinfield suggests, these texts repeatedly focus on issues, such as gender relations, and institutions, such as marriage, that were at a point of crisis during the early modern period. So the representation of women repeatedly produces a disruption in these scripts: 'we should observe and reflect upon the activity of scripting the plays, rather than simply helping the text into a convenient plausibility . . . So Shakespearean texts need not be pinpointed as either conservative or radical; they are stories through which analysis and discussion can disclose the workings of power' (Sinfield, 'Othello', pp. 14-26).

To read these plays either as straightforward documents of women's liberation or elaborate patriarchal devices for containment is to erase the conflicts and complexities of the Renaissance politics, discourses on women, the position of the popular theatre and that of playwrights. Sinfield says that the scripting of women in Shakespeare suggests 'a sadly conservative body of stories', although these stories can be contested by us (p. 24). But we should consider why the drama becomes increasingly preoccupied with the disorderly woman; why woman can no longer be presented as a stable entity; and why the stories themselves become deeply contradictory and contestable. The individual author may not be 'feminist', but the ideological effects of his fragmented female protagonist are radical precisely because she is presented as a discontinous being. If on the one hand, she is the product of a mobile and fast-changing society, on the other, she becomes the means of the interrogation in this drama of the series of boundaries induced by dominant paradigms: between male and female, private and public, emotional and political, natural and artificial, Europe and its others, which are not only interrelated but can be seen as concurrently produced and emphasised from the Renaissance onwards.

These boundaries are intensified by both patriarchal and colonial discourses at the same time as they are apparently erased, as was seen in the case of Othello. Institutionalised readings of Jacobean drama have legitimised such manoeuvres by emphasising either its supposed 'quest for moral order' (see Ribner; Ornstein) or its spiritual chaos measured against such an order. Thus, even as T. S. Eliot concedes that Middleton and Dekker's *The Roaring Girl* may be seen to illustrate 'the transition from government by landed aristocracy to government by a city aristocracy', he is anxious to add that 'as literature, as a dispassionate picture of human nature, Middleton's comedy deserves to be remembered chiefly by its real – perpetually real – and human figure of Moll the Roaring Girl' (p. 169). Moll is thus detached from the disturbing implications of the Jacobean controversy over female transvestism and cross-dressing; her questioning of gender boundaries is negated by invoking a timeless femininity and humanity.

Let us return to the question of internalisation and to the resultant schisms in female subjectivity. Beatrice-Joanna is taught to think of herself as both sublime and degraded. Her name indicates a dual personality: Beatrice is a Petrarchan name meaning purity and recalling Dante's chaste passion, and Joanna was apparently one of the commonest names among servant girls at the time. Her initial role is that of goddess: tragically unaware of her sexual vulnerability, arrogantly sheltering behind her spoilt and privileged upbringing that nourishes an illusion of power, and callous with all the innocence of her own distance from violence. Both naïvety and arrogance are stripped from her by DeFlores's reminder that as a woman she is displaced from the privileges of her own class:

> Push! Fly not to your birth, but settle you
> In what the act has made you, y'are no more now.
> You must forget your parentage to me:
> Y'are the deed's creature; by that name
> You lose your first condition, and I challenge you,
> As peace and innocency has turn'd you out,
> And made you one with me. (*The Changeling*, III.iv.134-40)

Men appear to function beyond the reach of money as far as women are concerned and thus approximate Fate itself: 'Can you weep Fate from its determin'd purpose? / So soon may you weep me' (III.iv.161-2). These conflicts of class and gender in *The Changeling* were indicated in the previous chapter.[1] In *Women Beware Women* they tear apart Livia, whose wealth and power derive from and can only be used in the interests of her male patrons; the briefest attempt at autonomy strips her to ordinary and vulnerable femininity.

Such contradictions also problematise our critical practice. Newton and Rosenfelt indicate the difficulty of combining gender and class as analytical parameters when they refer to Terry Eagleton's dismissal of Lucy Snow's desire for self fulfilment in Charlotte Brontë's *Villette* as 'an overriding need to celebrate bourgeois security'. This reading, they say, ignores the potential radicalism of even a middle-class woman's desire for autonomy (p. xxv). This is surely correct, but it is then necessary to go beyond such polarisation to grasp the ways in which a middle-class woman's desire for autonomy may be experienced and expressed as a need for bourgeois security; on the other hand, a woman's economic independence spills over into a gesture for autonomy. Similarly, different interpretations are possible of the assertion of Webster's heroine – 'I am the Duchess of Malfi still' (IV.ii.142). Is she here affirming her identity as a member of the aristocracy which she has threatened by marrying her steward and which, in turn, has tried to punish her, or is she asserting her feminine self who has rebelled against patriarchal control? Are the two incompatible, or mutually reinforcing? As we saw in relation to Othello, patriarchy is transformed and modified by racial or class tensions. Here I want to emphasise that these complexities are not just reflective of the conflicting positions women necessarily occupy in patriarchal societies, but are also experienced as painful confusions by the women themselves. Beatrice's split as a member of the 'superior' class but the 'inferior' sex is internalised and includes her various 'beliefs'. For example, her initial faith in romantic love was contrary to but coexistent with the new individualist ethic which had taught her that even love marriages are not made in heaven, but cruelly and coolly manipulated. She is not treated as goddess by any of the men – even Alsemero treats her as a potential whore whose virginity must be clinically proved. Yet till the end she cannot relate to the word 'whore', for she retains a sense of her own being as a woman who only desires a loving husband and is therefore innocent:

> What a horrid sound it hath!
> It blasts a beauty to deformity;
> Upon what face soever that breath falls,
> It strikes it ugly: oh, you have ruin'd
> What you can ne'er repair again. (V.iii.31-5)

As the product of patriarchal myths and the victim of their judgement she continues to reiterate her 'love' for Alsemero: 'Forget not, sir, / It for your sake was done' (V.iii.77-8). She can lie to protect the dream of domestic bliss which she knows is illusory; 'Remember I am true unto your bed' (V.iii.82). This is not just simple duplicity or deceit, for Beatrice conceives of herself both as innocent goddess and a degraded whore: she participates in her relationship with DeFlores, and is not just its victim, so she is alienated from Alsemero; at the same time she also lives by the domestic ideal and continues to be repulsed by DeFlores. This is not to suggest, of course, that Middleton has some strange

intuitive understanding of female psychology. Beatrice's relationship
with DeFlores at one level conveys shades of Miss Julie, Lady Chatterley's
Lover, A Streetcar Named Desire and of The Paradine Case. As Hitchcock remarks
in relation to that film, for a male audience there is a particular thrill in
seeing an immaculately dressed, upper-class woman messed up by the
end of the scenario, especially by a 'manure-smelling stablehand, a man
who reeked of manure' (Truffaut, p. 210), a thrill deriving from a fantasy
of male power. Equally for women audiences there may be a pleasure
in this situation, deriving from the idea of a double transgression.
Middleton and Rowley's play exploits the first, maybe the second; but
by allowing the contradictions of Beatrice's position to develop, posits
her as a heterogeneous, split self, not as an aberrant sinner.

Women beware women   Division into 2

The experience of dichotomous existence results also in women
becoming their own enemies. This is graphically portrayed by Middleton's Women Beware Women but not limited to that play. Both Dusinberre
and Jardine have referred to the loneliness of the female tragic hero in
the texts of the period (Shakespeare and the Nature of Women, p. 92; Still
Harping, p. 69). Isolation is not simply the result of their confinement in
a male world but indicates also the impossibility of these split beings
realising female solidarity and companionship. On the one hand the
attempts at female friendship constitute 'a secret space in the midst of
male society, a haven where the normal modes of subjection are cancel-
led and where a version of traditionally male substantiality is annexed
– what we might now hope to call human intimacy' (Whigham, p. 172).
In the context of Indian culture, Sudhir Kakar has suggested that the
female companionship within the extended family can serve a similar
purpose; this idea also crops up in Fatima Mernissi's analysis of Muslim
zenana, or female quarters. Certainly women's folk songs, even marriage
lyrics, jeer at men's notion of their own power, and female companionship affords a perspective on their own subordination; potentially even
a subversive space.[2] On the other hand, I think that both in Indian
society, and in the plays, these spaces are unable to be realised as female
havens because they are subject to, not only the contradictions of class
and race, but also the power relations resulting from women's patriarchal positioning – they manifest women's internal schizophrenia as
well. Germaine Greer's idealisation of the extended family as opposed
to the nuclear one is perhaps possible from the perspective of women's
isolation in the Western family; it may be seen as a well-intended
response to those who argue that such families are more 'developed'

than other kinds of households. However, it ignores the tortuous reality of situations where mothers and sisters in-law provide no support to the young bride or mother, and instead connive in her murder for dowry or contribute to her daily harrassment. Communities of women are not inherently free of, and may reproduce patriarchal power relations. For example, Beatrice and Diaphanta may be partners in conspiracy, but the relationship is essentially exploitative. Beatrice plays the male in it, testing Diaphanta's virginity and reproducing the structures of male legality:

> She will not search me, will she,
> Like the forewoman of a female jury. (*The Changeling*, IV.i.97-8)

Finally Diaphanta is destroyed by Beatrice and the secret space of their fellowship is violated by the rules that govern women in patriarchal class society. That the recurrent mistress-maid friendships in Renaissance drama are acts of desperate loneliness is evident in Beatrice's rather pathetic response to DeFlores's question as to how she could ever trust her maid: 'I must trust *somebody*' (V.i.15; emphasis added). They are also based on the concept of feudal loyalty, which is now exposed to the tensions of a world where all 'natural' ties including those between servants and their superiors are fast eroding (see Whigham for the Duchess's relation to Cariola).

Women often operate from what may crudely be defined as male positions: Livia acts on behalf of men as procuress so that Bianca's last words are that 'like our own sex, we have no enemy' (*Women Beware Women*, V.ii.215). Whereas in Shakespearean drama female solidarity is undermined by lack of power (Beatrice cannot defend Hero as a woman, Emilia defends Desdemona but both die anyway), Middleton's female changelings cannot even establish contact with each other. Their loneliness, isolation, and fissured relationships do not emerge as warnings against their depraved natures but indicate the contradictions imposed upon them within the patriarchal and class confine. Livia, who claims both power and intelligence, betrays other women on behalf of either the Duke or Hippolito; but the one time she acts out of her own desire for Leantio and reverses gender positions in the sexual market, she signals her own end. Beatrice-Joanna may betray Diaphanta, but she herself is hopelessly trapped between several men. By disallowing independent female agency in conditions of their subordination, the plays refuse the possibility of idealising the oppressed subject. Read in a situation where female participation, willing and unwilling, in the oppression of other women is a painful reality, these texts foreground the fissures of the honorary male, who is nevertheless both a victim and a potential rebel.

A 'giddy turning'

The discontinuity of Jacobean heroines has long presented a critical puzzle, as Belsey indicates (*The Subject of Tragedy*, p. 160), but it had been ingeniously reconciled to the concept of a fixed human nature; for example: 'Middleton seems to have grasped the principle . . . that the more generously a nature is endowed, especially perhaps a woman's, the more bitter is its corruption, if it is thwarted or maimed in the full course of its development' (Ellis-Fermor, p. 142). Nathaniel Richards, Middleton's first critic, observed that, 'he knew the rage / Madness of women *crossed*; and for the stage/ fitted their humours' (see Gill's edition of *Women Beware Women*, p. 379; emphasis added). Despite their underlying assumptions of a unifying concept of female nature, even traditional readings acknowledge this repeated crossing and thwatting of female desires in Renaissance drama.

One significant movement in the plays is that restriction is increasingly accompanied by a fundamental dislocation of identity. Despite their appropriation of male clothing or even roles and despite their assertion of female independence, Rosalind or Portia do not approach the dichotomy of disorderly women of later drama such as the Duchess, Beatrice-Joanna, Vittoria or Bianca. The difference may in part be attributed to genre, but even within tragedy there is such a movement: no longer is it possible to posit the unified subject of liberal-humanism as the experience of survival becomes a discontinuous one. In short, there is no pure opposition of idealised subject and oppressive structures despite the increasing violence of their contact; the violence reaches out and slashes the psyche and self-conception of the woman and no longer remains simply an act committed upon her.

It has been pointed out that the title of *The Changeling* could apply to nearly every character in the play (see Randall, pp. 348-9). The heroine's near schizophrenia is therefore latent in those who regard themselves as stable. Repeatedly human relationships too emerge as changeable. DeFlores reminds Beatrice that she is defined not by her birth but by her actions: 'Y'are the deeds creature' (III.iv.137), something that is constantly being made. However, recognition of change is resisted by the characters: Jasperino asks Alsemero if he has changed. Alsemero replies: 'No, friend / I keep the same church, same devotion' (I.i.34-5). Shakespeare's Parolles affirms 'Simply to be the thing I am / Shall make me live' (*All's Well That Ends Well*, IV.iii.310-11). The Duchess asserts that she is the 'Duchess of Malfi still', in spite of what has been done to her (IV.ii.139). Antony repeatedly affirms his identity even as it is constantly being eroded: 'I am / Antony yet' (III.xiii.92-3; see also chapter 5).

These are desperate attempts to sustain the eroding beliefs in the 'essential' selves which are being increasingly battered. Discontinuous identity in the drama has been previously analysed (see Dollimore, *Radical Tragedy*; Belsey, *The Subject of Tragedy*). I want to suggest that such an interplay of stability and change in texts that foreground disorderly women has the effect of qualifying, indeed questioning, received notions of feminine identity. The plays move towards increasing female fluidity. Desdemona may be actually divided by her various positions in relation to the status quo, but she perceives herself as a unified person when compared to Beatrice-Joanna who acknowledges the 'giddy turning' inside her (I.i.152). In both *Women Beware Women* and *The Changeling*, the conventions of romantic love are evoked to be swiftly undermined. Leantio and Bianca are initially a successful version of Romeo and Juliet, and are flushed with the excitement of their runaway marriage. Matrimony is evoked by both as an end to movement, a stability. It marks for Leantio the end of his restlessness and the promise of eternal pleasure in his newly acquired treasure. For Bianca it is a willing effacement of her previous identity:

> I have foresook friends, fortune and my country
> And hourly I rejoice in't. (I.i.131-2)

Alsemero and Beatrice's relationship opens in a temple with reverberations of love as mystical and everlasting. Alsemero's 'inclinations to travels' have now paused. The lovers are transformed by their love; initially this transformation is evoked in the manner typical of romantic love conventions where passion leads to a new stability of self-conception. Romeo and Juliet's new identities are as firm and unchanging as their love. But with Alsemero and Beatrice, discordant notes are struck early: there is a constant play on verbal and conceptual change and terms related to these – 'will', 'judgement', 'eyes', 'seeing'. This makes for a sense that all perception is flawed, all relationships subject to change. To Alsemero's first declarations of love, Beatrice replies:

> Be better advis'd, sir.
> Our eyes are sentinels unto our judgements,
> And should give certain judgement what they see;
> But they are rash sometimes, and tell us wonders
> Of common things, which when our judgements find,
> They can then check our eyes, and call them blind. (I.i.68-73)

Women Beware Women is a 'mocking parallel to Shakespeare's tragedy of star-crossed love' (Ornstein, p. 160) precisely because there too love is not a unified or static category. There are not one but many ways of

loving, and all of them are fluid. Bianca's mobility has brought her from
her parents to Leantio, but the movement will not cease with marriage.
Othello is racked with the contradictions attendant upon female
mobility; similarly Leantio demands from Bianca that she both defy the
stability of her initial positioning and guarantee her subsequent stillness.
But whereas Desdemona is only imagined to transgress further, Bianca
actually does so, and the difference has to do with the effect that violence
on the female body now has on the female mind. Desdemona is in a
sense inviolate, and violence also remains external to Lavinia. But Bianca
graphically internalises the crime committed upon her:

> Now bless me from a blasting! I saw that now,
> Fearful for any woman's eye to look on . . .
> Yet since my honour's leprous, why should I
> Preserve that fair that caus'd the leprosy?
> Come poison all at once! . . . I'm made bold now,
> I thank thy treachery; sin and I'm acquainted,
> No couple greater . . . (II.ii.420-41)

In patriarchal thought, the slide of woman from goddess to whore is
premised simultaneously upon her potential for sexual activity, and
upon her passivity as a receptacle for sin. Even when passive, the woman
is irrevocably polluted by illegitimate sexual contact; therfore sin can
be regarded as both outside of the female self and at the same time its
most definitive constituent. In Renaissance tragedy, however, female
propensity for sin is restructured: firstly, as socially induced rather than
a moral attribute and secondly, as no longer static, but constituting a
dynamic interaction between women's subjectivity and the social conditions of their existence. Therefore, in plays such as The Changeling, or
Women Beware Women, female immorality is imposed upon the subject,
but also incorporated into the individual's self-perception. It is no longer
either alien or intrinsic to women, therefore it is no longer able unambiguously to carry the connotations of its patriarchal usage. The contradictions imposed upon women are internalised, but then they catalyse an
alienation which radically disrupts all notions of social or psychic stability: the 'giddy turning' experienced by 'This changeable stuff' (The
Changeling, IV.ii.46) is not containable within the dominantly defined
notion of female dichotomy.

Bianca's rape is not the focal point or the climax of the play; it intersects
with a dialogue between Guardiano and Livia, an episode with the Ward,
and a chess game between the Mother (supposedly the guardian of
Bianca's virtue) and Livia (the agent of her seduction). After the rape,
the chess game continues until dinner is served as usual. Thus, instead
of being sensationalised, sexual violence is placed firmly in the context

of the play's concern with enforced marriage, state power, family relationships, and the contact between women.

Patriarchy and class power constitute the warp and the weft of violence against women in these plays. If Middleton focuses on the grey area between seduction and rape, on the nebulous zone where Bianca is both victim and participant, both shocked and adaptive, it is because Bianca herself occupies several intersecting positions – she is simultaneously the young runaway bride who wants to believe in romantic love, the glamour-struck girl obsessed by the splendour of the 'noble state' (I.iii.103), the bored wife beginning to chafe at the bondage of marriage, the daughter of 'parents great in wealth' who desires to be the virtuous wife rich in her husband's love but who is already tired of squalor. Leantio wooed her as a romantic lover but the Duke's language is explicitly commercial, playing on her own desires for wealth: 'Come, play the wise wench and provide for ever' (II.ii.383). The rape becomes part seduction because it plays on her dissatisfaction; yet it remains a rape because of her continuing participation in the illusions of romance and fidelity. Therefore Bianca moves away in sexual as well as class terms and yet perceives both transgressions as wrong. Finally of course, she moves from one bondage to another, as indeed does Isabella, and the question is raised whether anything else is possible for women in such societies.

The rape comes to mark Bianca's alienation from the ideology of faithfulness and honour by which she has been expected to live; this alienation is not translated into any supreme and penultimate moment of 'recognition' but rather into a deepening discontinuity of perception and behaviour. Like Bianca, Beatrice-Joanna is 'forced' into submission. And like Bianca, the process of coercion is never outside her. If Bianca's seduction depends on an awareness of what is denied her in terms of wealth, glamour and freedom, Beatrice's transgression depends on an illusory perception of what is possible, by the combination of arrogance and naïvety that her class position confers on her. The effect of events upon character is reiterated. Beatrice changes twice – first she begins to love Alsemero, then DeFlores. She had declared both undying love for Alsemero and her eternal hatred of DeFlores; but then,

> I'm forc'd to love thee now,
> 'Cause thou provid'st so carefully for my honour. (V.i.47-8)

Each change does not simply negate the previous state of being; Alsemero notes that 'there's scarce a thing but is both lov'd and loath'd' (I.i.122). Beatrice is simultaneously attracted and repelled by DeFlores, and both alienated from and attached to Alsemero. However, at no

point does she stand neatly outside patriarchal ideology; she needs and
exploits Diaphanta, she desperately lies to Alsemero, she is truly
wretched at being called whore. Sigrid Weigel, in an interesting essay
called 'Double focus', has argued that the latent schizophrenia of woman
consists in the fact that those elements of the model of femininity which
earn her *moral* respect (for example motherliness, understanding, socia-
bility) are also the basis for her social subordination (p. 80). This is
certainly true of women in the plays who necessarily experience themselves through male eyes, but even so their 'giddy turning' puzzles the
men in the play for they are no longer the stable female subjects desired
by dominant thought.

The unstable divide

In Jacobean drama female transgression is no longer simply a spectre
conjured up by the male imagination. Lisa Jardine is correct in protesting
against the attempt of critics to exonerate the female heroes of these
plays from the 'sexual slur'. The progression towards a dichotomous
identity accompanies women's active sexuality which is no longer able
to be expressed within patriarchal norms. Rosalind (*As You Like It*) or
Portia (*The Merchant of Venice*) or Beatrice (*Much Ado About Nothing*) can step
out of female clothing or roles, but their desires are reconciliable to the
masculine will:

> Women are released from their usual habits, and the sexes from usual relations,
> in order to ... justify these customs ...Shakespeare's magnificient comic
> heroines thrive in facilitating marriages ... ones that restore the 'natural' sex
> roles. Shakespeare's women are at their best, then ... when they function to
> believe in or to deliver men from their own best selves or to die in trying.
> (Andreson-Thom, p. 276)

Finally the women choose perfectly acceptable lovers; in fact their
selection often coincides with the will of the patriarch, as in *The Merchant
of Venice*, although the process confers an illusion of free choice. They
remain chaste until the marriage rites are formalised, and their defiance
does not challenge the boundaries of either race or class. Even so, it is
possible that the play on gender identity opens up the issue of women
in a new way; on the whole, however, these are the texts (rather than
The Duchess as Belsey suggests) where the liberal notion of marriage is
glowingly evoked. In the case of Desdemona there is a radical conflict
between her own perception of love, which is well within the limits of
chastity and patriarchal transfer of woman from father to husband, and
its political connotations, which clothe it with the implications of sexual

impurity. In *The Duchess of Malfi* female sexuality hovers on the borders of acceptable limits: widow remarriage is licentious but technically permissible.[3] In *The White Devil*, Vittoria's desire is clearly unchaste, but she is faithful to her lover, as is Cleopatra; in Middleton's plays female sexuality makes a final break from the confines of romanticism as Bianca and Beatrice-Joanna oscillate between different men. In Ford, sexual transgression can only be expressed by incest, which is already evident in *Women Beware Women*. Therefore, the general distinction between Elizabethan and Jacobean drama is that in the latter the assertive woman does sexually transgress and is not only imagined to do so

The shift is significant. As Woodbridge comments in relation to *The Duchess of Malfi*: 'Any defender of women could show a widow remaining chaste. But to turn a widow who does not remain chaste into a tragic hero was revolutionary' (p. 260). But precisely because of this, the ideological implications of female disobedience in the drama are still under debate, as the criticism of *The Duchess of Malfi* reveals. Lisa Jardine argues that in Webster's play male assessment of the Duchess is fraught with explicitly sexual innuendoes; that this controls the audience's judgement of her; that the Duchess's secret marriage would be regarded by them much as it is by her brothers – as a typically female act of cunning, duplicity and sexual waywardness, and that her punishment serves to exorcise the spectre of female rebellion (*Still Harping, 'The Duchess of Malfi'*). Such a reading telescopes the ideological effect of the play into the attitudes of the male adversaries of the Duchess. There is an obvious emotional weightage accorded to the Duchess, but this only compounds the problems in assessing her, which Shepherd effectively sums up: 'If we indict her lechery we side with the vicious brothers; if we want a chaste heroine we share the credulous ignorance of Antonio' (p. 117).

Catherine Belsey avoids a simple equation of male positions within the play with the ideology of the text (*The Subject of Tragedy*). She points to the positive portrayal of the Duchess's relationship with Antonio and its deliberate contrast to the horrors of the brothers' wrath. This difference warns us that the sexual slur which the brothers confer upon the Duchess cannot be taken as the moral tone of the play itself, as Jardine seems to do. But precisely such a contrast between the Duchess and her brothers is located by Belsey in liberal-humanist oppositions between public and private, political and domestic. By marking the woman's place within the latter, 'the affective ideal which is so glowingly defined in *The Duchess of Malfi* collapses into the sad history of collaboration between liberalism and sexism which defines the western family from the seventeenth century to the present'. The play, concludes Belsey, is a perfect fable of emergent liberalism' (*The Subject of Tragedy*, pp. 197-200).

I would like to suggest firstly, that the Duchess's duplicity is handled very differently than in a medieval sterotype of female hypocrisy; and secondly, that the play does not subscribe to but questions the division between private and public – it exposes the ideological and political thrust of such a division. Whereas other defences of the period such as Anger's pamphlet or Middleton's *More Dissemblers Besides Women* argue that men, not women, are duplicitous, *The Duchess* – and *The White Devil, The Changeling, Women Beware Women,* and *Antony and Cleopatra* – offer an alternative examination of female duplicity which begins by acknowledging instead of denying it. In Painter's *Palace of Pleasure* (1567) which contained a translation from Matteo Bandello's original story of the Duchess, she is a 'fine and subtile dame', who lusts for Antonio in order to 'make hir way to pleasure, which she lusted more than marriage', and her marriage itself is a 'Maske and coverture to hide her follies and shameless lusts' (p. 184). Webster does not deny either the Duchess' duplicity or her active sexuality, but female pleasure is no longer a dirty word in the new text.

Its liberal connotations are questionable on the very grounds that Belsey uses to point to them. It is true that the Duchess remains firmly within the domestic arena. So do Vittoria, Bianca, Beatrice-Joanna, Desdemona, Annabella and Isabella; none of them overtly seeks to usurp male authority, they remain within the spaces that have been patri-archally defined as personal and assigned to women. I have already indicated the massive effort in early modern society to confine women, ideologically and physically, into domestic areas; we also have seen that it is not coincidental that the issue of absolutism arose at the same time as increased restrictions on women (see Shepherd, p. 119). The Duchess is literally enclosed in the male-dominated castle. Denied individual identity and even a name, she is merely 'the Duchess'. Not only are most Jacobean heroines banished to the domestic sphere (Cleopatra is an exception), but they often aim only for concessions patriarchally granted to them:

> Why might I not marry?
> I have not gone about, in this, to create
> Any new world or custom. (III.ii.110-12)

Despite their pitifully domestic urges, these women are thwarted, not merely within the family, but as in *The Duchess of Malfi* or *The White Devil,* by public authority, by all the institutions of feudal and mercantile patri-archy; their transgression evokes a political disarray, even a chaos of cosmic proportions. Instead of demarcating the private world from the public, the impossibility of the first isolating itself is underlined. Feminists have not invented the connection between the personal and the political; patriarchal thought recognises it and attempts to disguise it. Thus a dowry murder in India is officially referred to as a 'dowry death', which lifts it from the category of an ordinary murder and seeks implicitly to exclude it from the realm of common criminality and justice. It becomes a 'family problem', but of course the effort to hush it up is not merely familial, but requires the complicity of police, public opinion and legal structures. The most passive and confined of female lives works as a crucial link in the political and public hierarchies. Although the Duchess is a good wife and mother she violates some of the notions of ideal femininity, as indeed she must, for such notions are total only within a stereotype. Precisely because she is so compliant, she cannot be demonised as a totally deviant woman. Yet she is destroyed even as a witch would be. It is this combination of the normal and the radical, the domestic and the political, that makes the implications of the story so deeply disturbing, particularly in a situation where the most everyday normal woman is subject to the most violent fate.

The effect of a play like The Duchess is to highlight the violent underpinnings of the domestic. Active female sexuality is not merely a breach of decorum but also a flagrant breach of the public and political order, as feminists know and seek to reveal, and as patriarchy knows and seeks to hide. Precisely because most of these women do not conceive of or articulate their demands as political, the violent and public reaction to their aspirations serves, not to subscribe to, but to lay bare the division between domestic and political, personal and public, emotional and rational.

Again, in the 'sister-tragedy' of The White Devil (the term is J. R. Brown's, The Duchess of Malfi, p. xxxi), Vittoria publicly confronts the judiciary as well as the Church, but only because her adultery, like the Duchess's remarriage, is not treated as a private issue. Vittoria recognises and exposes the attempt to divide the personal and the public by calling her trial a 'rape'; by claiming that the State and Church have 'ravish'd justice' (III.ii.271, 273). Patriarchal legality conceives of female sexuality as criminal, so she seizes on its own analogy and inverts it by employing the language of sexuality to describe a legal procedure; thus she is the first to employ the connection between sexuality and power in favour of the woman. In a society where the nuclear family and its ideals are still evolving, as in India, the effect of Jacobean tragedy can be read as interrogation instead of closure. At the same time, such a reading is, I believe, not contrary to the sexual politics of the Renaissance, where the language of patriarchy is also the vocabulary of political control.

Vittoria *articulates* the connections between private and public; the
Duchess does not. But the politics of these texts cannot be collapsed
into the consciousness of the individual heroine: to search for a
consciously political protagonist to carry the burden of an anti-patriarchal text would be to replicate the terms of idealist criticism. In search-
ing for the perfect and unified female revolutionary, feminists may themselves be guilty of underlining the terms of heroic or liberal drama,
which are denied by Jacobean tragedy. The *Duchess of Malfi* is not an elaborate patriarchal device to contain female rebellion; on the contrary, it
takes a woman who is a misogynist's delight – duplicitous, sexually
active, defiant – and then proceeds, not by defending her along the lines
that misogynists are familiar with and know how to counter, but by
asking questions which are hard to answer in the language of patriarchy.
The fissures of the female changeling are patriarchally imposed upon
her and yet serve to expose the politics of her subordination. It can be
suggested that by rupturing the linkage of heroism and morality, these
plays achieve for female identity what Dr *Faustus* or *Macbeth* had for the
notion of man. But such a rupture becomes harder to acknowledge in
the case of a woman, hence the dominant critical silence about its
implications in these plays.

Restriction and resistance

In chapter 3, I discussed the slide of meaning from physical and spatial
to sexual and ideological mobility in Renaissance texts. But the correspondence between them is not necessarily straightforward: for example,
the most physically mobile female roles are those of Rosalind, Viola or
Portia but here the mobility is dependent upon disguise and, I have
shown, involves an ideological fixity of female behaviour. Moll Cutpurse
is more mobile, more obviously defiant than the physically enclosed
Duchess, or Beatrice-Joanna who is finally locked in a cupboard, or
Vittoria who is confined to a reformatory; but she is not necessarily
more resistant to patriarchy. Moll roams the city, resists the confine of
marriage, but is also keeper of the law and, above all, doesn't raise the
problem of uncontrollable female sexuality because she remains chaste.
Partly, these differences can be related to those of the genre: generally
speaking comedy foregrounds physical movement, while Renaissance
tragedy increasingly concerns itself with its conceptual implications,
resulting in duplicity and schizophrenia of the women. The tragic
heroine is located within the estate, or castle, or home (Juliet cannot
even consider running away with Romeo to Mantua, but must await
him in the tomb of her forefathers) and her attempts at external or

internal movement result in her violent end; her comic counterpart travels around, either into fictitious worlds like Arden or actual spaces of streets and shops of London, but is finally reinstated within the social order.

If Moll questions the spaces allotted to women by straying out of them physically, appropriating masculine dress that allows for more spatial freedom and refusing the confine of home and marriage, the Duchess interrogates social and sexual boundaries from within traditionally alloted female spaces and thus threatens their very separation from the masculine, the public, and the political arenas. Women's speech spans both physical and conceptual movement, but not all speech is disruptive – for example, The Taming of the Shrew involves not Kate's silencing but her schooling, so that her longest speech is a tribute to her husband; as a shrew she actually spoke less, but disobedience conferred the illusion of excess upon her words. But at other times, female speech epitomises rebellion (Cleopatra is the most verbose of Shakespeare's women), hence the injunction to women to obey in silence (see Belsey, The Subject of Tragedy, pp. 149-91).

In a society where stability was invoked to maintain monarchism and its attendant hierarchies, the interrogation of both physical and ideological boundaries is subversive. In the seventeenth century both sorts of movement threatened a status quo which had to accommodate the potential for literal movement in urban culture; so the ideology of privacy had to accomplish what the castle wall had hitherto done. Since the texts we have been looking at posit the division between private and public, inner and outer, emotional and political as constructed and unstable, such a divide is unable to serve its ideological function of keeping women 'in their place', and instead catalyses their movement away from their usual sphere. It becomes evident that on the one hand there is evidence of female resistance, and on the other, the slightest female movement is magnified by its political repercussions.

We are now in a position to consider the correlation between physical and conceptual mobility and coercion more fully, in order to approach further aspects of recurrent female duplicity in the texts. Men have a private as well as public existence, whereas women are taught to function within men's private lives only.[4] They lack a public life of their own – they are denied participation as producers and controllers of wealth or authority. But, correspondingly, they are denied a dimension comparable to men's private lives, since all aspects of their lives are controlled and in that sense public. It is significant that although 'private' dominantly refers to the sexual, woman's sexuality is publicly structured. Therefore, lacking both public and private space, physically as well as

ideologically, woman has had to retreat further into her 'inner' being
in order to find spaces that are not publicly controlled. We may identify
the act of writing by women as an attempt to replace privacy with literary
space.[5] Such attempts may exist alongside the effort to find actual spaces,
but are prioritised precisely when the former are not available. As such
they are contradictory enterprises, doomed to failure because there are
no free inner spaces in the absence of outer ones; creative writing is
possible only when some realms of privacy are physically granted to
upper-class women (see Thorne, 'Women's Creativity'). At the same
time, secrecy and withdrawal can be seen as strategies to protect an
inner life. It is in this context that the dissembling and duplicity of the
Duchess and her sisters should be placed.

Let us return briefly to the example of Elizabeth I, who repeatedly
attempted to appropriate a masculine identity in order to consolidate
authority. In this she was not unique: for a latter-day female authority
like Indira Gandhi also felt compelled to claim that she had been brought
up as a boy and felt no different from a man: she thought it a compliment
when referred to as 'the only man in the cabinet' and said that 'certain
qualities are associated with men, such as decision making' (see Kishwar
and Vanita, p. 254). No doubt the comparison can be extended to
include other women, such as Margaret Thatcher, who rule as what
Heisch has called honorary men and extend patriarchal rather than
female power. Of course such assertions are strategic, but it is significant
that Elizabeth simultaneously evoked her femininity, sheltering behind
it to procrastinate on marriage, which her Parliament was pressuring
her towards: 'The weight and greatness of this matter might cawse in
me being a woman wantinge both witt and memory some feare to
speake, and bashfulness besides, a thing appropriat to my sex ...'
(Heisch, 'Queen Elizabeth I: parliamentary rhetoric', p. 34). Therefore
she oscillated between her status as honorary male and weak female;
while this may indicate at one level the internalisation of female inferiority, at another it was a brilliant strategy both to appropriate the public
spaces denied to women and repudiate the 'private' realm allocated to
them. Similar strategic employment of both masculine virtue and femininity will be noted in the case of Cleopatra's oscillation between
'president of my kingdom' (III.vii.17) and 'no more but e'en a woman'
(IV.xiv.73).

These 'movements' allow us to consider the subversive aspects of
female 'hypocrisy'. Isabella in Women Beware Women has no option but
to enter into a forced marriage with the foolish Ward. Her only choice
is that of the attitude with which she will do it. Now, when she begins
to love Guardiano, she finds her marriage can accommodate her secret

affair. Since the former involves emotional hypocrisy anyway, she finds it easier to dissemble. The marriage does not require, or even consider the whole of her being, therefore it initiates the split between appearance and reality. Whereas men can be legitimately two-faced (the public and the private man), in the case of women, the colonisation of the dark continent of interiority must be protected by duplicity.

For the men in The Duchess of Malfi, the Duchess is typed as duplicitous even before they know of her marriage. In the very first scene she is told that her 'darkest actions will come to light'; the Cardinal's fears anticipate, and perhaps contribute to the formulation of, her plans:

> You may flatter yourself
> And take your own choice: privately be married
> Under the eaves of the night. (I.i.316-18)

Beatrice-Joanna is assumed to be duplicitous by Alsemero even as he thinks of her as his goddess and the goal of his existence. By appropriating his virginity test, substituting Diaphanta for herself, Beatrice is attempting to protect herself but is also exposing the premises on which any marriage would be founded. The Duchess, Vittoria, Beatrice-Joanna merely adopt the dichotomy that patriarchal thought has conferred upon them anyway. The difference is that whereas women's anticipated duplicity or sexual activity is a patriarchal attempt to demonise and exorcise them, actual transgression is subversive of this control.

The increasing secrecy of rebellion also indicates the extent to which women are divided subjects whose public and private lives are forced apart and who are under male, public gaze. The fact that they are forced to experience themselves only in relation to men works like a knife, so that they can never be unified subjects in any sense, and experience the dichotomies of virgin/whore, intellect/body, reproductive vessel/decorative object. Male objectification is not only a placement of women in relation to men, but a specific female experience:

To be born a woman has been to be born within an allotted and confined space, into the keeping of men. The social presence of women has developed as a result of their ingenuity in living under a such tutelage within such a limited space. But this has been at the cost of a woman's self being split in two . . . her own sense of being appreciated as herself by another . . . Men act and women appear. Men look at women. Women watch themselves being looked at. This determines not only the relations between men and women but also the relation of women to themselves. The surveyor of women in herself is male: the surveyed female. Thus she turns herself into an object. (Berger, p. 47)

Women's criteria for self appraisal are male. Beatrice-Joanna thus experiences herself precisely as the combination of goddess and whore that she had been told all women are; she is at once the all powerful goddess whom all men desire and whose will is law, and the whore whom all men hate and who begs father and husband not to come near her for fear she will taint them.

Secondly, if 'male and female differences are seen as the product of symbolic structures encoded in the language of the pre-existing culture into which one is born, it can be argued that all women have suffered some degree of speech impediment in trying to communicate female experience with a phallocentric tongue' (Ardener, p. 206). What Kristeva calls the 'hysteric's voice' is, according to Juliet Mitchell, 'women's masculine language talking of feminine experience'. Thus concludes Ecker, who quotes the others, 'Women are seen to speak from within the patriarchal discourse rather than from a source exterior to phallocentric symbolic forms' (p. 21).

Duplicity as a strategy is both born of and flawed by the dichotomies of women's own experience. It raises the question of false consciousness, which has also been asked in connection with women's cross-dressing. Here it has been argued that women dressing as men only confirm male-imposed criteria of freedom, and that their rebellion is therefore not 'the real thing' (see Dollimore, 'Subjectivity, sexuality and transgression'). The question takes us right back into the debates around ideology: Lenin, who needed to theorise the basis for the growing revolutionary consciousness in Russia, needed to go beyond Marx's definition of ideology as just 'false consciousness'. If ideology is necessarily rooted in material reality, and this reality is oppressive, then where are the sources of a revolutionary consciousness? Lenin extended the concept of ideology to a consciousness which is various, and includes different oppositional versions, such as the bourgeois or the socialist (*What is to be Done*). Althusser's further distinction between a general ideology (whose function is to ensure social cohesion) and specific ideologies (deriving from various class positions) is extremely useful here, for it allows us to see that cross-dressing, or women's dichotomies in the drama, are neither pure revolutionary consciousness nor merely false, but rather are representative of the powerful clash of ideas played out on the arena of subjectivity. In her notes on feminist theory, Joan Kelly concluded that an oppositional consciousness arises out of 'the discrepancy between the real and the ideal' experienced by those who stand on the boundary of the dominant culture: 'like Hegel's slave, woman experiences an "unhappy consciousness", a form of alienation that makes her at once a participant in the culture that oppresses her and a stranger to it' (p. xxv): such an unhappiness informs the duplicitous changeling of the drama.

Receiving the disorderly woman

Dominant readings of Renaissance tragedy have moved towards a closure, a sealing off of its disturbances to authority and hence of its radical potential (see Dollimore, *Radical Tragedy*). In the colonial context this has implied an effacing of the various contradictions experienced by the readers, both in relation to their own culture and to the colonial text. The binary oppositions imposed on women are analogous to and reinforce those of colonial discourse; thus in the case of Indian women the erasure extends to both powerfully interlinking sets of contradictions, each of which may otherwise serve as a vantage point for grasping the interrogation of various boundaries that I have traced in the texts, and vice versa.

It has been suggested that Indian women experience social space along the binary oppositions imposed by patriarchal thought – private/public, danger/safety, pure/polluted (Sharma, p. 227). Instead of a static dichotomy, however, I suggest that the experience of Indian women is far more volatile. To begin with, Indian religions and culture contain powerful matriarchal myths, or myths of female power. Such myths, as we are repeatedly warned, may only confirm male superiority by either demonising female strength, or working as a safety-valve to let out anti-patriarchal steam.[6] However, as Natalie Davis suggests, the image of the disorderly woman, *even when contained and demonised*, 'opens out behavioral options for women' (pp. 154-5). Female strength and female disorder are not interchangeable; the images sometimes cited to glorify Indian traditions as proto-feminist in fact function to underline a male conception of female energy: 'The feminist movement has no relevance in India, none at all, because our whole background is different ... Take for instance Savitri – she is typically in the line of strong women. She challenged even death and persevered in doing so because she was exercising her natural feminine quality'.[7]

Savitri's power is derived from and is in the service of her husband. She had married Satyavan despite the knowledge that he was fated to die within one year. When the god of death Yama came to claim him, Savitri insisted on accompanying her husband since his wife's place was always with him. She refused to accept Yama's assurances that with her husband's death all her wifely obligations had expired. Finally Satyavan was returned to Savitri in acknowledgement of her devotion so that the two of them could beget 'a century of sons possessed of strength and prowess and capable of perpetuating our race' (Kakar, p. 67). Here we have a powerful legitimisation of the ideologies that inform *sati*; and a

woman's strength is as a wife and as a reproducer of the patriarchal
family. Even in the evocation of the story to assert an indigeneous tradition of female power (cited above), there is not only a rejection of
feminism but, via the affirmation of wifely power as a 'natural' attribute
of women, an implicit negation of a whole counter-tradition of powerful
and disturbing femininity, subversive of precisely those norms upheld
by Savitri.

This tradition has slowly begun to be uncovered, although large areas
of it can be seen as assimilated into, demonised by, or clouded over by
dominant histories, myths and cultures (see Babb, 'Marriage and
malevolence'; Chattopadhyay, Lokayata; Ponniah, 'Ideology and the
status of women in Hindu society'). Liddle and Joshi suggest that this
tradition, including worship of the mother goddess, constitutes 'a matriarchal culture, in the sense that it preserves the value of women as life-
givers and sources of activating energy, and it represents the acknowledgement of women's power by women and men in the culture' (p.
55). Although this concept is somewhat vague, and it is doubtful whether
Indian culture today can be called matriarchal in any sense of the term,
the presence of this counter-tradition makes available a powerful and
potentially radical ambivalence and dichotomy, which is not so easily contained as dominant culture may suggest. In popular culture, the early
figure of the powerful, malevolent, unmarried goddess is woven into
images of everyday life female disobedience and vice versa; both are
sought to be ritually exorcised but survive as powerful behavioral
options. These may be bolstered by a wide array of contemporary images
– for example, those provided by the growing women's movement;
conversely, feminist movements or education may strategically seize
upon the latent dichotomy of popular culture.

In the folk festival of 'Bandamma Panduga' in Andhra, for example,
one may find a disturbance, an interrogation of desired female
behaviour, through theatrical representation.[8] The festival is designed
to propitiate the goddess Bandamma, who is single, powerful and therefore evil. Her active sexuality is linked to fears of female authority in
general and to widows, disobedient wives and promiscuous women in
particular. During the first four days of the festival, she is worshipped
in her powerful and malignant aspect, and on the final day is represented
as propitiated, tamed and domesticated. Two different kinds of theatrical
performances are therefore held: the first are skits, which revolve around
the theme of the world turned upside down and reversals of social,
particularly sexual, hierarchy; the second is formal drama emphasising
female loyalty, male protectiveness and social stability. As Tapper notes,
the reversals in the skits are closely linked to actual fears of disorderly

women:

These skits are also interesting guides to the suspicions about female character which are a part of the ideological rationale for male dominance. Among the issues raised in them are the problem of the lack of male heirs, the role of female economic activity, the need for wives to respect their husbands, adultery and other aspects of marital breakdown. (p. 24)

I will quote briefly from one such skit:

Wife: (brags, gossiping with another woman) Do you have a husband who is equal to mine? (Long pause) Well, perhaps our husbands are similar after all . . . Your husband has a crooked mouth and mine has a crooked arse. (Enters the house and begins ordering her husband to help her take a heavy basket off her head) Come on, help me take this basket off my head. Do it slowly, be careful. (As he helps her she uses the opportunity of his bending over to step on his head.) Due to my devotion to you as a loyal wife, if I put my foot on your head, I will go straight to heaven.
Husband: Hey! Are you putting your foot on my head?
Wife: Yes, doesn't every wife? Hold on, I'll take my leg down (said as she steps on him even more emphatically). Ah, I am so loyal to you. From the day I was born I never desired any other man. (Aside) Except Penta Rao! (Tapper, pp. 24-5)

The audience laughs at the reversals and these are finally 'righted' by the drama.

But as with the instances of disorder analysed by Davis, their containment is not complete; both the daily experience of oppression of women and the linkage with the power of the single goddess makes such images desired rather than totally negative. If Indira Gandhi encouraged representations of herself as Kali, the goddess of destruction, she was playing upon the ambivalence allowed by such an image. During the independence struggle, women's resistance was glorified and channeled into patriarchally accepted images of active women. For example, the legendary Rani of Jhansi, celebrated for her resistance to the British Raj during the 1857 uprising, is popularly represented as *mardani* or mannish; at the other end of the spectrum the Gandhian movement enlisted mass female participation, but on the premise that woman is 'a giver whose giving extends beyond the family but does not exclude it; a mother and sister not to a few individuals but to the country and to the world' (Vanita, 'Ravana', p. 189).

My point simply is firstly, that the ambivalence of such histories must be amplified. We must deny the supposed homogeneity of culture and position the Indian female readers as occupying diverse and contradictory heritages. Secondly, of course, the radical potential of such heterogeneity is not inherent but is catalysed in conjunction with subsequent developments – for example, growing articulation of female

discontent and the women's movement. So one may suggest that the
images of female disorder in Renaissance drama and in, say, Indian
culture and contemporary reality, can be made to become mutually
illuminating, can be made to interact in specific classroom situations.

We have spoken of the various contradictions which operate in the
case of the Jacobean heroine. The final one is of course between the
male author and the female creation. Whose voice do we hear? The
woman protagonist or the male author? Do the heroines experience
greater interiorisation of male behaviour than is usual because they are
the products of the masculine pen? Or are they able to resist male domination more than real life women precisely because they do not suffer
all the handicaps of the latter? Catherine Belsey's argument is that male
actors playing women disguised as men produced a subject that is able
to resist/transcend usual gender divisions ('Disrupting sexual difference'). Can we extend this, to suggest that because male writers speak
as women who are trying to appropriate male prerogatives, there is
even a greater disruption of the purely uni-gendered standpoint – such
that the female subject is able to occupy the area between the real life
woman and the conventional heroine, between the stereotypical
woman and the monstrous one?

The question still remains as to why male writers should foreground
the issue of female transgression. I have suggested that the idea of a
patriarchal conspiracy reduces the complexities of the ideologies that
inform the plays and and also ignores their political thrust. An author's
attitude to gender relations is to be seen as part of his/her other politics,
not simply coexisting with them; to use the sex of the author uncritically
as an indicator of his/her feminism or patriarchalism would be as great
a mistake as to accept the class background of an individual as sufficient
for determining their politics – although we may grant that a feminist
perspective is in principle far more readily available to women. On the
other hand, the plays are far more contradictory and complicated than
just simple defences of women.

Instead gender becomes also the metaphor (though not merely in a
crudely representative sense) for a series of relationships between
authority and its 'others'. Such metaphors are not limited for the use of
those in power and it can be suggested that they are crucial for a drama
which has increasingly been seen to focus on the complexity of power
relations. As I shall suggest in the next chapter, women also become a
vehicle for the theatre's exploration of its own complicated relationship
to the status quo.

Finally, a constant harking back to the question of authorial intention
may serve only to insist on a single and stable meaning; on the contrary

to explore the different effects of the play is not only to uncover its meanings within specific situations, but also to amplify aspects of its inception which have been historically clouded by its dominant deployment. The radical interrogation possible via the duplicitous woman, then, may only be one meaning which attaches to Renaissance drama from the perspective of the situation obtaining in contemporary English studies in India; nevertheless it serves to focus both on Renaissance sexual politics and some of the subsequent histories of these texts.

Notes

1 Ornstein finds that DeFlores 'was her fate because he realised the potentialities of her nature . . . Like Middleton's other heroines Beatrice must be betrayed in order to know herself, for only he can free her from the chains of convention and of family and duty. He is her Petrarchan love; his single-minded, reckless, consuming sexual hunger is the closest approximation she will find to the literary dream of absolute passion'(p. 187).

But does Beatrice ever 'know herself', and is she ever 'freed'? Here the terms of heroic drama are reproduced and romanticised, and there is no analysis of the interlinkage of class and gender in this 'consuming sexual hunger'. T. S. Eliot claimed that Middleton 'understood woman in tragedy better than any of the Elizabethans' excluding (of course!) Shakespeare. For Eliot such an understanding is a patronising, almost intuitive, act possible by the man of genius, because there are permanent human feelings and a universal femininity (p. 166).

For an analysis of a recent adaptation of Middleton's Women Beware Women see my 'Disorderly Women', chapter six.

2 See Kakar, The Inner World; Mernissi, Beyond the Veil. One such folk song is in Punjabi; a woman narrates her experiences after marriage to her friends: whenever she goes to eat, she finds her husband Girdhari Lal's plate next to hers; when she goes to bathe, his underclothes; when she goes to sleep, his bed and if she goes to the toilet, his wash bowl appears next to her own. The song becomes bawdier, and is punctuated by the friends chanting 'O, wonderful Girdhari Lal'. The tone or flavour are untranslatable but since Girdhari's achievement consists of a rather irritating proximity, the song hilariously undercuts the romance of marriage or even the supposed sexual prowess of the bridegroom. Some other songs are more unkind, or even downright abusive.

3 Citing the pronouncements of Vives, Cornelius Agrippa, Stephen Guazzo and William Heale in favour of remarriage, Frank Wadsworth argues that 'the evidence suggests that when Webster decided to dramatise the story of the Duchess of Malfi, he would not have had to assume that his audience would immediately and automatically condemn the Duchess for remarrying' (p. 398). While there is evidence to suggest that widow remarriage is technically permissible in the eyes of religion and law, I think Wadsworth is wrong to assume that remarriage was tolerated because the widow of substance was a desirable economic proposition. In fact he himself notes that the King's widows (i.e. those women who inherited property held by him) were allowed to remarry as long as they did not claim this property or paid the necessary fee for it. Wadsworth concludes that the attitude towards widow remarriage was economic instead of moral. However a crude separation of the two is not possible: hence while it may be suggested that the richer the widow the more the disapproval, it is also true that the disapproval would bolster itself by the moral tones of religion and misogynist prejudice and filter downwards to all widows. On the other hand this suggests a debate over the question of remarriage, a tension rather than a confirmed and unequivocal indictment from all

sections of society.

4 I am deeply indebted to Judith Blair's brilliant essay 'Private parts in public places' for my analysis of duplicity. This article and others in Ardener's collection, *Women and Space* provided an introduction to spatial analysis generally and directed my attention to the social and sexual *placement* of women.

5 See Rashmi Bhatnagar's 'Genre and gender' for an analysis of woman's loneliness and literary space in Tagore's novel *The Broken Nest*. Anne Thorne's dissertation on women's creativity and architectural space brings together similar issues with useful documentation on medieval and Renaissance housing.

6 For analysis of the patriarchal basis of various apparently feminist myths see Joan Bamberger 'The myth of matriarchy: why men rule in primitive society'; Mandy Merck, 'The city's achievements: the patriotic Amazonomachy and ancient Athens'; William Blake Tyrell, *Amazons: a study in Athenian myth-making*. Marina Warner's *Monuments and Maidens* is also useful with respect to the meaning of iconography of the female form.

7 Kamladevi Chattopadhyay, *Times of India*. Chattopadhyay is a veteran freedom-fighter and author of *Indian Women's Battle for Freedom*; she typifies the post-colonial dilemma of third world women, which Mernissi talks of in *Beyond the Veil*, where an indigenous heritage and mode of struggle becomes imperative and yet leads into the pitfalls, indicated by Fanon, of asserting some of the most retrogressive elements of tradition.

8 This festival is specific to a particular region, so the precise disturbance does not apply to urban readers of the texts, but I am here interested in indicating the duality in what has been dominantly claimed as a closed and static tradition. Such a disturbance in urban areas may be provided by the militancy of the growing women's movement or by agit-prop theatre. Interestingly, as a result of the mass-scale involvement of women during the independence struggle, women's political (but not necessarily feminist) activity is more acceptable in India than in many Western European contexts.

5

'Travelling thoughts':
theatre and the space of the other

Negative capability reconsidered

The assumption of dominant Anglo-American criticism, that tragedy must arrive at 'some comprehensive vision of the relation of human suffering to human joy' (Ribner, p. 1) and must lead via catharsis to moral certainity, was central in both bringing the privileged text to a closure and in institutionalising this by framing a hierarchical canon of 'great' art. The exalted stature of Shakespearean drama, its affirmation of a moral (i.e conservative) order and its movement towards a final and unquestionable truth are interdependent claims which are invoked to confirm one another (see also Heinemann, p. 203). On the other hand, Middletonian drama (for example) was dismissed as 'not the highest kind of tragedy' because its protagonists do not arrive at any 'recognition of truth' (Muir, pp. xiii-xiv). Truth-telling was an attribute of the Godlike and 'detached' artist, and yet this criterion was selectively applied on a slanted principle: precisely what was celebrated as 'negative capability' in the case of Shakespeare was dismissed as an 'ironically detached unheroic view of life not attuned to the heroic passions of early tragedy' in the case of Middleton.[1]

Bertolt Brecht has increasingly been used to re-read the plays of the period because he found a 'complex, shifting, largely impersonal, never soluble' conflict, a 'disconnectedness' of both structure and perspective that approximated to his own (*Brecht on Theatre*, p. 161) in what had been regarded as a omniscient authorial detachment. This has radical implications, not only for the reading of the plays, but for 'democratising' the Renaissance canon, with its Shakespearean apex, for Brecht observed similar characteristics in at least twenty of Shakespeare's contemporaries.

Brecht's analysis was important also for focusing in a new and self-conscious way on structure and form as an aspect of textual meaning and perspective. The blurring of distinctions between comedy and tragedy had often been disparagingly noted by critics in relation to the plays of Middleton; *Women Beware Women*, for example, has been called an 'unsuccessful attempt to create tragedy out of the materials and conventions of satiric comedy' , its central theme 'more appropriate to a broadside balladeer than the tragic poet' (Ornstein, p. 140). Brecht read such 'impurities' in the context of the various ways in which Renaissance drama resisted artistic isolation into the world of make-believe. He noted that its language incorporated the speech of the beer-hall audiences; that daylight performances and open stages prevented hypnotic illusion, that the dramatisation of material familiar to the audience encouraged a critical approach; that the collective nature of the theatre companies and their life-style encouraged montage and epic construction which opposes the idea of drama as a self-sufficient microcosm. All this, says Brecht, led to a 'naive surrealism', practised not only by Shakespeare but also by other dramatists of the period (see Heinemann, p. 209).

Robert Weimann has demonstrated that 'the basis of Shakespeare's "negative capability" is itself socio-historical', located partly in the 'freedom, the detachment, and the imagination made available to him by the popular tradition in the theater' and partly in the fact that while older feudal values could already be questioned, those of capitalism 'were not yet their *necessary alternative*'; the 'myriad-mindedness' of Shakespeare's art is contextualised by Weimann in terms of the positioning of both artist and the playhouse (pp. 176-7), and is interwoven with the structural looseness of the plays. More recently, Jonathan Dollimore has elaborated the implications of the Brechtian connection by drawing upon Brecht's critical and dramatic approach to identify the materialist 'realism' of Renaissance drama, its emphasis on discontinuity of form and character and its radical questioning of the philosophical and political status quo (*Radical Tragedy*; see also Heinemann, 'How Brecht read Shakespeare').

My own purpose here is to insert the dimension of gender more fully into such proto-Brechtian multiplicity and montage, and to suggest that the epic structure is at least partly derived from and closely related to the drama's interrogation of gender roles and patriarchal authority. Conversely, the non-teleological form itself becomes an important vehicle for resisting closure: it suggests, as Brecht claimed, the open-endedness of a situation – that if things could happen one way, they could also have happened in a totally different manner. Open-endedness in this sense does not connote a free-wheeling vaccuum: 'true realism has to do more than just make reality visible on the stage . . . One has to be able to see the laws that decide how the processes of life develop' (*Brecht on Theatre*, p. 27).

An invocation of the sanctity of a linear and teleological structure was crucial for the colonial deployment of the Western canon. On the one hand, it ensured that questions of form and structure flooded (and still do) the examination papers, inviting the reader yet again to squeeze the text into a strait-jacket and to erase the possible fractures of experience in reading it. On the other, it imposed Western aesthetics (for example, the Aristotelian demarcation of tragedy from comedy) upon traditions, such as that of Indian drama (both classical and folk) , which had acknowledged the intermingling of moods and genres. Westernised theatre groups, and imported British troupes (often playing melodramatic versions of Shakespeare; see chapter 1) ensured the hegemony of such ideas in actual performance, and generations of actors were taught to forget the proto-Brechtian epic traditions of the Indian theatre.

Today there have been some efforts to revive such a heritage, and to enrich it by infusing it with contemporary relevance. This has included adaptations of Western drama; and when Habib Tanvir, for example, has performed Brecht's plays in the style of folk theatre from Chattisgarh, using the latter's actors and music, it has illustrated, among other things, the extent to which much Indian drama had worked on assumptions and techniques analogous to Brecht's. There is not the space here to consider the ways in which third world literatures, both traditional and modern, both writers unknown to the West and those who have become current objects of its gaze, like Rushdie, Márquez, and recently, Ghosh, step out from the model of linear time and space and transgress the dominant Western literary model. It may be said, however, that such a movement cannot be explained simply by analogies to Western rejections of linearity (such as those of Miller or Beckett) for it refers specifically to the disjunctures and complexities of a non-Western experience (see Datta, for example).

However, it will not do simply to demarcate the two either; for the refusal of a Western text to comply with the structural or ideological unity demanded of it by dominant criticisms is equally useful for questioning the preferred textual model. Hence to seize upon what Brecht saw as the 'disconnectedness' of Renaissance drama is one way to contest its institutionalised usage as the barricade around a series of privileged positions. Finally, since the patriarchal gaze on women and the colonial one on its others is one-dimensional, because it aims both to obscure their depth and to deny their potential for mobility, we may usefully consider how montage, as a structural and thematic perspective, can challenge the dominant portrayals of women and other colonised peoples. At the same time, by identifying these perspectives and techniques as not exclusive to the hitherto privileged author or text and by bringing excluded ones into related focus, we may question the sanctity of the Western syllabus as it has been inherited and preserved by Indian departments of English.

Montage

Middleton's frequent collaborations with other writers possibly contributed to the loose and episodic structure of his plays. For example, the comic scenes in The Changeling, supposedly the work of Rowley, are interspersed with Middleton's tragic scenes. Many readings have been at pains to establish the harmony between the two. But the two plots also serve to puncture and comment upon each other. In that sense, they do not merely 'blend' into one another, but create a collage which serves to demystify certain issues.

Both the main plot and the sub-plot reinforce the different ways in which people change. In both the heroine is tempted to be unfaithful: whereas Beatrice actually succumbs and changes, Isabella remains faithful. But this does not serve to condemn Beatrice; rather the almost surrealistic treatment of madness in the sub-plot serves to alienate us in the Brechtian sense from the 'madness' of Beatrice's story. Bradbrook notes that the masque of madmen reinforces the idea of love as madness, as something that confounds discretion and darkens reason. On the contrary, the madhouse splices the main story to create a montage which prevents us from reacting hypnotically to a romantic and mystical conception of love, which even within the main plot is not a fixed category, but expands, erodes and changes as people do: it is both socially created and affects events, but is never absolute.

The point here is that montage expresses what I have previously considered as the unresolved tensions of Beatrice's 'giddy turning'. Measured against the contingency of character and social construction of subjectivity which the plays emphasise, the 'spectacular catastrophe(s)' of Jacobean tragedy noted by critics (Gibbons, p. xviii) do not constitute the 'revelation' which is considered the proper end of drama, for they only confirm what the almost cool depiction of violence in the earlier acts has relentlessly underlined. Hence to Muir's complaint that Beatrice does not attain knowledge we may reply that this is precisely the point: neither the protagonists nor the plays arrive at that famous final moment of closure. Examining this in relation to The White Devil, Dollimore cites a passage from Brecht which is worth re-quoting at this point:

The tragedy of Mother Courage and of her life . . . consisted in the fact that here a terrible contradiction existed which destroyed a human being, a contradiction which could be resolved, but only by society itself and in long, terrible struggles . . . It is not the business of the playwright to endow Mother Courage with final insight . . . his concern is, to make the spectator see. (Radical Tragedy, p. 246)

I have earlier commented on the rape scene in *Women Beware Women* where Bianca internalises the violence committed upon her and, at the same time, is alienated from the beliefs by which guilt is measured. The rape is inserted into a long scene, framed by the chess game and broken up by clusters of smaller scenes of courtly life. The chess game has been used elsewhere in the drama as a political metaphor, as for example in Middleton's own *A Game at Chess;* what is especially important in the case of *Women Beware Women* is that he employs it to de-sensationalise the rape. Violence on the female body has become a sort of courtly game in which those outside the royal circle are pawns. What lifts the scene from being just a cynical comment on power is the violence and unexpectedness of Bianca's reaction: even as she adapts to her status as victim, she retains a sense of her own agency. Bianca is one of the three women involved in the rape scene – Livia's machinations and the Mother's helplessness place women in a series of different relationships with patriarchal power. As the three interact with each other we glimpse the relativity and contigency of each relationship – the Mother seeks to confine her daughter-in-law but is herself ensnared in the chess game, Livia will shortly be out-manoeuvred. Again, none of the three attain any final insights; Bianca's dying belief – 'Like our own sex, we have no enemy' (V.ii.215) – is pitifully inadequate in explaining her fate.

The non-linear, non-climactic, episodic structure, and montage, usually disclose the construction of identity and social relations. For example, as we saw in *Othello,* Iago's downstage position serves to hoist popular notions of racism or misogyny onto the stage itself, where they become particular and contested perspectives instead of confirmed truths. In Webster's *The White Devil* characters repeatedly overhear, watch and secretly observe each other, so that at most points we watch the action through a series of eyes, not just our own. Such successive framings have been often regarded as 'stock-devices', stereotypical versions of a play within a play. But their effect is far from stereotypical. Consider, for example, Vittoria's first 'private' interchange with Brachiano, which is watched by Zanche, Flamineo and Cornelia. Whereas Romeo and Juliet's balcony scene fills the entire arena, this affair is interrupted and interpreted for the audience by different comments:

Brachiano.	Excellent creature.
	We call the cruel fair, what name for you
	That are so merciful? (Embraces her)
Zanche.	See now they close.
Flamineo.	Most happy union.
Cornelia.	(aside) My fears are fall'n upon me, oh my heart!
	My son the pander: now I find our house
	Sinking to ruin. (I.ii.202-8)

Zanche invests the liaison with her own desire for romance, which is ridiculed by others because she is black (see V.iii). Flamineo's comment is ironic, for he is hardly concerned with the lovers' *happiness*, and yet, his own viciousness can be seen as a consequence of his poverty and marginalisation (see Dollimore, *Radical Tragedy*, pp. 322-5). Cornelia's remark serves to swerve the gaze away from Vittoria's transgression to her brother's part in it. Montage here insists that the relationship is no privatised ideal of spontaneity and instant attraction, it is something planned and manipulated, and *always public*. The act of watching constantly punctures the illusion of privacy and individual agency; the resultant 'broken' focus ties in with Vittoria's public trial and punishment and thus prepares us for the interplay of private and public, which is the main theme of the play:

Lawyer.   My lord Duke and she have been very private.
Flamineo. You are a dull ass; 'tis threat'ned they have been very public. (III.i.17-19).

Spatial politics

Let us examine the effects of montage more closely by focusing on a text that is supposed to achieve the kind of tragic harmony that is seen to elude *The Changeling*. Three centuries of critical opinion, from Samuel Johnson onwards, has been preoccupied with 'overcoming' the heterogeneous nature of both the form and the content of Shakespeare's *Antony and Cleopatra*: the focus has variously been on its disjointed structure, mingling of tragic and comic, flux in character; its divisions between private and public, male and female, high and low life; on what Danby has called the 'dialectic' of the text.[2] However, a correlation of these various binaries – the thematic oppositions, the broken structure, its treatment of fluid gender and racial identity – has yet to be attempted. An 'epic effect' has been noted, but in the classical sense of the word (see Mark Rose, p. 2); we might more usefully employ the term in its Brechtian sense to analyse these various schisms. 'The continual hurry of the action, the variety of incidents, and the quick succession of one personage to another ... the frequent changes of scene' (Johnson, quoted J. E. Brown, p. 26) then emerge as contradicting the classical elevation of character or teleological progression towards catharsis, as achieving a Brechtian alienation from character to posit a radical interrogation of the imperial and sexual drama.

The geographical turbulence of the first three acts involves a redefinition of femininity and of female space: patriarchal Rome contests

Egyptian Cleopatra for her geographical and sexual territory. Into the contest is woven the theme of imperial domination. Dominant notions about female identity, gender relations and imperial power are unsettled through the disorderly non-European woman. These ideas appear to be reinstated as the quick shifts of scene are abandoned in favour of a more orthodox climax at the end of the play, an apparent resolution of the dilemma. Whereas in the first three acts of the play there are twenty-three changes of scene, and shifts of location within each as well, as the play proceeds there is a change in the quality and quantity of movement: in Act IV alone there are fifteen changes of locale, but all within Egypt. Act V contains only two scenes, and both are confined to the area of Cleopatra's monument. Alongside this, different characters strive to rise 'above' their earlier turbulence and assert an inner unity of being. However, this harmony is precarious; the manner of its achievement conveys the very opposite of a resolution and the various sets of oppositions noted by critics are not subscribed to but eroded by the play.

The issues of imperial expansion, political power and sexual domination are dramatically compressed into spatial and geographical shifts and metaphors. The almost cinematic movements – 'panning, tracking, and playing with the camera' (Danby, p. 197) – are designed to reveal the complexity of the terrain on which men and women move as well as of their inner spaces. They penetrate into different aspects of power, which is at once something concrete – land, kingdoms, wealth – and something relatively abstract – emotions, ideology, and sexuality. Theatrical space is not just an inert arena but interacts with the texts' treatment of social and psychological space.

Not only does the locale constantly shift, but in each setting we are reminded of another. In Egypt, Rome is evoked, and vice versa. While leaving for Rome, Antony tells Cleopatra: 'thou, residing here, goes yet with me, / And I, hence fleeting, here remain with thee' (I.iii.103-4). This is a common enough lovers' platitude but it serves to remind us that in addition to the purely geographical shifts of terrain, there are also those of conceptual settings; the lovers' private world is constantly contrasted to the political space. Antony identifies the former with Egypt, and in preferring it to Rome is trying to privatise love, to locate his relationship with Cleopatra in a domestic arena. But he also attempts to expand this space so that it excludes the other, threatening world of masculine politics, and crowds out other concerns:

> Cleopatra.   I'll set a bourn how far to be belov'd.
> Antony.   Then must thou needs find out new heaven, new earth. (I.i.16-17)

This is what Donne's lovers are also trying to do as they seek ever more expansive metaphors for their relationship and for each other: 'She's all States, and all Princes I'; their room becomes an 'everywhere' (p. 73).

Roman patriarchy demonises Cleopatra by defining her world as private (Antony is no longer a serious general by entering it); as female (Egypt robs Antony and his soldiers of their manhood); and as barbaric (Antony is now a slave of gypsies). But both Antony and Caesar are aware that Egypt is not merely a private space and that its female, non-European nature only intensifies its challenge to imperial Rome:

> Antony.   My being in Egypt, Caesar
>   What was't to you?
> Caesar.   No more than my residing here at Rome
>   Might be to you in Egypt. Yet, if you there
>   Did practice on my state, your being in Egypt
>   Might be my question. (II.ii.39-44)

Objective space is always invested with political or emotional connotations; as Caesar indicates, Egypt is a place from which subversion can be practised, and as such it can never be merely a lovers' retreat. Antony too courts Cleopatra with territorial and political gifts: he will 'piece / Her opulent throne with kingdoms; all the East / . . . shall call her mistress' (I.v.45-7). Caesar complains precisely of this:

> Unto her
> He gave the establishment of Egypt; made her
> Of Lower Syria, Cyprus, Lydia,
> Absolute queen. (III.vi.8-11)

Passionate as the relationship between Antony and Cleopatra is, 'the language of desire, far from transcending the power relations which structure this society, is wholly informed by them' (Dollimore, *Radical Tragedy*, p. 203). These relations are both sexual and racial. In the beginning Antony thinks he is in control of what he regards as the opposition between politics and pleasure; therefore he assumes that he can simultaneously possess the Roman matron Octavia through the legal bonding permitted by imperial patriarchy, and the oriental seductress Cleopatra, through a sexually passionate and 'illicit' relationship:

> I will to Egypt;
> And though I make this marriage for my peace,
> I'th' East my pleasure lies. (II.iii.39-41)

He alternately views Egypt as his retreat from Roman politics and a place to consolidate his bid for power. In short, he oscillates between Cleopatra's territory and Caesar's, both literally and otherwise. As the play proceeds he is no longer in command of such a divide: his position in both Rome and Egypt becomes unstable and manifests itself as a dislocation of personality: 'I / Have lost my way for ever', 'I have fled myself', 'I have lost command' (III.x.3-4, 7, 23). 'Authority melts from me', he cries, but like Faustus, the Duchess of Malfi, and Parolles, he invokes his lost 'essential' self: 'Have you no ears? I am / Antony yet' (III.xiii.90-3). Even as Antony complains that Caesar keeps 'harping on what I *am*, / Not what he knew I *was*' (III, xiii, 142-3; emphasis added), he is aware of the change in himself. Without power, without space, without Rome and without Cleopatra, Antony disintegrates.

It is important that Cleopatra's transformation into the 'whore' and 'witch' occurs precisely at this point: the language of what Antony perceives as a betrayal reduces Cleopatra's 'infinite variety' to both patriarchal and racist stereotypes. Helen Carr has pointed out that 'although the substitution of "witch" for "whore" as the primary image of the deviant woman signifies a greater degree of horror at the possibility of female sexuality, at the same time it represses the idea of a consciously sexual woman (the witch's fantasies are alien and evil intruders in her mind' (p. 51). Cleopatra, I have argued, is both: her sexuality is an aspect of her blackness and as such can only be erased later, when she herself adopts token Roman-ness. Whereas, in falling from Othello's favour, Desdemona became 'begrim'd' and morally black and false to her true self, Cleopatra as the 'foul Egyptian' only realises her 'true' position as the complete outsider. As Antony perceives that he is only nominally the site of the conflict which is actually between Cleopatra and Caesar, the latent struggle for power between him and Cleopatra escalates. The metaphors for this three-way struggle become those of the land and the sea. Whether the fight should take place on the Roman element, the land, or Cleopatra's medium, the water, is at once a matter of military strategy and a measure of Antony's emotional and political affiliations. The erosion of the absolute space of love stems from his increasing perception of his own marginality, and Cleopatra's refusal to share her space. With all worlds being lost, Antony's vacillations cease, and so do the structural shifts.

Such a movement is also dependent on the play's treatment of Cleopatra. If Cleopatra's political being threatens patriarchy it also catalyses the contradictions within her, which are inherent in the position she occupies as a sexually active non-European female ruler. Although she is unique among the independent women in Renaissance drama, for she appears to command her own spaces, these are precariously constructed: as the ruler of Egypt her space is threatened by the expansionist designs of the Roman empire, and as a woman, by the contradictions of heterosexual love. Her insecurity, her fear of invasion

– not just as a ruler, but also as a woman who is threatened even (or especially) by her lover – is evident in her physical stasis, her reluctance to move from her territory. However slippery, inconstant and variable Cleopatra may be, however she may threaten the boundaries between male and female, political and private worlds, she remains geographically stationary. She resents the intrusions of Roman messengers who remind her not only of Antony's wives, first Fulvia and then Octavia, but also of the imperial threat.

Cleopatra fluctuates between establishing her emotional and her political spaces: a vacillation without end for she cannot simultaneously occupy both. She finds it much harder to locate her own territory in relation to Antony than vis-à-vis Caesar. She can either function within the private life of a man, or enter politics as a honorary man and chaste woman, like Elizabeth. In any case it is a double bind. As 'foul Egyptian' she will always stand outside Roman society: Antony can never fully trust her and will marry safe and obedient Roman women like Octavia to ensure his stability within that society. Her gender renders her politically unacceptable, her political status problematises her femininity, and her racial otherness troubles, doubly, both power and sexuality. To the extent that she acts as a ruler, she is perfectly comprehensible to Caesar: he even praises her for concealing her treasure from him; 'nay, blush not, Cleopatra; I approve / Your wisdom in the deed' (V.ii.148-9). But whereas he will not haggle over 'things that merchants sold' (V.ii.83), he refuses to grant her autonomy even in respect of her death.

The last act appears to 'resolve' the various tensions of the play; the style now changes from montage and a mingling of comic and tragic to that of classical tragedy. It appears that Cleopatra is tamed; the wanton gypsy becomes Antony's wife, the queen is stripped to an essential femininity that attaches to all women irrespective of class: 'no more but e'en a woman, and commanded / By such poor passion as the maid that milks / And does the meanest chares' (IV.xv.73-5). The variable woman is now 'marble constant'; the witch gives way to the penitent goddess as Egypt tries to do 'what's brave, / what's noble . . . after the high Roman fashion' (IV.xv.86-7).

Several aspects of this resolution serve to contradict its apparent implications. Firstly, Cleopatra is able to capitulate to Roman matrimony only after Antony has died, and when one aspect of her conflict has dissolved rather than being resolved. The prospect of sharing power with Antony no longer exists, and she begins to approximate the lovers in Donne's poems, or Antony's own earlier expressions of absolute emotion. After his death Antony can fill her world in a way that Antony alive could never be allowed to do:

> His face was as the heav'ns, and therein stuck
> A sun and moon, which kept their course and lighted
> The little O, the earth . . .
> His legs bestrid the ocean; his rear'd arm
> Crested the world. (V.ii.79-83)

The poetry has been seen as sublime. Cleopatra's words display an effort to cloak personal and political loss in the language of a transcendental, eternal romance. Given the conditions of its utterance, the poetry reveals the politics of sublimation, rather than a transcendence of politics. Antony can now comfortably be called 'husband' (V.ii.285) without the risk to freedom that actual matrimony implies.

Cleopatra also lets her own fierce identification with Egypt slip for the first time. Literally, of course she still does not accept Caesar's Rome, which remains a threat:

> Shall they hoist me up,
> And show me to the shouting varletry
> Of censuring Rome? Rather a ditch in Egypt
> Be gentle grave unto me! (V.ii.55-8)

But Rome was also Antony's space and as his wife she can adopt the 'Roman fashion'.

Secondly, if these moves reflect Cleopatra's contradictions, they are also strategic and constitute the unruly woman's last performances. Having lost power, it now becomes 'paltry to be Caesar' (V.ii.2); it is now time to speak of things other than power. Her suicide clouds her political defeat with mystic glamour and a show of autonomy. Her own body is the last 'space' to be wrested from Roman control. The asp will bring her 'liberty' in the absence of real territory. The maternal image of the snake at her breast tames her own earlier identification with the serpent, replacing the deadly Eastern inscrutibility with a comprehensible version of the Madonna. Of course, both are patriarchal constructions of women. The first demonises the alien woman while the second seeks to domesticise her.

Till the end, Cleopatra attempts to maintain some vestiges of power even as she acknowledges Caesar as 'the sole sir o'th' world' (V.ii.119). It is only when every effort has failed that she has 'immortal longings' (V.ii.279). Without power 'What should I stay – / In this vile world?' (V.ii.311-12).

As Cleopatra achieves these false resolutions, the play also abandons the cinematic montage that so adequately expressed the discontinuity of character, the dialectic between inner and outer, political and personal, male and female spaces. The shifts of scene which conveyed both the vacillations of Antony and the unruly theatricality of Cleopatra give way to the elevation of the 'Roman' suicides; to the conventional 'climax' and the stock devices of formal drama, as patriarchal roles and divisions are apparently reinstated. If Cleopatra's fluid identity and play-acting demanded one kind of theatrical form, her new role as Antony's marble-constant wife employs the more classical technique. The Roman theatre takes over from the volatile Egyptian one. The closed space of the monument, the measured actions and tones, the slow, drawn-out scenes and the elevated language all tone down the fiery and unpredictable performances of the earlier Cleopatra. The narrative of masculinity and imperialism regains control but Cleopatra's final performance, which certainly exposes her own vulnerability, not only cheats Caesar but denies any final and authoritative textual closure.

Another purpose of playing

Robert Weimann has suggested several reasons for perceiving an approximation of the Brechtian epic in Renaissance drama; an increasing focus on discontinuous identity and on female changeability may be another. In the play just discussed, elements of the disorderly woman are identified with those of the popular stage, and therefore the foregrounding of such women also interrogates the controls and limitations of theatrical space. If there are two styles and forms in the play, they also explore the popular drama's own position within an authoritarian state.

Louis A. Montrose's important essay, 'The purpose of playing' suggests a relationship between authority and Renaissance theatre which we can trace as analogous to that between authority and women. The public theatre and the professional player resisted the drive towards fixity in several ways: their profession was based on a kind of duplicity, or temporary donning of identity; players were upwardly mobile in real life; their costumes were often the discarded clothes of the nobility and defied the dress code (see Jardine, *Still Harping*, p. 141-2); and the plays themselves reveal a pervasive concern with 'fictional situations in which human characters are confronted by change within the self, the family, the body politic, the cosmos' (Montrose, p. 63). The protean nature and concerns of the theatre are placed by Montrose against the background of the desperate attempt of the authorities to contain – ideologically, economically and spatially – the enormous and varied mobility of various sections of society; I have suggested that this scenario is also the ideological and political backdrop for the foregrounding of female changeability, duplicity, mobility in the drama.

The drive to limit and contain theatre space was concurrent with and similar to the effort to limit and contain women. In both cases transience, mobility, alteration, disguise and changeability are seen as subverting a dominant need for stability. Contemporary tracts explicitly connect actors with other unruly social groups; conversely, theatre becomes acknowledged as a disruptive force. As Jean Howard has shown, women figure 'prominently in the antitheatrical narrative of social disruption ... (they) are constructed in these texts as the duplicitous, inherently theatrical sex' ('Renaissance antitheatricality', p. 168) Both Howard (p. 168) and Peter Stallybrass ('The history of sexuality', pp. 1, 12) quote from Philip Stubbes, in whose writings this comparison becomes very clear: his suspicion of the 'painted sepulchres' of the stage employs the language common in the theme of the white devil. Conversely, he accuses women of proteanism ('Proteus, that Monster, could never chaunge him self into so many fourmes and shapes as these women do') and goes on to level the same charge against actors. Attacks on changeable fashion and clothing draw together the threats of female cross-dressing as well as theatrical disguise – interestingly, transgressive women are accused of being masculine, whereas popular theatre is accused of being effeminate. In both cases the fears are that social and sexual boundaries will be erased. The woman who puts on male clothing is warned '... if you will walke without difference, you shall live without reverence: if you will contene order, you must endure the shame of disorder; and if you will have no rulers but your wills, you must have no reward but disdaine and disgrace' (Haec-Vir).

Both women and theatre are seen to stray from their allotted spaces in various ways. The physical confines of the home and the playhouse are challenged: for example, Elizabeth fears the subversive potential of Shakespeare's Richard II not merely because of its timing before the Essex rebellion, not merely because 'I am Richard II. Know ye not that?' but also because the play, she complains, was performed in 'open streets and houses' (Greenblatt, The Power of Forms, pp. 3-4; see also Dollimore, 'Shakespeare, cultural materialism', p. 8). Social and political boundaries are defied by the drama and women as they dress in the garments of their superiors, and if women are seen as attempting to usurp authority, the players are accused of inciting political trouble or rebellion. Ideologically, women threaten the demarcation of the 'private' sphere and popular theatre resists the confinement of dramatic performance.

We may pursue the connections further. The theatre of the period involves not just the general disguise that all drama calls for, but specifically an interchange of gender roles, both literally by boy-actors and thematically by the further exchange of male-female roles. At the same time, female cross-dressing functions as a version of theatricality that extends disguise from the playhouse to social space. Again, parallel to the theatre's growing concern with women, the public controversy on gender-roles becomes increasingly theatricalised: the authors of the pamphlets speak from within adopted roles such as that of the masculine woman, Haec-Vir, or the effeminate man, Hic Mulier. The pamphlets are also a self-consciously dramatic public dialogue between the authors whose pseudonyms confer a particular identity upon them: thus Esther Sowernam replies in 1617 to Joseph Swetnam's *Arraignment of Lewde, Idle, Unconstant and Froward Women* published two years earlier also by letting her name (sour-name) play on the ironies of his (sweet-name). The controversy finally culminates in a straightforward play *Swetnam the Woman-Hater Arraigned by Women* (1620), in which Swetnam is brought on trial before an all-female jury. Shepherd points out that this 'is probably the nearest women of the time got to writing a publicly performed play . . . (which is also) the first case of a female mob sympathetically treated on the Jacobean stage' (*The Women's Sharp Revenge*, p. 55).

During James's reign there was a drive towards formalising theatre, which can be seen as an attempt precisely to contain and define the audience-theatre relationship. James himself had likened the king to 'one set on stage, whose smallest actions and gestures, all the people gazingly do behold' (Dollimore, 'Shakespeare, cultural materialism, p. 8). The effort to make theatre as well as architecture a part of James' statecraft implicitly acknowledged not only the power of theatre but the theatricality of power.[3] Wotton testified that the Banqueting House at Whitehall, planned by Inigo Jones, James's chief architect, as a place where masques were performed and where ambassadors and royal guests were received, was a place where 'Art became a piece of State' (Goldberg, *James I*, pp. 40-4).

Jones created elaborate masques and imported European Palladianism and the Italian proscenium stage with its perspective scenes. The latter relied heavily on arches, which were designed to separate audience from performer, and to reinforce the impression of power and grandeur through formality and distance.

No spatial structure is free of social implications, including those of gender: architecture (and theatre design) is not ideologically inert.[4] The arch was increasingly being used as an emblem of state power; Inigo Jones was exploiting its potential as a symbol of order and grandeur both in the theatre and in public construction. There were arches for James's entrances into London which were carefully designed to be 'triumph(s) in the high Roman style' (Goldberg, p. 33). Stephen Harrison's *Archs of Triumph* (1603-4), which Ben Jonson described as 'the expression of state and magnificience' were typical of such usage. They can be contrasted to the *ad hoc* stages that were constructed for Elizabeth I's earlier entrances (Bergeron, pp. 75-8). If the arch effected a separation between the royal actor and his audiences, it also served the purpose of distancing the events of the stage. Formal theatre enacted on the picture frame stage sought to exalt the power of the state as much as the public theatre was seen to threaten it. Later the arch was repeatedly used in colonial architecture as emblematic of imperial might. Hence it is significant that as Antony repudiates Rome in favour of Cleopatra, he uses the arch as a symbol of the Roman empire:

> Let Rome in Tiber melt, and the wide arch
> Of the rang'd empire fall! Here is my space. (I.i.33-4)

In this context, the opposition of Caesar and Cleopatra in the play can be seen as partially deriving from the contrasting *styles* of James and Elizabeth. The arch here becomes one of the various spatial signifiers of the conflict between the Egyptian theatre and the Roman, one more way of establishing the dimensions of Cleopatra's theatricality, of suggesting that Egypt and Rome are invested with implications deriving from theatrical practice.

James' anti-woman bias was also picked up by the new architecture and theatre. Inigo Jones conceived of his own architecture and theatre design as 'solid, proportional, *masculine* and unaffected' (Thorne, p. 57; emphasis added). If masculinity connotes order and power, then the variety and disorder of the popular theatre is connected yet again to the disturbance offered by unruly femininity.

The volatile stage

Webster's preface to *The White Devil* confesses that 'this is no true dramatic poem'; that it was written for an 'open and black' stage which lacked 'a full and understanding auditory' and on whose audience, resembling 'ignorant asses', 'the most sententious tragedy ... observing all the critical laws' would be wasted (p. 491). Jonson's note to the readers of *Sejanus His Fall* makes a similar excuse for writing 'no true poem': 'Nor is it needful, or almost possible, in these our times, and to such auditors ... to observe the old state, and splendour of dramatic poems, with preservation of any popular delight' (p. 247; emphasis added). While formally deferring to the superior status of classical art and deprecating the very audiences they invoke to justify their own departures from it, both these notes indicate the liberating influence of the same open stage that had terrified Elizabeth, and of an interactive audience. Montrose has suggested that

the actual process of theatrical performance, marked off from the normal flow of social activity, offers its audience (and of course, its performers) an imaginative experience which temporarily removes them from their normal places. In this sense, to go to the playhouse to take part in a play is voluntarily to undergo a marginal experience; it is to cross the interstices of the Elizabethan social and cognitive order. ('The purpose of playing', p. 63)

If the subversive potential of any theatre depends to some degree on such a removal, it also requires, conversely, an *intersection* with social reality. The dynamics of audience participation, as Brecht's dramaturgy demonstrated, generates a certain power in itself. For example, the involvement of the entire population of a town may be elicited by traditional theatre performances in India. Anuradha Kapur describes the annual *Ramlila*, or dramatisation of the epic *Ramayana*, as staged in the town of Ramnagar. Here the city becomes the stage, and all the audience who await the return of the hero-god Rama from exile become actors. Rama's return is endowed with enormous emotional power by the mass participation which renders the stage 'volatile' and 'there is then the hope of great happenings'. The opposite, suggests Kapur, is the effect of a stage where the spectator is isolated:

... the auditorium, and especially the picture-frame stage, creates a series of *calculable* relationships: the enclosed space, the static set and the imprisoned spectator. Short of jumping on to the stage there is scarcely any possibility of transgression ... naturalistic theatre, under the tyranny of certain architectural features is unable to make its space anything other than versimilar. (p. 57; emphasis added)

The power of theatre therefore derives from its ability to employ strategically both its privileged *removal from* and *extension into* social space. Such a duality is also responsible for the dialectic of its own position – playwrights and players may transgress the social order but are also constituted by it. Thus drama may simultaneously question and confirm normative behaviour; it may both challenge and reinforce the prescriptions for order (see Montrose, 'Renaissance literary studies', pp. 9-11). The three-way intersections of theatrical, social and female spaces during the Renaissance allow a simultaneous examination of all three.

'Travelling thoughts'

The rigidity of the Western canon, especially as it operates in the colonial situation, was discussed in the first chapter. Reverence for the bard has led to a devaluation of other dramatists of the period. Marlowe leads up to Shakespeare and Webster and Jonson down from him, but almost no one else is admitted to the charmed circle. In relation to the Romantic poets, Marilyn Butler proposes that 'poets we have installed as canonical look far more interesting individually, and far more understandable as groups, when we restore some of their lost peers' (p. 1349).

I will therefore turn to a somewhat later and almost totally neglected writer, Richard Brome, in order to suggest that some of the issues just discussed are brilliantly focused by his play The Antipodes; it could well be a key-text in an alternative curriculum.[5] But Brome's play is useful beyond providing a gloss on Shakespeare. As Walter Cohen points out, one serious limitation of current 'political approaches to Shakespeare' is their almost exclusive emphasis on that dramatist (p. 20). Pragmatic concerns, even those which have to do with re-reading what we are made to read in the classroom, inevitably lead to such a bias; one of my purposes in interlacing key issues raised by Shakespeare's plays with those of others has been precisely to disallow such a prioritisation. Of course, from the perspective of post-colonial education, the validity of replacing one master-text with another can be questioned, a problem which requires full discussion but is outside the scope of my argument at this point (see chapter 6).

More self-consciously than the texts previously considered here, The Antipodes looks forward to Brechtian theatre politics – not only preferring fragmentation and multiplicity to the definitive statement, employing various alienation devices, combining the didactic and the comic but also explicitly positing the formation of identity and the function of theatre as related issues. It is truly 'in advance of its time as a contribution to criticism and aesthetics, albeit in a somewhat disguised form' (Davis, 'Richard Brome's neglected contribution', p. 527). Even more significantly, the play considers the interrelation of social and psychic space by locating the production of male and female fantasies in the different spaces occupied by men and women. Although focusing neither on the disorderly woman, nor any actual black person, it brings together the issues of race and gender by showing geographical expansion and the attendant production of travel mythology as profoundly gendered.

Criticism of the play (at least prior to Martin Butler's Theatre and Crisis) has been, like the label generally attached to Brome, conservative, and

has largely ignored the radical thrust of the method as well as the subject
of the play. The plot is fairly simple, and revolves around the cure of
Peregrine Joyless, a young man so obsessed with 'travelling thoughts'
(I.ii.27), with the wonderful lands, strange peoples, and other 'strangest
doings' (I.iii.10) portrayed in travel books, that he has lost all contact
with his actual existence, and most crucially with his wife Martha, who
is still a virgin after three years of marriage.

Peregrine's name, also used by Jonson in *Volpone*, is derived from the
Latin *peregrinus* meaning 'foreign' and means also 'outlandish; . . . an alien
resident: a pilgrim or traveller in a foreign country' (*Chambers 20th Century
Dictionary*). His sickness in this play dramatises the hold of the enormous
range of travel literature during the early years of colonial expansion
upon the public imagination. Such literature, as I have remarked in
relation to *Othello*, combined myth and facts, entertainment and enquiry,
and was filtered through cultural, political and religious prejudice. The
ideological effects of the images of strange lands and peoples were not
necessarily expansive, but often strengthened existing chauvinism. The
racist implications of this have been considered; *The Antipodes*
demonstrates the psychological effects of such literature.

In 1555 there appeared Richard Eden's accounts of the first two
English voyages to Africa, which combine actual description with
fantastic stories. In 1577 Richard Willes's *The History of Travayle* and in 1589
Hakluyt's *Principal Navigations* contributed to the growing fund of travel
account-fantasies. Peregrine's visions of 'monsters / Pigmies, and giants,
apes and elephants, / Griffins, and crocodiles, men upon women, / And
women upon men, the strangest doings' are, however, more specifically
drawn from *The Travels of John Mandeville* and especially from the notion
therein of an antipodal land (see Brome, pp. 16-17)

For Peregrine fantasy results in alienation from his reality, especially
from Martha. If his mind soars beyond the colonial horizons, hers with-
draws and shrinks to a preoccupation with her bodily fertility in what
amounts to a classic case of womb hysteria. Both husband and wife are
neurotic, but the 'disorder' of their minds is derived from typically
defined gender roles – his is based on the male colonial fantasy of travel
power and excitement; hers on the female one of domesticity and children. Earlier I have considered how the spatial and ideological ghetto-
isation of women indicates their subordination and conditions their
subjectivity; in *The Antipodes* its psychological effects are related to those
of colonial expansionism. Once again imperialism and sexism reinforce
the prescribed spaces of the female mind. Also typically, whereas
Martha's fantasy is dependent upon Peregrine's co-operation, his has
no room for her at all. In Christian allegory, ironically, Martha's name

symbolises the active life; in the play, we witness her inabilty even to fantasise about it.

One may here refer usefully to modern studies on the spatial behaviour of the sexes, which have documented how boys' play is obsessed with movement and exterior landscapes whereas girls tend to concentrate on still objects and interior spaces (Erikson, 'Inner and outer space'). There is a tendency to explain this by biological differences alone, by referring to girls' awareness of the inner spaces of their bodies instead of seeing how gender differentials in spatial perception are socially induced (see Ardener, Women and Space, passim). Brome's play allows us to locate female hysteria in relation to the gradual expulsion of woman from outer arenas until only her womb remains for her to act her fantasies upon. Even more importantly, it addresses the usually glamourised male sense of 'adventure' as a form of hysteria. Peregrine's disorders are the predecessors of Gulliver's alienation and Kurtz's madness. Significantly, his relationship with his wife emerges as a measure of his cure; 'real knowledge of a woman' will indicate his readiness to adjust to English society. At the end of Avt IV, Peregrine consents to embrace Martha because he has been led to believe that she is transformed into a Princess of the Antipodes; so she is integrated into his fantasy.

The Antipodes has been called 'a dramatization of psychiatric therapy' (Shaw, p. 123); apart from Corax in Ford's The Lover's Melancholy, Doctor Hughball, to whom Peregrine's father Joyless brings him, is 'the first practicing psychiatrist to appear on the English stage' (R. J. Kaufmann, p. 65).[6] Hughball lives with Letoy, a 'Phantastic Lord' whose house 'in substance is an amphitheater of exercise and pleasure' (I.v.52-3). The two form a sort of director-producer partnership whereby theatre becomes the medium of psychotherapy. They stage a show in which Peregrine is made to live out his fantasy – made to believe that he is actually in Mandeville's 'world of Antipodes', where the people

> In outward feature, language and religion,
> Resemble those to whom they are supposite:
> They under Spain appear like Spaniards,
> Under French Frenchmen, under England English
> To the exterior show; but in their manners,
> Their carriage, and condition of life
> Extremely contrary. (I.vi.107-13)

By Brome's time, the phrase 'to act the antipodes' had become a proverbial expression for a reversal of the expected order of things (Shaw, p. 127). Brome is also generally drawing upon a long tradition of the world turned upside down which was recurrent in satiric or Utopian literature (see Morton, *The English Utopia*). There are Shakespearean echoes too in the theme of finding one's 'true' self after a temporary sojourn into the madness of the inverted world. *The Antipodes* in fact draws together various common Saturnalian strands – madness, dislocation, eventual cure, flouting of hierarchy and social criticism. Reversal can be used for a variety of political ends and can serve either as a safety-valve to maintain the status quo or as a radical critique of society, as in More's *Utopia*. In Brome's text, as Martin Butler argues, inversion operates as a 'brilliant structural and analytical tool' for a specifically political critique of Charles's government (pp. 215, 220) and also for a more general indictment of all hierarchical societies.

First Hughball describes the Antipodes and its principle of reversal by which 'the people rule / The Magistrates', 'the women over-rule the men' and 'As parents here, and masters, / Command there they obey the child and servant' (I.vi.119-27). The doctor tells Diana, Joyless's young wife, that it is nature, not art that enables Antipodian women to rule over men. Diana's comment, 'Then art's above nature, as they are under us', not only holds art responsible for male domination in her own world but opens up the play's consideration of another sort of theatre and art which can work as therapy, correctively. The ability of art to intervene in both private fantasy and social existence, to mould identity, is repeatedly emphasised. Joyless fears the possible effects of theatre upon Diana and is adamant that she shall not see a play. The Doctor insists that 'she must, if you can hope for any cure' (I.vi.201). Art has an effect on nature, ideas can shape reality.

As Butler has pointed out, there are two categories of reversal in the Antipodean world. The first are simply amusing and confirm our social beliefs – such as those where old men go to school or merchants ask gentlemen to cuckold them. But the second are more disturbing, firstly because they offer a deeper and more political critique of existing social and gender relations, and secondly because they reveal that a large part of what goes on in the Antipodes actually exists surreptitiously in London. In other words, reversal here is not pure fantastical inversion but part of actual suppressed subversion, as for example when servants rule masters, or women hunt and 'deale abroad / Beyond seas, while their husbands cuckold them, / At home' (I.vi.169-71). Peregrine is most shocked by sexual inversion:

> Can men and women be so contrary
> In all that we hold proper to each sex? (IV.v.31-2)

At another point, we see a courtier who is a beggar; Diana's repeated comments that such things are the *opposite* of reality only serve to ques-

tion whether they really are so far removed from the truth. Is it not that
courtiers *are* a variety of beggars and churchmen are usurers? So while
some illusions here point to the upside-down quality of Charles'
England (see Martin Butler, p. 217) others depict what is lacking in that
society.

There are several aspects of Brome's handling of reversal which lifts
it above the common-play-within-the-play device. One is that unlike
usual reversals or escapes from reality, neither the Antipodes nor the
real world are simply idealised or maligned. Of course the didactic purpose is obvious: just as Letoy and Hughball cure their patients so Brome
the doctor-playwright hopes to cure his audience through what has
been called comic catharsis. Brome probably drew upon Burton's
Anatomy of Melancholy, which explained that 'perturbations of the mind'
may be rectified by 'some feigned lie, strange news, witty device, artificial
invention' and particularly recommended the utility of mirth (see J. L.
Davis, p. 524). Brome refuses to allow the spectator/reader to regard
the Antipodean critique of reality as Utopian fantasy; social criticism is
not dependent upon idealisation but is made part of a more complex,
wry and pluralist approach – such as we encounter in a more self-conscious and polemical way in Brecht. Swinburne was not far from the
truth when he commented that the play reveals that life is always and
everywhere 'an incongruous congruity of contradictions' (quoted J. L.
Davis, p. 524).

An aspect of the reversals that has been ignored by existing criticism
is the manner in which the relation between England and the Antipodes,
and hence of imperial power and its others, is subjected to examination.
The scholarly discourses pursued by Peregrine construct it as a land of
'monsters more', but the Antipodes is in fact far from the fantasy land
of the grotesque, of all that is alien to European and Christian civilisation:
the theatrical enactment visualises it as uncomfortably like England.
Moreover, both its similarities and differences are determined by the
actors, or the participants in the imperial drama: it is a constructed and
not an actual world, created by the imagination of the white traveller,
Peregrine, the Doctor, or anyone else who cares to participate in myth-
making. Thus the play comes close to apprehending the process
whereby cultural, racial and geographical differences are transposed
into that curious blend of fact and fiction, fantasy and fears that one
finds not just in the travel literature of the period but in most Orientalist
writings.

The free interplay of the actors and spectators in *The Antipodes* is also
important. Actually, there is not one but three plays: the first is the
staging of the Antipodal world for Peregrine's benefit ; in the second

Letoy pretends to court Diana, the young wife of Peregrine's intensely
jealous father Joyless and by witnessing her refusal, the old man is cured;
finally there is the masque of the last scene celebrating the triumph of
harmony over discord. None of the plays is presented naturalistically –
we are never allowed to forget that they are staged, that spectators and
participants mingle and interchange positions. Consider the first show,
which is primarily put on to cure Peregrine. Besides being the principal
spectator, he is also the most crucial actor, for the effect of the drama
depends upon his participation. At the same time, the presence of Letoy,
Joyless, Diana, Martha and Barbara is a constant reminder that this is
but a play. An alienation effect is achieved, not only through the spectators, but also through the Doctor, who is both director and actor in
the Antipodean theatre and also in the stage of Peregrine's mind. Letoy
similarly punctures the illusion by stepping in and out of the drama:
the actors are his men and he plays director to them. The audience are
his guests and he plays host to them. At the same time he initiates the
second play while the first is still on by beginning to flirt with Diana.
The two plays are interwoven, preventing any total absorption in or
totalising effect of either of them. The audience is made aware of the
significance of its participation; in the manner of epic theatre they are
invited to step in and to comment on the action.

There is no tight story either, so that the total effect is one of fragmentation. The Antipodes could be said to return, like Brecht's own plays are
seen to do, 'to the theatre's simplest elements instead of trying to foster
an illusion of reality' (Ridless, p. 56). It is, finally, claiming quite a lot for
art – in fact no less than Brecht himself: ideological practices and theatre
particularly have a definite and material effect on reality and are agents
of its change. One might argue that this is not special to Brome, that the
notion of comedy as criticism dates back to ancient Greek drama. But
Brome goes further than that, for art is a corrective practice only if the
audience accepts its diagnosis – the participation of the patient is essential. Theatre then is lifted fom a minority entertainment and, again
anticipating Brecht, derives its power from audience involvement.

Finally, the play takes a dig at its own practice, for the world it has
brought Peregrine back to is not much better than his illusory one.
Fantasy also has the power to distort perception in a retrogressive way,
as in Peregrine's case. But most importantly, neither kind of imagination
is arbitrary but is based on what is available or denied to human beings.

The Antipodes, then, suggests that the basis for male and female spatial
fantasies, expansive and contractive respectively, is the gender roles that
are socially defined for them, and the desires and fantasies of an entire
culture, as they are organised by its mobility or stasis. In other words

Brome is examining the formation of subjectivity, including its most elusive and 'private' aspects – through powerfully imposed ideologies, and more self-conscious alternative fantasies that deliberately engage with and subvert them.

Notes

1 Ornstein, The Moral Vision. Some thirty years earlier T. S. Eliot had found that Middleton 'has no point of view, is neither sentimental nor cynical; he is neither resigned nor disillusioned nor romantic; he has no message' (p. 162); Una Ellis-Fermor detected in him a 'belittling of those human figures which his contemporaries exalt', 'a pitiless abstemiousness' (p. 152). It had been generally concluded, as Eliot did, that Middleton is merely a 'great recorder', 'merely a name which associates with six or seven great plays' (p. 162). So whereas Shakespeare's detachment was seen to stem from a positive morality, that of others was made to neatly tie in with the 'hectic portraits of vice and depravity' to be found in Jacobean drama (Ornstein, p. 3).

2 L. C. Knights comments: 'In Macbeth we are never in any doubt of our moral bearings. Antony and Cleopatra, on the other hand, embodies different and apparently irreconciliable evaluations of the central experience' (quoted J. R. Brown, Antony and Cleopatra, p. 172). Adelman; Belsey, The Subject of Tragedy; Jardine, Still Harping; Holloway; Mack; Markels; Mark Rose; Rozett; Simmons and Stella Smith all emphasise different aspects of the heterogeneity foregrounded by the play.

3 Architecture and stage design are only one aspect of the interrelation between power and theatricality during the Renaissance, which has been richly focused, for example, by Greenblatt, Renaissance Self-Fashioning; Goldberg, James I; Montrose, 'The purpose of playing'; Tennenhouse, 'Strategies of State' and Power on Display.

4 The ideological loading of spatial structures has to do with the contexts in which they are created, with associations that gather around them, with their settings and usages. The dome, for example, was a symbol of perfection under the Mughals: the Taj Mahal confered upon it multiple associations of love (it was built by Shah Jahan for his wife Mumtaz Mahal); of might (it took twenty years, much wealth and a vast army of labour to construct it); and of ruthless power (the master-craftsmen who executed it had their thumbs cut off on completion so that they could never build another such monument and the exclusivity of the Taj could be preserved). Coleridge's dome in 'Kubla Khan' carries Orientalist connotations of the glamour, pleasure as well as despotism of the east. It may be conjectured that the arch codes for power because its shape, like that of the dome, required careful planning and meticulous execution.

5 Richard Brome, described in the title page of the 1658 version of his comedy, The Weeding of the Covent Garden, as 'An Ingenious Servant and Imitator of his master: that famously renowned poet Ben Jonson', wrote mainly comedy. The Antipodes was composed in 1637 for a new company, Queen Henreitta's and was first acted at the Salisbury Court playhouse in 1638. Martin Butler has argued that Caroline drama did not break with the concerns of earlier drama, and 'did persistently engage in debating the political issues of the day' (p. 1). Institutionalised criticism tends to rigidly demarcate literature of different periods (and to classify these according to the prevailing monarch) – hence Elizabethan, Jacobean and Caroline dramas are often treated as three completely distinct types of theatre.

6 As John Drakakis has suggested to me, Pinch in Shakespeare's The Comedy of Errors might be considered as another predecessor of Hughball.

6

Seizing the book

The contaminated text

It is perhaps appropriate to conclude with Shakespeare's *The Tempest*, whose varied stage and critical history has explicitly foregrounded the question of appropriations of dominant culture. This history reveals a struggle over textual truth and value, but also alerts us to the problems of 'seizing the book'; hence the following discussion is not a 'conclusion' at all, but more in the nature of a speculation on some of these difficulties.

McLuskie, writing on Shakespeare, quotes Eagleton, writing on ideology: 'The aesthetic is too valuable to be surrendered without a struggle to the bourgeois aestheticians, and too contaminated by that ideology to be appropriated as it is' ('Feminist deconstruction', p. 33). It is this 'contamination' which makes appropriation rather than just another interpretation of the text necessary; a demarcation between the two terms is in one sense false, for they spill into one another, and yet it marks the distinction between a criticism that explicitly acknowledges its own partisanship and another that defends itself by claiming that it is objective, and not 'devoted to special purposes' – which is how the *Oxford Illustrated Dictionary* defines 'appropriation'.

So often the first step of our devotion to special purposes is to expose those of others – to treat institutionalised readings as appropriations too: 'If Shakespeare can be appropriated by these conservative standpoints, there is scope for intervention also for an oppositional politics' (Sinfield, 'Reproductions', p. 132). *The Tempest* lends itself easily to such an exposé.[1] Western criticism and productions of the play have differed from those of *Othello* in their earlier and more explicit acknowledgement of the play's involvement with the colonial theme. One reason for this difference is that Caliban's status (confirmed by the list of *personae* as a 'savage and deformed slave') does not threaten common-sense notions about black people or slaves in the same way as does Othello's emphasised nobility and heroism. While much critical effort was expended to prove both Othello's non-negroid lineage and his moral whiteness – despite abundant references to his blackness – there has been no parallel concern about the precise shade of colouring of

Prospero's 'thing of darkness'; even though *The Tempest* is more ambiguous about Caliban's colour and race. Not until 1934 was he represented as black on the British stage, but most previous productions had presented him as animalistic and, after the publication of Darwin's *Origin of the Species* in 1859, as an ape, hideously deformed and grotesque, a sort of 'half monkey, half coco-nut' representing the missing link, half-seal, half-man, fishlike, and so on. Simultaneously he was projected as a colonised native of varying descriptions (see Griffiths, pp. 163-9). Such explicitly social-Darwinist, racist and imperialist productions indicated Caliban's *political* colour as clearly *black*.

It is true that the play's connection with the 'New World' (acknowledged as early as 1808) was, until fairly recently in Western criticism, relegated to background material and not allowed to become part of the play's ideological and historical 'con-texts' (see Barker and Hulme, p. 195). Such a closure negatively acknowledged and actively utilised material which was formally marginalised. Hence in Kermode's introduction to the play, for example, sources are painstakingly logged but kept at bay; we are told that the play is primarily concerned with an opposition between Nature and Art ('as all serious pastoral poetry always is') and that 'there is nothing in *The Tempest* fundamental to its structure of ideas which could not have existed had America remained undiscovered' (p. xxv). Any illusions we might have about the political innocence of such efforts to close off the text from what Barker and Hulme have called 'contextual contamination' are dispelled by what follows:

If Aristotle was right in arguing that 'men . . . who are as much inferior to others as the body is to the soul . . . are slaves by nature, and it is advantageous for them to be always under government' . . . then the black and mutilated cannibal must be the natural slave of the European gentleman, and *a fortiori*, the salvage and deformed Caliban of the learned Prospero. (p. xlii)

It is no accident that Kermode's text is widely used in India or that in that context its obvious bias is inserted into notions of the play as a romance, an almost mystic piece of enchantment. Although appropriations occur all the time, in every reading or staging of the text, it is only when they become subversive that questions of *authenticity* -- historical or thematic 'correctness' – surface sharply.

For example, generations of white Othellos are permitted while a single black Antony provokes an outrage. In a letter to the *Guardian*, Brigid Larmour refers to the paper's disparaging review of her casting a black man as Antony: 'How is authenticity being infringed? Would it be authentic to have an Italian, toga'd Antony and a boy Cleopatra . . . Does it strain authenticity to have a blonde Cleopatra like Helen Mirren or a tall one like Vanessa Redgrave?' (30 May 1987). From an editorial in *Plays and Players* entitled 'Multi-racial humbug' it is obvious that theatrical authenticity is a way of holding on to a lost empire:

Far from taking pride in one of the most complex, consistent and individual cultures in Europe, apologetic Brits are welcoming the (in many cases artificial) grafting of new elements of varying suitability or relevance on to the indigenous growth. Politics, we suspect, have more to do with this than art; quotas rather than quality.

Referring to Hugh Quarshie, a black actor who speaks of Enobarbus being played by a Caribbean actor as 'a real coup', the editor continues: 'Too true, Hugh. It will also be coup when played by a Chinese midget, nude on rollerskates, and just as relevant. Of course, there could be a production (any day now, to judge by the RSC's slavish addiction to updating for dumb dumbs) in which this would be valid' (July 1986, p. 2). It is not entirely accidental that I found this review, which ends by referring to alternative theatre practices as 'the new colonialism', in the library of the British Council at Delhi, nor that a few days later a prominent professor of English literature at Delhi introduced a talk on Shakespeare by declaring that she was 'a diehard conservative' whose love for Shakespeare had distanced her from 'new-fangled theories and writers' in whom her students seemed unfortunately very interested.

To return to *The Tempest*; while social-Darwinist depictions of Caliban as ape-man were greeted with exclamations of wonder at Shakespeare's prophetic anticipation of Darwin's scientific analysis, the *Financial Times* complained after Jonathan Miller's anti-imperialist production that 'colonialism, the dominion of one race (as opposed to one nation) over another, is something that Shakespeare had never heard of' (Griffiths, p. 178). Caliban stands more clearly and self-consciously in opposition to dominant culture than does Othello. For this reason, it was an easier text to appropriate for anti-imperial purposes; since the early fifties African and Caribbean intellectuals 'chose to utilise (it) . . . as a strategy for (in George Lamming's words) getting "out from under this ancient mausoleum of (Western) historic achievement". They seized upon *The Tempest* as a way of amplifying their calls for decolonization within the bounds of the dominant cultures' (Nixon, pp. 557-8).

Whereas Western readings had acknowledged Caliban as 'the core of the play' only in order to concur with Prospero's reading of him as a an inherently inferior being 'on whose nature / Nurture can never stick' (IV.i.188-9), this other history seized upon Caliban to articulate its own bondage and rebellion; at the same time it also initiated a debate on the psyche of the colonised subject. Significantly, during the years following Britain's forced retreat from Empire, as such anti-imperialist appropriations became frequent, there were very few productions of the play on the British stage (Griffiths, p. 176).

The history of The Tempest, therefore, clearly reveals a contest over textual truth and value, and exposes dominant Shakespearian criticism as part of that struggle rather than the guardian of some irrefutable core of meaning. That both racist and anti-colonialist appropriations and interpretations of the play exist does not argue for the simultaneous validity of contradictory meanings; pluralism seeks to deflect the fact that 'different readings struggle with each other on the site of a text, and all that can count, however provisionally, as knowledge of a text, is achieved through this discursive conflict' (Barker and Hulme, p. 194).

But what makes it possible for The Tempest to be read in these different ways? A recent article by Thomas Cartelli, entitled 'Prospero in Africa', suggests that the reasons why particular readings arise in relation to a specific text are not entirely extraneous to the text itself. Centring his argument on Ngugi Wa Thiong'o's A Grain of Wheat, Cartelli argues that the Kenyan writer's association of Prospero with Conrad's Kurtz by combining them in his central character, Thompson, is not a misreading of the play but is historically justified by the inevitable collapse of imperialist 'idealism', which we might identify with Prospero, into coercive brutality, which is so clearly revealed by Kurtz. Prospero's rhetoric of noble intentions combined with his coercive actions was the strategy employed by later colonialists as well.

Recent criticism of the play has been concerned with a historically determined ambivalence in the text; Paul Brown's incisive analysis concludes that The Tempest 'serves as a limit text in which the characteristic operations of colonial discourse may be discerned – as an instrument for exploitation, a register of beleaguerment and a site of radical ambivalence' (p. 68); Barker and Hulme have shown that 'Prospero's play and The Tempest are not necessarily the same thing' (p. 199). Cartelli's article suggests that this ambivalence has been central in establishing The Tempest's 'as a privileged text in the history of colonialist discourse'. He maintains that since the play is not 'simply anticolonialist' and allows Prospero a certain privileged status, it is 'a responsible party to its successive readings and rewritings in so far as it has made seminal contributions to the development of the colonial ideology through which it is read' (p. 100-1). The text thus becomes, at least partly, the source of the ideological contamination of which Eagleton speaks.

It seems to me, however, that Cartelli emphasises only half the implications of this position, and of recent criticism of The Tempest. If there is a connection between the ambivalence of the play and its usefulness for the construction of later paternalistic colonialism, is there also not one between the same ambivalence and anti-colonialist appropriations? Cartelli's article suggests that alternative readings are only possible in relation to the The Tempest's original contexts but that later history of the play has unfolded its latent imperialist elements: 'the position which The Tempest occupied at its moment of production may not . . . have been as decidedly colonialist as Thompson and Ngugi consider it to be at its point of reception' (p. 106). But here, surely, we are talking about only one, dominant and institutionalised, point of reception. There have been others, as I have indicated by recounting the already well-known features of its African and Carribean appropriations. Because he ignores these, Cartelli goes on posit too drastic an opposition between the original and subsequent contexts of the play:

For Ngugi, a historically or critically 'correct' reading of The Tempest that isolates the play 'at its originating moment of production' would serve merely an anti-quarian interest, documenting an alleged 'intervention' in colonialist discourse that made no discernibly positive impact on the subsequent development of colonial practices. His own variety of historicity would, on the other hand, focus less on the text's status as a historically determined literary artifact, now open to a variety of interpretations, than on its subordination to what history has made of it. (p. 107)

If we consider the issues raised by anti-colonialist appropriations alongside those that emerge when we assess the 'originating moment of the play', then a 'historically correct reading' of a text need not be pitted against locating 'what history has made of it': radical readings are not about investing a text with what isn't there at all. Can we suggest, instead, that the struggle over meaning is intensified in the case of a text which is itself polyphonic and that the contradictions within the text and the struggle between its different appropriations are inter-related? This would mean that the difficulties of appropriating the play should be looked at alongside the limits of its 'radical ambivalence'. Moreover, one cannot read the political interests of all oppositional readings, even those that emerge at the same time, as identical. These two propositions need to be examined together, and I shall do so by looking at the ways in which the representation of gender in The Tempest marks the limits for its appropriation in the Third World context today.

'The imperishable empire'

The play's history in India alerts us against reading the encounter of Third World readers with the white text as a uniform one. A recent production of The Tempest on the Delhi stage worked hard at excluding the imperial theme. It attempted to make the spectators identify with Prospero instead of Caliban by elaborating the 'magical' effects desired by Prospero so that the Calibans in the audience would be hypnotised into complicity with the colonial closure which is part of the play's contradictory enterprise. Such productions have been largely ignored as semi-amateur, incompetent theatre playing to a relatively small urban elite, but they serve to uncover ways in which different colonised peoples bring varying histories to bear upon their contact with Western literature. If identification with Caliban came strongly for African and Caribbean audiences, it was because their own blackness and racial difference were overtly emphasised by colonial rule. In India, as I argued in chapter 1, the Aryan myth was invoked to disguise the specifically racist aspects of Empire, and can be seen to 'persuade' the readers/ spectators of *The Tempest*, already holding strong colour prejudices that permeate caste and communal politics within India, and unfortunately perceiving themselves as somehow less black than Africans, that in fact they are closer to noble, white Prospero than monstrous, black Caliban.

Moreover, Shakespeare's last plays, and particularly *The Tempest*, had been the focus of Orientalist comparisons of Shakespeare to Kalidasa, the most famous of ancient Sanskrit playwrights. This analogy was picked up by Indian criticism of Shakespeare, which invoked both the stereotype of a spiritual India and dominant assumptions about the universality of art, fixed Indian literary achievement in the distant past, excluded the question of present relevance (or irrelevance) and lifted both dramas from their respective historical contexts. Both Shakespeare and Kalidasa (and by implication all great art) value order, suffering and passivity:

The theme is more or less the same, destruction of domestic happiness, separation, suffering and finally reconciliation and reunion. In all these plays there is regeneration achieved through patient suffering and repentance ... at the highest level of poetic experience, all barriers that divide peoples disappear, revealing the essential unity of art and unity of poetic experience itself. (Acharya, pp. xii-xiii)

An earlier book, written jointly by an Indian, H. H. Anniah Gowda, and an Englishman, Henry W. Wells, claims to be 'a monument to hearts and hands across the seas' on the basis of its comparisons between Shakespeare's last plays and some classical plays of India. A comprehensive critique of these books is tempting but beyond my scope here. Notable, however, are the ways in which they combine an Orientalist conception of India ('with the possible exception of Egypt . . . the supreme mother of myth', p. 30), patriarchal identification of female with instinct and male with reason ('both Shakuntala and Miranda represent

an instinctive harmony with nature; their lovers the King Dushyanta
and Ferdinand, merely add understanding to intuition', pp. 122-3), and
an essentialist idealism (these plays deal with the 'basic and outstanding
realities in the human condition', p. 65).

It might be argued that such writings are extreme examples, but their
assumptions are certainly normative in the Indian classroom. The complex histories behind books such as Wells and Gowda's are also at work
when an Indian audience in 1987 is told to accept The Tempest as a drama
of forgiveness, patience and magic, or research students at Delhi University are asked to study the play as part of 'The Romance Tradition' in
English literature, with connections with Daphnus and Chloe prioritised to
'erase' the imperial theme. The point, however, is that with varying
degrees of sophistication, these histories and pedagogic traditions underline the colonial history of the play: they work to ensure what one critic
had frankly admitted, that 'the imperishable Empire of Shakespeare will
always be with us' (Narasimhaiah, p.v).

The black rapist

One of the reasons for the play's declining pertinence to contemporary
third world politics has been identified as

> the difficulty of wresting from it any role for female defiance or leadership in a
> period when protest is coming increasingly from that quarter. Given that Caliban
> is without a female counterpart in his oppression and rebellion, and given the
> largely autobiographical cast of African and Caribbean appropriations of the play,
> it follows that all the writers who quarried from The Tempest an expression of
> their lot should have been men. (Nixon, p. 577)

It is true that the play poses a problem for a feminist, and especially a
nonwestern feminist appropriation, if by 'appropriation' we mean an
amplification of the anti-colonial voices within the text. But such a difficulty does not arise simply from the lack of a strong female presence,
black or white, in the play, but also from the play's representation of
black male sexuality.

Caliban contests Prospero's account of his arrival on the island but
not the accusation of attempted rape of Miranda. Identifying the political
effects of Prospero's accusation, Paul Brown comments that 'the issue
here is not whether Caliban is actually a rapist or not, since Caliban
accepts the charge' (p. 62). On the contrary, I suggest that this acceptance
is important for assessing both colonial and anti-colonial readings of
the play. An article written in 1892, which later became what Griffiths
calls 'a standard defence of Caliban' speaks of the rape as 'an offence,

an unpardonable offence, but *one that he was fated to commit*' (p. 166; emphasis added) and goes on to see Caliban as unfortunate, oppressed, but 'like all these lower peoples, easily misled'. This implies that sexual violence is part of the black man's inferior nature, a view that amalgamates racist common-sense notions about black sexuality and animalism, and sexist assumptions about rape as an inevitable expression of frustrated male desire.

These notions were complexly employed in the influential *Psychologie de la colonisation* (1948) by Octave Mannoni, who seriously reassessed the play in order to propound a controversial view of the psychology of the colonised subject. Mannoni advocated the notion of the 'Caliban complex' which he analysed as the desire for dependency on the part of the native. Caliban (and the Madagascans, whose uprising of 1947-48 provided the impetus for the work) revolts not against slavery but because he is abandoned by Prospero. Analysing Caliban's speech in Act II, Mannoni came to the conclusion that 'Caliban does not complain of being exploited: he complains of being betrayed'. As other Caribbean and African intellectuals pointed out, Mannoni posited Caliban as an eager partner in his own colonisation (Nixon, pp. 562-5). Crucially, Mannoni traces the roots of racism to sexual guilt. The antagonism between Caliban and Prospero hinged on Miranda's presence as the sole woman on the island. Accordingly, a definition of the coloniser's psyche, or what Mannoni called the 'Prospero complex' was based on the notion of racism as a pseudo-rational construct used to rationalise feelings of sexual guilt.

Both dependency and racism by this account are connected to politics of sexual desire, but in a way that preserves the patriarchal exclusion of sexuality from economics as well as the racist assumption that Caliban's subordinate status will naturally lead him to desire (and hence rape) Miranda. The supposed desire of the native for European care has been advanced by nearly every imperialist regime. That Mannoni's theories could be used to legitimise colonisation was demonstrated by the publication of Philip Mason's *Prospero's Magic: Some Thoughts on Class and Race* in 1962 (see Nixon, pp. 564-5). Mannoni was severely criticised for his psychological reductionism by, among others, Frantz Fanon, who pointed out that economic motivations for plunder were omitted in the former's account.

Fanon's own explanation of the sexual encounter between the black man and white woman in *Black Skins, White Masks*, which has already been cited in connection with *Othello*, attributes both sexual insecurity and racist hatred to the white father who is antagonised by the black lover of his daughter. Fanon also describes the ways in which a black

man who has internalised the value system of white society may view
his liaison with a white woman as a pathway to acceptance and I have
used this explanation to describe Othello's love for Desdemona (see
chapter 2). A Fanonian explanation of black men's desire for white
women is useful only in specific situations and with some qualifications.
Firstly, to extend it to the consciousness of all black men would be to
assume 'too readily that black men have necessarily internalised the
white man's view of things' (see Lawrence, 'Just plain common-sense',
p. 71). Secondly, in Fanon's account, the white woman is only an *object*
of the black man's desire; her own subjectivity is markedly absent. This
is a serious limitation of Fanon's work, for racist common-sense
(although from a totally different perspective) also posits that black men
lust after white women, and also erases the desire of white women. By
doing so, racism moves from the black man's desire to his bestiality and
concludes that black men will seek to *enforce* a liaison upon white
women. Hence the myth of the black rapist. In *Othello*, such a myth
hovers on the margins of Brabantio's accusations, but is undercut by
Desdemona's own powerfully articulated desire for Othello.

In *The Tempest*, Prospero's accusation of rape and its corroboration by
Caliban upholds such a myth, which derives from the idea that, aware
of the damage they can do by making sexual advances towards white
women, black men have all conceived 'a peculiar lust for white womanhood' (Lawrence, p. 71). Of course, rape has been articulated as a
weapon by black militants: Eldridge Cleaver called it an 'insurrectionary
act' against white society. Imamu Baraka wrote: 'Come up, black dada
nihilismus. Rape the white girls. Rape their fathers. Cut the mother's
throats' (cited Angela Davis, p. 197). If varieties of feminism are guilty
of racist practices, it needs hardly to be detailed here that sexist versions
of anti-racism abound as well. The result of these has strengthened the
fiction, often presented as 'facts', of black animalism. Susan Brownmiller's influential study of rape, *Against Our Will*, has argued that black
men's historical oppression has placed many of the 'legitimate' expressions of male supremacy beyond their reach, resulting in their open
sexual violence. Quoting Jean McKellar's *Rape: The Bait and the Trap*, which
claims that ninety per cent of all reported rapes in the United States are
by black men, Angela Davis points out that even official FBI figures place
it at forty per cent (p. 179). The point here is not that black men do not
rape, but that their dominant fictional representation has legitimised
both patriarchal and racist myths of female and black sexuality.

Gerda Lerner rightly says that 'the myth of the black rapist of white
women is the turn of the myth of the bad black woman – both designed
to apologize for and facilitate the continued exploitation of black men

and women' (quoted Angela Davis, p. 174). And of white women, one may add – the construction of the black rapist also includes that of the passive white woman, whose potential desire for black men is thus effaced. In *The Tempest*, therefore, we must read Caliban's rapacity as set against Sycorax's licentious black femininity and the passive purity of Miranda, whose own desire, like Portia's, corroborates the will of the father; although Miranda can be seen to 'slip away' from Prospero (see Paul Brown, p. 67; Fiedler, p. 206), this slippage does not erode fatherly authority in the same way as Desdemona's passion for Othello. Moreover, this juxtaposition of Miranda, Sycorax and Caliban focuses both on the economic aspects that were erased by Mannoni, and on the gender politics that have been ignored in some other appropriations.

Sycorax

Mannoni, significantly, edited out these opening lines of Caliban's version of Prospero's arrival on the island:

> This island's mine, by Sycorax my mother,
> Which thou tak'st from me. (I.ii.331-2)

These lines had elicited the first recorded anti-imperialist response to the play in 1904, which found that in them 'the whole case of the aboriginal against aggressive civilisation (was) dramatised before us' (Nixon, pp. 561-2). They were also focused by subsequent Caribbean and African appropriations, but although some of these indicated the matrilinear nature of many pre-colonial societies, gender was hardly ever seized upon by anti-colonial intellectuals as a significant dimension of racial oppression.

Sycorax is more than the justification for Caliban's territorial rights to the island – she operates as a powerful contrast to Miranda. Both Prospero and Caliban testify to her power; the former draws upon the language of misogyny as well as racism to construct her as a 'foul witch' (I.ii.258), the latter invokes her strength to express his hatred of his master (I.ii.321-3, 339-40). Prospero's descriptions of Sycorax emphasise both her non-European origins – she's 'from Argier' – and her fertility – 'This blue-ey'd hag was hither brought with child' (I.ii.265, 269). She is also 'so strong / That could control the moon, make flows and ebbs, / And deal in her command without her power' (V.i.269-71). Hence she stands in complete contrast to the white, virginal and obedient Miranda. Between them they split the patriarchal stereotype of woman as the white devil – virgin and whore, goddess (Miranda is mistaken for one by Ferdinand) and witch.

But Sycorax is also Prospero's 'other'; his repeated comparisons between their different magics and their respective reigns of the island are used by him to claim a superior morality, a greater strength and a greater humanity, and hence legitimise his takeover of the island and its inhabitants; but they also betray an anxiety that Sycorax's power has not been fully exorcised, and for Caliban still invokes it for his own rebellion: 'All the charms / Of Sycorax, toads, beetles, bats, light on you!' (I.ii.339-40). As George Lamming pointed out in The Pleasures of Exile, while Miranda is like many an African slave child in never having known her mother, 'the actual Caliban of The Tempest has the advantage . . . of having known the meaning and power of his mother Sycorax' (p. 111).

Prospero's takeover is both racial plunder and a transfer to patriarchy. The connections between witches and transgressive women, between witch-trials with the process of capital accumulation, and between the economic, ideological and sexual subordination of native women by colonial rule, have already been discussed (chapters 1 and 3). The restructuring of the colonised economy not only involved the export of raw material to factories in England, but also a redefinition of men and women's work, which economically dislocated women, and cal-cified patriarchal tendencies in the native culture (see Lawrence, 'Socio-logy and black "pathology"' pp. 113-14). In Burma, for example, British colonialists acknowledged that Burmese women had property and sex-ual rights unheard of in England. Accordingly, Fielding Hall, Political Officer in the British Colonial Administration in Burma, suggested that in order to 'civilise' the Burmese people:

1. The men must be taught to kill and to fight for the British colonialists.
2. Women must to surrender their liberty in the interests of men. (Mies, quoted by Rughani, p. 19)

Colonised women were also subjected to untold sexual harassment, rape, enforced marriage and degradation, both under direct slavery and otherwise. Sycorax's illegitimate pregnancy contrasts with Miranda's chastity and virginity, reminding us that the construction of the pro-miscuity of non-European women served to legitimise their sexual abuse and to demarcate them from white women.

Therefore Prospero as colonialist consolidates power which is specifically white and male, and constructs Sycorax as a black, wayward and wicked witch in order to legitimise it. If Caliban's version of past events prompts us to question Prospero's story, then this interrogation should include the re-telling of Sycorax's story. The distinctions drawn by generations of critics between his 'white magic' and Sycorax's 'black magic' only corroborate Prospero's narrative. African appropriations emphasised the brutality of Prospero's 'reason' and its historical suppression of black culture, but they did not bring out the gender-value of these terms; they read the story of colonised and colonising men but not of colonised and colonising women, which is also told by Miranda's lonely presence on the island.

Miranda's schooling

It is ironical but not entirely inappropriate that one of the oldest of Delhi's colleges for women should have been called 'Miranda House', after the daughter of the university's colonial founder, Sir Maurice Gwyer. Miranda's schooling in *The Tempest* demonstrates the contradictory position occupied by white women in the colonial adventure. Paul Brown has discussed how 'the discourse of sexuality . . . offers the crucial nexus for the various domains of colonialist discourse' (p. 51) and the ways in which control of his subjects' sexuality is crucial for Prospero's exercise of power. Patriarchalism alternately asserts its *knowledge* (the father's wisdom: Prospero's magic, his schooling of Miranda, his civilising of Caliban); its *humanity* (parental concern and love: Prospero's re-iteration of his 'care' of Miranda, his liberation of 'my Ariel', and of his 'humanely taken' pains over Caliban); its *power* (the father's authority: Miranda cannot choose but obey Prospero, he can torture both Caliban and Ariel); and often all three together (Prospero's aside to the rebels that he will 'tell no tales' is simultaneously a disclosure of his knowledge of their plans, a favour and a warning). In the colonial situation, patriarchalism makes specific, and often apparently contradictory demands of its 'own' women.

Miranda is the most solitary of Renaissance woman protagonists, and moves on an exclusively male stage – 'I do not know/ One of my sex; no woman's face remember' (III.i.48-9) – where references are made to only three other women. She indicates the apparent exclusion of women from the colonial arena, but at the same time, their actual and sinister inclusion, together with other images of femininity in the play, propels the narrative even when posited as an absence. Miranda provides the ideological legitimation of each of Prospero's actions; at the beginning of the play he tells her that his 'Art' is prompted by his concern for her : 'I have done nothing but in care of thee' (I.ii.16). Next, in the same scene, he claims that his enslavement of Caliban was prompted by the latter's attempted rape of Miranda (I.ii.345-8). Later she is described by him as 'a third of mine own life, / Or that for which I live' (IV.i.3-4); therefore after she is married he will 'retire me to my Milan, where/ Every third thought shall be my grave' (V.i.310-11).

Prospero's complaint against Antonio is that he 'new created / The creatures that were mine, I say or chang'd 'em, / Or else new form'd 'em (I.ii.81-3). His own enterprise is precisely the same, and Miranda is the most successful of his creations. For twelve years 'have I, thy schoolmaster, made thee more profit/ Than other princess' can, that have more time / For vainer hours, and tutors not so careful' (I.ii.171-4). This education has had two main and diverse purposes. On the one hand it has schooled her to <u>obedience</u>; Prospero proudly affirms that Miranda is 'ignorant of what thou art; nought knowing / Of whence I am'. She obeys in silence and has been taught not to question why, despite the fact that Prospero has left his story tantalisingly incomplete: 'More to know / Did never meddle with my thoughts' (I.ii.17-22). She has therefore been well prepared to accept his version of the past (unlike Caliban, who questions it). Gratitude to her father mingles with a self-depreciation and she repeatedly perceives herself as a nuisance to him (I.ii.63; I.ii.151-2). Prospero never takes this control for granted, however, and is anxious to secure her attention and obedience. His story-telling is punctuated by repeated orders to 'sit down', 'Obey, and be attentive', 'Dost thou attend me', 'I pray thee, mark me', 'Thou attend'st not?', 'Dost thou hear?' (I.ii). Miranda is ordered to sleep, awake, come on, see, speak, be quiet, obey, be silent, hush and be mute. She is his property, to be exchanged between father and husband: 'Then, as my gift, and thine own acquisition / Worthily purchas'd, take my daughter' (IV.i.13-14).

On the other hand, Miranda's schooling calls upon her to participate actively in the colonial venture. Although she does not 'love to look upon' Caliban, she must be educated about the economics of the situation:

> We cannot miss him: he does make our fire,
> Fetch in our wood, and serves in offices
> That serve us. (I.ii.311-15)

Editors of The Tempest have often sought to transfer Miranda's verbal assault on Caliban beginning 'Abhorred slave' (I.ii.351-62) to Prospero on the grounds that Miranda is too delicate and not philosophical enough to speak so harshly (see Kermode, p. 32; Barton, 'Leontes', p. 137). On the contrary, these lines underline Miranda's implication in the colonialist project. She has been taught to be revolted by Caliban ('abhorred slave'); to believe in his natural inferiority ('thy vile race') and inherent incapacity to be bettered ('which any print of goodness will not take'); to feel sorry for the inferior native ('I pitied thee') and to try and uplift him ('took pains to make thee speak'); and to concur totally in his 'deserv'd' confinement. Miranda thus conforms to the dual requirements of femininity within the master-culture: by taking on aspects of the white man's burden the white woman only confirmed her own subordination.

'Miranda House' was a school for Indian women and its naming was not a careful colonial conspiracy. I do not want to ignore the contradictions of such institutions, and the space for alternative stances within them ; yet the name betrays some of the assumptions underlying female education in the colonies and indicates the effort to create a native female intelligentsia which be schooled to ignore its gendered and racial alienation from the prevailing status quo.² Two other women are mentioned in The Tempest, and the references to them reinforce racial and sexual power relations. The first of these is Miranda's mother, who is dismissed as 'a piece of virtue' (I.ii.56) and remembered solely for her capacity to ensure the pure descent of the Duke of Milan. Later we hear of Claribel, daughter of Alonzo, King of Naples, who has been married to the King of Tunis. The tempest wrecked the ship while it was returning from the wedding celebrations. While he laments the death of his son, Alonzo is told:

> Sir, you may thank yourself for this great loss,
> That would not bless our Europe with your daughter,
> But rather loose her to an African. (II.i.117-19)

Thus women and black men, and particularly a combination of the two, are posited as the cause of misfortune. We are also told that Claribel herself, 'the fair soul', oscillated between 'loathness' at this union and 'obedience' to her father (II.i.123-4). Her marriage is abnormal and the source of ill-luck but she, a true European daughter, is subservient to patriarchal will. The references to the marriage also serve to distinguish between different non-Europeans, between the King of Tunis and Caliban, underlining the way that class positions, power and regional differences can alter the meaning of racial difference. In this respect, one may recall also that whereas Cleopatra's status can allow her frankly to acknowledge her dark colour – 'Think on me, / That am with Phoebus' amorous pinches black' (I.v.27-8) – Zanche as a lowly servant girl must attempt, with a dowry of 'a hundred thousand crowns', to 'wash the Ethiop white' (The White Devil, V.iii.256, 259; see also Newman, p. 142).³

A doomed dialectic?

The 'rape' amplifies the doomed dialectic which might be detected in Caliban's ability to curse in the coloniser's tongue, which exerted the greatest

fascination for anti-colonial appropriations and became a symbol both
for the internalisation of European values by the African and Caribbean
intellectual and for his subversion (hers was not considered) of them.
George Lamming's *The Pleasures of Exile* points out that the 'gift' of language
is 'not English, in particular, but speech and concept as a way . . . (it) is
the very prison in which Caliban's achievements will be realised and
restricted' (pp 109-10). Caliban presents the rape as his attempt to
'people . . . This isle with Calibans' (I.ii.350-1). But even by positing
himself as worthy of duplication, Caliban's revolt boomerangs to confirm the shaping power of dominant culture. Lamming wonders why
Caliban is so sure that his children by Miranda would be like him, and
not like her or Prospero. But he does not consider the phallocentricism
of Caliban's confidence, nor how it is ironically undercut by his subordinate racial position. Moreover, he constantly simplifies both Caliban
and Miranda: 'Caliban is in his way a kind of Universal. Like the earth
he is always there, generous in his gifts, inevitable, yet superfluous and
dumb . . . Caliban can never reach perfection, not even the perfection
implicit in Miranda's privileged ignorance' (pp. 108-10). The political
effect of Prospero's accusation and Caliban's acceptance is to make the
potential revolutionary a rapist, and I have tried to suggest that it is
crucially interrelated with the other ways in which Caliban's spaces are
limited by the boundaries of colonial discourse. Although the connection between Caliban's linguistic and sexual rebellion is hinted at by
Lamming, it is not fully developed; this ommission is typical of the
gender-blindness of many anti-colonial appropriations and criticism.

   Can Caliban ever exist outside the territories allowed him by *The Tempest*? Feminists have found the 'masculine will' of disorderly women in
Renaissance drama unsatisfactory, and I have tried to show that no other
pure feminist consciousness is possible from within the masculine arena
available to them. Homi Bhabha writes: 'it is always in relation to the
place of the Other that colonial desire is articulated: that is, in part, the
fantasmatic space of "possession" that no one subject can singly occupy
which permits the dream of the inversion of role' (Introduction, *Black
Skins, White Masks*, p. xv). This implicates both the coloniser and the
colonised: while it would be idealist to imagine spaces outside such a
dialectic in the colonial situation, the interlocking is increasingly dissatis-
fying in the post-colonial reality. Even within the colonial struggle, the
evocation of native culture has been important – Aime Cesaire, for example, tried to locate his Caliban in indigenous space – he is rooted in
African religion and culture and draws on traditions uncontaminated
by colonialism.

   Here *The Tempest* brings us to the centre of a crucial controversy surrounding current theories of colonial discourse. Benita Parry has suggested that recent work in this area has concentrated on the complexity, ambiguity and 'hybridity' of colonial discourse at the expense of obscuring what Fanon called the 'murderous and decisive struggle between two protagonists' (Parry, p. 43). This problem has been identified in relation to The Tempest by Thomas Cartelli. In an essay which I have referred to earlier, he counterposes those 'who quarrel with the notion of a Tempest that speaks the predatory language of colonialism' and 'another nonwestern interpretative community for whom The Tempest has long served as the embodiment of colonial presumption'. As he sees it, the first group 'problematize(s) the traditionally stereotyped critical estimate of the relationship of Prospero and Caliban', while the second resists this 'by recuperating the starkness of the master/slave configuration' (p. 101).

It is true that the limits of the 'radical ambivalence' of The Tempest are marked by the confinement of Caliban to the space structured by the coloniser; the play does not allow him, to visualise what Parry calls 'another condition beyond imperialism'. But we can question a simple opposition between the two groups identified by Cartelli by arguing that the play functions as 'the embodiment of colonial presumption' only when the tensions and ambivalence which Brown points to are erased. What do we mean by 'the starkness of the master / slave configuration'? Surely not that either of the two opponents, their stances and psyches are simple or monolithic? The harshness of the colonial conflict cannot be stressed by ignoring the complexity of the adversaries.

This project has tried to emphasise this point in relation to our own encounter with the European text, including the agenda for its alternative teaching. The colonial conflict intersects with others – those of class, gender, caste and ethnicity and 'the colonial subject' is not a simple being. Moreover, three centuries of colonial history have shaped complex institutions, such as the Indian education system, which cannot be dismantled unless we take into account the interpenetration of colonial, indigenous and patriarchal power structures. But this is precisely the point at which Parry's criticism becomes crucial: she attributes the concentration on 'hybridity' to a 'programme marked by the exhorbitation of discourse and a related incuriosity about the enabling socio-economic and political institutions and other forms of social praxis' (p. 43). Whereas in The Tempest Caliban is simply left on his island, we know that in reality Prospero rarely simply sails away. To curse in 'your language' (I.ii.362) is not to appropriate the European text on its own terms or to limit ourselves to the spaces allowed by it. Not only will it centre around a disclosure of the similarity and dissimilarity, usefulness and irrelevance of the Western text, but it must extend to the economic, sociopolitical and institutional realities in which our academic practice exists.

Notes

1 I am indebted to work on The Tempest by Barker and Hulme, Paul Brown and Rob Nixon, all of which has made this chapter possible.
2 The English department of Miranda House has been instrumental in initiating (in Delhi) the critical examination of English studies in India (see chapter 1, note 1); it has also provided a forum for regular discussion of critical theory and its applicability in the Indian classroom and published feminist criticism by university lecturers in Delhi. This perhaps bears out my contention that, given the increasing feminisation of English studies, and women's alienation from the dominant concerns of the discipline, a Third World feminist criticism will play a central role in overhauling English studies in India.
3 Femininity and race are picked up in the references to other women, as in the apparently trivial banter about Dido 'which has never properly been explained' (Kermode, p. 46). This exchange both differentiates between African Tunis and Carthage, centre of the Old World, and introduces the idea of identification between the two worlds: 'Tunis, sir was Carthage' (II.i.78).

Bibliography of work cited

(* denotes editions of texts used for quotations)

Acharya, P. B., *Tragicomedies of Shakespeare, Kalidasa and Bhavabhuti* (New Delhi, Meharchand Lacchmandas, 1978).

Adelman, Janet, *The Common Liar: an Essay on Antony and Cleopatra* (New Haven, Yale University Press, 1973).

Advani, Rukun, 'The publisher in the market place. Some ideological aspects of publishing for English studies' (paper presented at Miranda House, University of Delhi, April, 1988).

Agrippa, Henry Cornelius, *A Treatise of the Nobilitie and Excellencye of Woman Kynde,* trans. Henry Care (London, 1542).

Altbach, Philip G, 'In search of Saraswati: the ambivalence of the Indian academic' in Altbach ed., *Comparative Perspectives on the Academic Profession* (New York and London, Praeger Publishers, 1977).

— 'Servitude of the mind? Education, dependency and neocolonialism' in Altbach, Arnove and Kelly eds., *Comparative Education* (New York, Macmillan and London, Collier Macmillan, 1982).

Altbach, Philip G. and Kelly, Gail, eds., *Education and Colonialism* (New York and London, Longman, 1978).

Althusser, Louis, *Lenin and Philosophy and Other Essays,* trans. Ben Brewster (London, New Left Books, 1971).

Amur, G. S. and Desai, S. K. eds., *Colonial Consciousness in Commonwealth Literature* (Bombay, Madras and New Delhi, Somanja Publications, 1984).

Andreson-Thom, Martha, 'Thinking about women and their prosperous art: a reply to Juliet Dusinberre's *Shakespeare and the Nature of Women', Shakespeare Studies* 11 (Columbia, University of South Carolina, 1978, pp. 259-76).

Anger, Jane, *Jane Anger her Protection for Women* (1589) in Simon Shepherd ed., *The Women's Sharpe Revenge.*

Ardener, Shirley ed., *Women and Space: Ground Rules and Social Maps* (London, Croom Helm, 1981).

Aston, Trevor ed., *Crisis in Europe 1560-1660: Essays from Past and Present* (London, Routledge, 1965).

Babb, Lawrence A., 'Marriage and malevolence: the uses of sexual opposition in a Hindu pantheon', *Ethnology* 9, 1970.

Babcock, Barbara ed., *The Reversible World. Symbolic Inversion in Art and Society* (Cornell University Press, 1978).

Bagchi, Jasodhara, 'Shakespeare in a loin-cloth: English literature and the early nationalist consciousness in Bengal' (paper presented at Miranda House, University of Delhi, April, 1988).

Bailey, Richard W. and Görlach, Manfred, *English as a World Language* (Cambridge University Press, 1982).

Baines, Barbara J. ed., *Three Pamphlets on the Jacobean Anti-feminist Controversy*, Scholars' Facsimiles and Reprints (New York, Delmar, 1978).

Baldick, Chris, *The Social Mission of English Criticism 1848-1932* (Oxford University Press, 1983).

Bamber, Linda, *Comic Women, Tragic Men: A Study of Gender and Genre in Shakespeare* (Stanford, Stanford University Press, 1982).

Bamberger, Joan, 'The myth of matriarchy: why men rule in primitive society' in Rosaldo, Michelle and Lamphere, Louise eds., *Women, Culture and Society* (Stanford, 1974).

Barker, Francis et al. eds., *Europe and Its Others* Volume 2 (Colchester, University of Essex, 1985).

Barker, Francis and Hulme, Peter, 'Nymphs and reapers heavily vanish: the discursive con-texts of *The Tempest*' in Drakakis, 1985, pp. 191-205.

Barrett, Michele, *Women's Oppression Today* (London, New Left Books, 1980).

— 'Ideology and the cultural production of gender' in Newton and Rosenfelt, 1985, pp. 65-85.

Barthel, Diane, 'Women's educational experience under colonialism: towards a diachronic model', *Signs* 11, no. 1 (autumn 1985).

Barton, Anne, 'The feminist stage', *Times Literary Supplement*, 24 October 1975.

— 'Leontes and the spider: language and speaker in Shakespeare's last plays' in P. Edwards, I. S. Ewbank and G. K. Hunter eds., *Shakespeare's Styles: essays in honour of Kenneth Muir* (Cambridge, Cambridge University Press, 1980), pp. 131-50.

— 'Was Shakespeare a chauvinist?', *New York Review of Books*,, 11 June 1981.

Basu, Aparna, 'Policy and conflict in India: the reality and the perception of education' in Altbach and Kelly eds., 1978.

Belsey, Catherine, *The Subject of Tragedy* (London and New York, Methuen, 1985).

— 'Disrupting sexual difference: meaning and gender in the comedies' in Drakakis, 1985, pp. 166-90.

— 'Constructing the subject: deconstructing the text' in Newton and Rosenfelt, 1985, pp. 45-64.

Berger, John et al., *Ways of Seeing* (London, BBC and Penguin, 1972; New York, Penguin, 1977).

Bergeron, D. M., *English Civic Pageantry 1558-1642* (London, Arnold, 1971).

Bhabha, Homi, 'The other question', *Screen* 24, no. 6 (Nov.-Dec. 1983), pp. 18-36.

— 'Representation and the colonial text. A critical exploration of some forms of mimeticism' in Frank Gloversmith ed., *The Theory of Reading* (New Jersey, Barnes and Noble/ Sussex, Harvester, 1984), pp. 123-46.

— 'Signs taken for wonders: questions of ambivalence and authority under a tree outside Delhi, May 1917', *Critical Inquiry* 12 (autumn 1985).

— 'Introduction' to Fanon, 1986.

Bhatnagar, Rashmi, 'Genre and gender: a reading of Tagore's *The Broken Nest* and R. K. Narayan's *The Dark Room*' in Chatterjee ed., 1986, pp. 172-87.

— 'Uses and limits of Foucault: a study of the theme of origins in Edward Said's *Orientalism*', *Social Scientist* 158 (July 1986).

Bhatt, B. D. and Aggarwal, J. C., *Educational Documents in India 1813-1968* (New Delhi, Arya book depot, 1969).

Bhavani, Kum Kum and Coulson, Margaret, 'Transforming socialist-feminism: the challenge of racism', *Feminist Review* no. 23 (summer 1986).

Blair, Judith, 'Private parts in public places: the case of actresses', in Ardener ed., 1981.

Blumberg, R. L. and Dwaraki, L., *India's Educated Women; Options and Constraints* (Delhi, Hindustan Publishing Corporation, 1980).

Boose, Lynda B., 'Father and the bride in Shakespeare', *PMLA* 93, no. 3, (May 1982).

Bradbrook, M. C., *Themes and Conventions of Elizabethan Tragedy* (Cambridge University Press, 1935).

Bradley, A. C., 'Shakespeare's *Antony and Cleopatra*' in J. R. Brown ed., *Shakespeare: Antony and Cleopatra, a Casebook* (London, etc., Macmillan, 1968).

Brecht, Bertolt, *Brecht on Theatre, the Development of an Aesthetic*, ed. and trans. John Willett (London, Eyre Methuen, 1964).

Bridenthal, Renate and Koonz, Claudia, eds., *Becoming Visible: Women in European History* (Boston, Houghton Mifflin Company, 1977).

Briggs, K. M., *Pale Hecate's Team: An Examination of the Beliefs on Witchcraft and Magic among Shakespeare's Contemporaries and His Immediate Sucessors* (London, Routledge, 1962).

*Brome, Richard, *The Antipodes*, ed. Anne Haaker (London, Edward Arnold, 1966).

Brown, J. E., *The Critical Opinions of Samuel Johnson* (London, Russell, 1926).

Brown, John Russell ed., *Antony and Cleopatra, A Casebook* (London, Macmillan, 1968).

— ed., *The Duchess of Malfi* (London, Methuen, 1964).

Brown, Paul, '"This thing of darkness I acknowledge mine": *The Tempest* and the discourse of colonialism', in Dollimore and Sinfield eds., 1985, pp. 48-71.

Brownmiller, Susan, *Against Our Will: Men, Women and Rape* (London, Secker and Warburg, 1975).

Brustein, Robert, 'The monstrous regiment of women' in G. R. Hibbard ed., *Renaissance and Modern Essays* (New York, Barnes and Noble, 1966).

Butler, Marilyn, 'Revising the canon', *Times Literary Supplement* (4-10 December 1987).

Butler, Martin, *Theatre and Crisis, 1632-1642* (Cambridge University Press, 1984).

Camden, Caroll, *The Elizabethan Woman* (Houston, New York and London, Elsevier, 1952).

Carby, Hazel V., 'White woman listen! Black feminism and the boundaries of sisterhood' in CCCS, 1982, pp. 212-35.

Carr, Helen, 'Woman/ Indian: "the American" and his others' in Francis Barker et al. eds., 1985.

Cartelli, Thomas, 'Prospero in Africa: *The Tempest* as colonial text and pretext' in Howard and O'Connor eds., 1987, pp. 99-115.

Castiglione, Baldassare, *The Book of the Courtier* (1561) trans. Thomas Hoby (London, J. M. Dent, 1928).

CCCS (Centre for Contemporary Cultural Studies), *The Empire Strikes Back: Race and racism in 70s Britain* (London, etc., Hutchinson, 1982).

Chakravarti, Uma, 'The development of the Sita myth: a case study of women in myth and literature', *Samya Shakti* I, no. 1 (July 1983), pp. 68-75.

Charney, Maurice, *Shakespeare's Roman Plays: the Function of Imagery in the Drama* (Cambridge, Mass., Harvard University Press, 1961).

Chatterji, Lola ed., *Woman Image Text: Feminist Readings of Literary Texts* (New Delhi, Trianka, 1986).

Chattopadhyay, Deviprasad, *Lokayata: A Study in Ancient Indian Materialism* (New Delhi, People's Publishing House, 1973).

Cherry, Caroline, *The Most Unvalued'st Purchase: Women in the Plays of Thomas Middleton* (University of Salzburg, 1973).

Clark, Alice, *The Working Life of Women in the Seventeenth Century* (London, Frank Cass, 1968).

Clark, Sandra, 'Hic Mulier, Haec Vir and the controversy over masculine women', *Studies in Philology* vol. 82, no. 2 (spring 1985), pp. 157-83.

Cohen, Walter, 'Political criticism of Shakespeare' in Howard and O'Connor, eds., 1987, pp. 18-46.

Cook, Judith, *Women in Shakespeare* (London, Harrap, 1980).

Coppola, Carlo ed., *Marxist Influences and South Asian Literature*, South Asia series occasional paper no. 23 (Asia studies centre, Michigan State University, winter 1974).

Coward, Rosalind, 'Sexual liberation and the family', m/f, no. 1 (1978).

Cowhig, Ruth, 'Blacks in English Renaissance drama and the role of Shakespeare's *Othello*' in Dabydeen, ed., 1985, pp. 1-25.

Dabydeen, David, ed., *The Black Presence in English Literature* (Manchester University Press, 1985).

Danby, John F., 'The Shakespearean dialectic: an aspect of *Antony and Cleopatra*, *Scrutiny* 16 (1949), pp. 196-213.

Dash, Irene G., *Wooing, Wedding and Power: Women in Shakespeare's Plays* (New York, Columbia University Press), 1981.

Datta, P. K., Review of A. Ghosh's *The Circle of Reason*, *Social Scientist*, October 1986.

Davies, Tony, 'Education, ideology and literature', *Red letters*, vol. 7, 1978, pp. 4-15.

Davis, Angela, *Women, Race and Class* (London, Women's Press, 1982).

Davis, Joe Lee, 'Richard Brome's neglected contribution to comic theory, *Studies in Philology* 40 (1943).

Davis, Natalie Zemon, 'Women on top: symbolic sexual inversion and political disorder in early modern Europe' in Babcock ed., 1978.

*Dekker, Thomas, John Ford and William Rowley, *The Witch of Edmonton* in Fredson Bowers ed., *The Dramatic Works of Thomas Dekker* (Cambridge, Cambridge University Press, 1958).

Dollimore, Jonathan, *Radical Tragedy; Religion and Ideology in the Drama of Shakespeare and his Contemporaries* (Brighton, Harvester, 1983).

— 'Shakespeare, cultural materialism and the new historicism' in Dollimore and Sinfield eds., 1985, pp. 2-17).

— 'Subjectivity, sexuality and transgression: the Jacobean connection' (forthcoming).

Dollimore, Jonathan and Sinfield, Alan, eds., *Political Shakespeare: new essays in cultural materialism* (Manchester University Press, 1985).

Donne, John, *The Elegies and Songs and Sonnets*, ed. Helen Gardener (London, Oxford University Press, 1965).

Doraiswamy, Rashmi, 'Western interpretations of Bakhtin', *Journal of Arts and Ideas* nos. 12-13 (Jan.-June 1987), pp. 93-122.

Drakakis, John ed., *Alternative Shakespeares* (London, Methuen, 1985).

Drakopoulou, Maria 'The Use of the Concept of the Sex-role in the Study of Female Criminality and Delinquency' (unpublished MA thesis, University of Sussex, 1985).

Dusinberre, Juliet, *Shakespeare and the Nature of Women* (London, Macmillan, 1975).

Eagleton, Terry, *William Shakespeare* (Oxford, Basil Blackwell, 1986).

Easlea, Brian, *Witch-hunting, Magic and the New Philosophy: an Introduction to the Debates of the Scientific Revolution 1450-1750* (Brighton, Harvester, 1980).

Ecker, Gisela ed., *Feminist Aesthetics* (London, The Women's Press, 1985).

Ehrenreich, B. and English, D., *Witches, Midwives and Nurses: a History of Women Healers* (New York, Feminist Press, 1973).

Eisenstein, Zillah R. ed., *Capitalist Patriarchy and the Case for Socialist Feminism* (New York and London, Monthly Review Press, 1979).

Eliot, T. S., 'Thomas Middleton' in *Selected Essays* (London, Faber, 1932).

Ellis-Fermor, Una, *The Jacobean Drama: an Interpretation* (London, Methuen, 1936).

Elyot, Thomas, *The Defence of Good Women* ed. Edwin Johnston Howard (Oxford and Ohio, The Anchor Press, 1940).

Empson, William, *Some Versions of the Pastoral* (London, Chatto and Windus, 1968).

English Historical Documents 1485-1558 (Volume V) (London, Eyre and Spottiswoode, 1964).

(The) English Studies Group, 'Recent developments in English studies at the centre' in Hall *et al*. eds., 1980, pp. 235-68.

Erickson, Peter B., 'Patriarchal structures in *The Winter's Tale*', *PMLA* 94 no. 5 (October 1982).

Erikson, E. H., 'Inner and outer space: some reflections on womanhood' in Lee and Sussman eds., *Sex Differences: Cultural and Developmental Dimensions* (London, Pluto Press, 1976).

Fanon, Frantz, *Black Skins, White Masks*, trans. Charles Lam Markmann (London and Sydney, Pluto Press, 1986).

Feminist Review no. 23 (Summer 1986; special issue: 'Socialist feminism out of the blue'.

Fiedler, Leslie A., *The Stranger in Shakespeare* (Hertfordshire, Paladin, 1974).

Figes, Eva, *Patriarchal Attitudes: Women in Society* (London, Faber, 1970).

Firestone, Shulamith, *The Dialectic of Sex: the Case for Feminist Revolution* (London, Cape, 1971).

Forbes, Geraldine H., 'In search of the "pure heathen": missionary women in nineteenth century India', *Economic and Political Weekly* 21, no. 17 (26 April 1986).

Ford, John, 'Tis Pity She's a Whore, ed. Brian Morris in *Elizabethan and Jacobean Tragedies* (Kent, Ernest Benn, 1984).

Forster, E. M., *A Passage to India* (London, Arnold, 1947).

Forum Against Rape, Leaflet (23 February 1980).

Foucault, Michel, *Power/Knowledge: Selected Interviews and Other Writings 1972-77*, ed. Colin Gordon (Brighton, Harvester, 1980).

French, Marilyn, *Shakespeare's Division of Experience* (London, Cape, 1982).

Friere, Paulo, *Pedagogy of the Oppressed*, trans. Myra Bergman Ramos (New York, Herder and Herder, 1972).

Garrett, Clarke, 'Women and witches: patterns of analysis', *Signs* vol. 3, no. 2, 1977.

Gibbons, Brian, 'Introduction', *Elizabethan and Jacobean Tragedies* (Kent, Ernest Benn, 1984).

Gilroy, 'Police and thieves' in CCCS, 1982, pp. 143-82.

Goldberg, Jonathan, 'The politics of Renaissance literature: a review essay', *ELH* 49, (1982), pp. 514-42.

— *James I and the Politics of Literature: Jonson, Shakespeare, Donne and their Contemporaries*

(Baltimore and London, John Hopkins University Press, 1983).

Greenblatt, Stephen, *Renaissance Self-Fashioning* (University of Chicago Press, 1980).

— ed., *The Power of Forms in the English Renaissance* (Norman, Oklahama, Pilgrim Books, 1982).

Greer, Germaine, *Sex and Destiny; the Politics of Human Fertility* (London, Secker and Warburg, 1984).

Griffiths, Trevor R., '"This island's mine": Caliban and colonialism', *Yearbook of English Studies* 13 (1983), pp. 159-80.

Hacker, Barton, 'Women and military institutions in early modern Europe; a reconnaisance', *Signs* 6, no. 4 (summer 1981) pp. 643-71.

Haec-Vir, or the Womanish-Man (1620) in Baines ed., 1978.

Hall, Stuart, 'Recent developments in theories of language and ideology: a critical note' in Hall *et al.* eds., 1980, pp. 157-62.

Hall, Stuart *et al.* eds., *Culture, Media, Language* (London etc., Hutchinson, 1980).

Hartmann, Heidi, 'The unhappy marriage of Marxism and feminism' in Sargant ed., 1981.

Heale, William, *An Apologie for Women* (1609), *The English Experience. Its Record in Early Printed Books Published in Facsimile*, no. 665 (Norwood, Walter J. Johnson, 1974).

Heinemann, Margot, 'How Brecht read Shakespeare' in Dollimore and Sinfield eds., 1985, pp. 202-30.

Heisch, Alison, 'Queen Elizabeth I: parliamentary rhetoric and the exercise of power', *Signs* 1, no. 1 (1975).

— 'Queen Elizabeth I and the persistence of patriarchy', *Feminist Review* no. 4 (1980).

Hic Mulier or the Mannish-Woman (1620) in Baines ed., 1978.

Hill, Christopher, *Society and Puritanism in Pre-Revolutionary England* (London, Panther Books, 1969).

— *The World Turned Upside Down: Radical Ideas During the English Revolution* (Harmondsworth, Penguin, 1975).

Hobsbawm, E. J., 'The crisis of the seventeenth century' in *Crisis in Europe 1560-1660: Essays from Past and Present* (London, Routledge, 1965).

Holloway, John, *The Story of the Night: Studies in Shakespeare's Major Tragedies* (London, Routledge, 1961).

Howard, Jean E. and O'Connor, Marion F., eds., *Shakespeare Reproduced: the text in history and ideology* (New York and London, Methuen, 1987).

Howard, Jean E., 'Renaissance antitheatricality and the politics of gender in *Much Ado About Nothing*' in Howard and O'Connor eds., 1987, pp. 163-87.

Hulme, Peter, 'Polytropic man: tropes of sexuality and mobility in early colonial discourse' in Barker *et al.* eds., 1985.

Hunter, G.K., *Dramatic Identities and Cultural Tradition, Studies in Shakespeare and his Contemporaries* (Liverpool University Press, 1978).

Jaggar, Alison M., *Feminist Politics and Human Nature* (Brighton, Harvester, 1983).

James I, *Political Works of James I* (New York, Russell and Russell, 1965).

Jardine, Lisa, 'The Duchess of Malfi: a case study in the literary representation of women' in Sussanne Kappeler and Norman Bryson eds., *Teaching the Text* (London, Routledge, 1983).

— *Still Harping on Daughters: Women in Seventeenth Century Drama* (Brighton, Harvester, 1983).

Jayawardana, Kumari, *Feminism and Nationalism in the Third World* (London, Zed

Books, 1986).

Jones, Ann Rosalind, 'Writing the body: towards an understanding of l'ectriture feminine' in Newton and Rosenfelt eds., 1985, pp. 86-101.

— 'Julia Kristeva on femininity: the limits of a semiotic politics', Feminist Review no. 18 (winter 1984).

Jones, Eldred, Othello's Countrymen: the African in English Renaissance Drama (Oxford Univerity Press, 1965).

Jonson, Ben, Epicoene, ed. Edward Partridge (New Haven and London, Yale University Press, 1971).

*— Sejanus His Fall ed. W. F. Bolton in Elizabethan and Jacobean Tragedies (Kent, Ernest Benn, 1984).

Jordan, Constance, 'Feminism and the Humanists: the case of Sir Thomas Elyot's Defence of Good Women', Renaissance Quarterly 36, no. 2 (summer 1983).

Joseph, Gloria, 'The incompatible ménage à trois: Marxism, feminism and racism' in Sargant ed., 1980.

Kahn, Coppelia, Man's Estate: Masculine Identity in Shakespeare (Berkeley, University of California Press, 1981).

Kakar, Sudhir, The Inner World: a Psychoanalytic Study of Childhood and Society in India (New Delhi, Oxford University Press, 1978).

Kanner, Barbara ed., The Women of England from Anglo-Saxon Times to the Present (London, Mansell, 1980).

Kapur, Anuradha, 'Actors, pilgrims, kings and gods: the Ramlila at Ramnagar', Contributions to Indian Sociology (new series) 19, no. 1 (1985).

Kaufman, Gloria, 'Juan Luis Vives on the education of women', Signs 3, no. 2, 1977.

Kaufmann, R. J. Richard Brome: Caroline Playwright (Columbia University Press, 1961).

Kelly, Joan, Women, History, Theory (Chicago, University of Chicago Press, 1984).

Kendal, Geoffrey (with Clare Colvin), The Shakespeare Wallah (Middlesex, Penguin, 1986).

Kernan, Alvin, 'Othello, an introduction' in Alfred Harbage ed., Shakespeare, the Tragedies: a Collection of Critical Essays (New Jersey, Prentice-Hall, 1964).

Kishwar, Madhu, 'Arya Samaj and women's education – Kanya Mahavidyalaya, Jalandhar', Economic and Political Weekly 21, no. 17 (26 April 1986).

Kishwar, Madhu and Vanita, Ruth, eds., In Search of Answers: Indian Women's Voices from Manushi (London, Zed Books, 1984).

Kishwar, Madhu and Vanita, Ruth, 'The burning of Roop Kanwar', Manushi nos. 42-3, Sept.-Dec. 1987, pp. 15-25.

Knox, John, The First Blast of the Trumpet Against the Monstrous Regiment of Women (1558), ed. Edward Arber (Westminster, Archibald Constable, 1895).

Krishnakumari, N. S. and Geetha, A. S., 'Dowry – spreading among more communities', Manushi 3, no. 4 (1983).

Kuhn, Annette and Ann Marie Wolpe eds., Feminism and Materialism: Women and Modes of Production (London, Boston and Henley, Routledge, 1976).

Lamming, George, The Pleasures of Exile (London and New York, Allison and Busby, 1984).

Lawrence, Errol, 'Just plain common-sense: the "roots" of racism' in CCCS, 1982, pp. 47-94.

— 'In abundance of water the fool is thirsty; sociology and black "pathology" in CCCS, 1982, pp. 95-142.

Lewis, Jane, 'The debate on sex and class', *New Left Review* no. 149 (Jan.-Feb. 1985).

Liddle, Joanna and Joshi, Rama, *Daughters of Independence: Gender, Caste and Class in India* (New Delhi, Kali/ London, Zed Books, 1986).

(The) Literature and Society Group, 'Literature/society: mapping the field' in Hall *et al.* eds., 1980, pp. 227-35.

Loomba, Ania, 'Disorderly Women in Jacobean Tragedy : Towards a Materialist-Feminist Critique' (DPhil thesis, University of Sussex, 1987).

Lown, Judy, 'Not so much a factory, more a form of patriarchy: gender and class during industrialisation' in Eva Gmarnikov *et al.* eds., *Gender, Class and Work* (London, Heinemann, 1983).

Lucas, F. L. ed., *The White Devil* (London, Chatto and Windus, 1958).

Mack, Maynard, '*Antony and Cleopatra*: the stillness and the dance' in Milton Crane ed., *Shakespeare's Art: Seven Essays* (Chicago and London, University of Chicago Press, 1973).

McLuskie, Kate, 'Feminist deconstruction: the example of Shakespeare's *The Taming of the Shrew*', *Red Letters* 12, 1981.

— 'The patriarchal bard: feminist criticism and Shakespeare: *King Lear* and *Measure for Measure* in Dollimore and Sinfield eds., 1985, pp. 88-108.

Macaulay, T. B., *Prose and Poetry* compiled G. M. Young (London, Hart-Davis, 1952).

Mahmood, Syed, *A History of English Education in India* (Aligarh, 1895).

Malory, Thomas, *Le Morte D'Arthur* (Caxton, 1485), ed. J. W. Spisak (University of California Press, 1983).

Mani, Lata, 'The production of an official discourse on sati in early nineteenth century Bengal', *Economic and Political Weekly* 21, no. 17 (26 April 1986).

Mannoni, O., *Prospero and Caliban: the Psychology of Colonization*, trans. Pamela Powesland (New York, 1964).

Markels, Julian, *The Pillar of the World: Antony and Cleopatra in Shakespeare's Development* (Columbus, Ohio State University Press, 1968).

*Marlowe, Christopher, *The Tragical History of Dr. Faustus* in *The Complete Works of Christopher Marlowe* (Cambridge University Press, 1973).

Marx, Karl and Engels, Frederick, *Manifesto of the Communist Party* (Moscow, Progress Publishers, 1971).

McCrum, Robert *et al.*, *The Story of English* (London and Boston, Faber, 1986).

Menezes, A., 'Has Shakespeare fallen on evil tongues?' in Narasimhaiah ed., 1964, pp. 12-19.

Merchant, Carolyn N., *The Death of Nature: Women, Ecology and the Scientific Revolution* (San Francisco, Harper and Row, 1980).

Merck, Mandy, 'The city's achievements: the patriotic Amazonomachy and ancient Athens' in Susan Lipshitz ed., *Tearing the Veil* (London, Routledge, 1978).

Mernissi, Fatima, *Beyond the Veil: Male-Female Dynamics in Muslim Society* (London, Al Saqi Books, 1985; revised edition).

*Middleton, Thomas, *More Dissemblers Besides Women*, in A. H. Bullen ed., *The Works of Thomas Middleton* (New York, AMS Press, 1964).

*— *A Chaste Maid in Cheapside* in Muir ed., 1975.

*— *Women Beware Women* in Muir ed., 1975.

*— *The Changeling* in Muir ed., 1975.

— *The Selected Plays* ed. David L. Frost (Cambridge University Press, 1978).

— *The Family of Love* ed. Simon Shepherd (Nottingham University Press, 1979).

— *Women Beware Women* ed. Roma Gill in *Elizabethan and Jacobean Tragedies* (Kent, Ernest Benn, 1984).

Middleton, Thomas and Dekker, Thomas, *The Roaring Girl*, ed. A. H. Gomme (London, Ernest Benn, 1976).

Mies, Maria, *Patriarchy and Accumulation on a World Scale: Women in the International Division of Labour* (London and New Jersey, Zed Books, 1986).

Miller, Barbara Diane, 'Prenatal and postnatal sex-selection in India: the patriarchal context, ethical questions and public policy' (Michigan State University working paper 107, December 1985).

Millett, Kate, *Sexual Politics* (New York, Avon Books, 1971).

Mitra, Ashoka, 'The status of women', *Frontier*, 18 June 1977.

Montrose, Louis Adrian, 'The purpose of playing: reflections on a Shakespearian anthropology', *Helios* no. 7 (1980) pp. 51-74.

— 'Renaissance literary studies and the Subject of History', *English Literary Renaissance* 16, no. 1 (winter 1986), pp. 5-12.

Morton, A. L., *The English Utopia* (London, Lawrence and Wishart, 1969).

Moorhouse, Goeffrey, *India Britannica* (London, Paladin, 1984).

More, Thomas, *Utopia*, trans. Ralph Robinson (Menston, Sedar Press, 1970).

Morley, Dave, 'Texts, readers, subjects' in Hall *et al.*, eds., 1980, pp. 163-73.

Muir, Kenneth ed., *Thomas Middleton, Three Plays* (London and Melbourne, Dent, 1975).

Mulde-Sacke: or the Apologie of Hic Mulier (1620) in Baines ed., *Three Pamphlets*.

Muliyil, G., 'Why Shakespeare for us?' in Narasimhaiah ed., 1964, pp. 5-11.

Munda, Constantia, *The Worming of a Mad Dogge or a Soppe for Cereberus the Iaylor of Hell* (1617) in Shepherd ed., 1985.

Nagarajan, S., 'The Englishman as a teacher of English literature abroad' in Amur and Desai, eds., 1984, pp. 4-22.

Narasimhaiah, C. D. ed., *Shakespeare Came to India* (Bombay, Popular Prakashan, 1964).

Narayana, Birendra, *Hindi Drama and Stage* (Delhi, Bansal, 1981).

Neely, Carol Thomas, 'Women and men in Othello: "What should such a fool/ Do with so good a woman" ' in Lenz *et al.* eds., *The Woman's Part: Feminist Criticism of Shakespeare* (University of Illinois Press, 1980).

Newman, Karen, '"And wash the Ethiop white" – femininity and the monstrous in *Othello*' in Howard and O'Connor eds., 1987, pp. 143-62.

Newton, Judith and Rosenfelt, Deborah, *Feminist Criticism and Social Change: Sex, Class and Race in Literature and Culture* (New York and London, Methuen, 1985).

Nixon, Rob, 'Caribbean and African appropriations of *The Tempest*', *Critical Inquiry* 13, (spring 1987), pp. 557-77.

Norris, Christopher, 'Post-structuralist Shakespeare: text and ideology' in Drakakis ed., 1985, pp. 47-66.

Ogundipe-Leslie, Molara, 'African women, culture and another development', *Journal of African Marxists* (February 1984).

Okri, Ben, 'Meditations on Othello', *West Africa*, (23 and 30 March 1987) pp. 562-4; 618-19).

Orkin, Martin, 'Othello and the "plain face" of racism', *Shakespeare Quarterly*, 38, no. 2, (summer 1987) pp. 166-88.

— *Shakespeare Against Apartheid* (Craighall, AD. Donker, 1987).

Ornstein, Robert, *The Moral Vision of Jacobean Tragedy* (Madison and Milwaukee,

University of Wisconsin Press, 1965).

Ortner, Sherry, B., 'Is female to male as nature is to culture?', *Feminist Studies* vol. 2, 1975, pp. 167-82.

Painter, William, *The Palace of Pleasure* (1567) in J. R. Brown ed., *The Duchess of Malfi* (London, Methuen, 1964).

Parker, Kenneth, 'The revelation of Caliban: "the black presence" in the classroom' in Dabydeen ed., 1985, pp. 186-206.

Parmar, Pratibha, 'Gender, race and class: Asian women in resistance' in CCCS, 1982, pp. 236-75.

Parry, Benita, 'Problems in current theories of colonial discourse', *Oxford literary Review* Vol. 9, Nos. 1-2, 1987, pp. 27-58.

Parthasarathy, R., 'Whoring after English gods' in Guy Amirthanayagam ed., *Writers in East-West Encounter: New Cultural Bearings* (London and Basingstoke, Macmillan, 1982).

Pathak, Zakia, and Sunder Rajan, Rajeswari, 'Shahbano', forthcoming.

de Pisan, Christine, *The Book of the City of Ladies*, trans. Earl Jeffrey Richards (London, Pan, 1983).

Ponniah, Gowrie, 'Ideology and the Status of Women in Hindu Society' (unpublished MA thesis, University of Sussex, 1976; forthcoming publication).

Pym, John, *The Wandering Company; 21 years of Merchant-Ivory films* (London, British Film Institute/ New York, The Museum of Modern Art, 1983).

Randall, Dale B. J., 'Some observations on the theme of chastity in *The Changeling*, *English Literary Renaissance* 14, no. 3 (autumn 1984).

Rao, V. V. Prakasa and Rao, V. Nandini, 'Sex role attitudes of college students in India' (Michigan State University, working paper 72, November, 1984).

Ribner, Irving, *Jacobean Tragedy: the Quest for Moral Order* (London, Methuen, 1962).

Richmond, Farley, 'The social role of theatre in India' in Coppola ed., 1974.

Ridless, Robin, *Ideology and Art: Theories of Mass Culture from Walter Benjamin to Umberto Eco* (London, Lang, 1984).

Ridley, M.I. ed., *Othello* (London, Methuen, 1958).

Robinson, Cedric J., *Black Marxism: the Making of a Black Radical Tradition* (London, Zed Books, 1983).

Rollo, J.C., 'Teaching Shakespeare in India' in Narasimhaiah ed., *Shakespeare Came to India*, pp. 1-4.

Rose, Jacqueline, 'Sexuality in the reading of Shakespeare: *Hamlet* and *Measure for Measure* in Drakakis ed., 1985, pp. 95-118.

Rose, Mark ed., *Twentieth-century Interpretations of Antony and Cleopatra* (New Jersey, Prentice-Hall, 1977)

Rose, Mary Beth, 'Women in men's clothing: apparel and social stability in *The Roaring Girl*', *English Literary Renaissance* 14 (autumn 1984).

— ed., *Women in the Middle ages and the Renaissance* (Syracuse University Press, 1986).

Rowbotham, Sheila, *Women, Resistance and Revolution* (Middlesex, Penguin, 1972).

Rozett, Martha Tuck, 'The comic structures of tragic endings: the suicide scenes in *Romeo and Juliet* and *Antony and Cleopatra*, *Shakespeare Quarterly* 36, no, 2 (summer, 1985).

Rughani, Pratap, 'Kipling, India and Imperialism' (unpublished paper).

Russell, Bertrand, *Marriage and Morals* (London, George Allen and Unwin, 1929).

Ryan, Michael, *Marxism and Deconstruction: a Critical Articulation* (Baltimore, John Hopkins University Press, 1982).

Rymer, Thomas, *A Short View of Tragedy* (1693) (Yorkshire, A Scolar press Facsimile, 1970).

Sadisivayya, 'Promotion of Indian solidarity through literature' in *Studies in Education and Culture* (Bangalore, Hosali Press, 1959).

Said, Edward, 'Raymond Schwab and the romance of ideas', *Daedalus* 105, no. 1 (winter 1976).

— *Orientalism* (London, Routledge, 1978).

Sangari, Kumkum, 'Marquez and the politics of the possible', *Journal of Arts and Ideas* nos. 10-11 (Jan.-June, 1985), pp. 37-58.

— 'What makes a text literary? The early nineteenth century in England and India' (paper presented at Miranda House, University of Delhi, April 1988).

Sargant, Lydia ed., *Women and Revolution: the Unhappy Marriage of Marxism and Feminism: A Debate on Class and Patriarchy* (London, Pluto Press, 1981).

Schochet, Gordon, 'Patriarchalism, politics and mass attitudes in Stuart England', *Historical Journal* 12, no. 3, (1969), pp. 413-41.

Serpieri, Alessandro, 'Reading the signs: towards a semiotics of Shakespearian drama' in Drakakis ed., 1985, pp. 119-43.

*Shakespeare, William, *The Complete Works of William Shakespeare*, ed. Peter Alexander (London and Glasgow, Collins, 1951).

— *The Tempest*, ed. Frank Kermode (London, Methuen, 1954).

— *Othello*, ed. M. I. Ridley (London, Methuen, 1958).

Sharma, Ursula, 'Purdah and public space' in Alfred de Souza ed., *Women in contemporary India and South Asia* (Delhi, Manohar Publications, 1975).

Shaw, Catherine M., *Richard Brome* (London, Twayne, 1980).

Shepherd, Simon, *Amazons and Warrior Women: Varieties of Feminism in Seventeenth Century Drama* (Brighton, Harvester, 1983).

— ed., *The Women's Sharp Revenge: Five Pamphlets from the Renaissance* (London, Fourth Estate, 1985).

Simeon, Dilip, 'Communalism in modern India: a theoretical examination', *Social Science Probings* vol. 4 no. 1 (March, 1987).

Simmons, J. L. , 'The comic pattern and vision in *Antony and Cleopatra*', *English Literary History* 36 (1969), pp. 483-501.

Sinfield, Alan, *Literature in Protestant England 1560-1660* (London, Croom Helm, 1982).

— 'Reproductions, interventions' in Dollimore and Sinfield eds., 1985, pp. 130-3.

— 'Give an account of Shakespeare and education, showing why you think they are effective and what you have appreciated about them. Support your comments with precise references' in Dollimore and Sinfield eds., pp. 134-57.

— *Alfred Tennyson* (Oxford, Blackwells, 1986).

— 'Othello and the politics of character' (paper given at the University of Santiago de Compostella, Nov. 1987; forthcoming publication).

Smith, Hilda, 'Feminism in Seventeenth Century England' (PhD dissertation, University of Chicago, 1975).

— *Reason's Disciples: Seventeenth Century English Feminists* (Urbana, University of Illinois Press, 1982).

Smith, Stella T., 'Imagery of union, division and disintegration in *Antony and Cleopatra*, *Clafflin College Review* 1, no. 2 (May 1977) pp. 15-28.

Sowernam, Esther, *Esther Hath Hang'd Haman* (1617) in Shepherd ed., 1985.

Spear, Percival, *A History of India* (Volume 2) (Middlesex, Penguin, 1966; rept. 1984).

Speght, R., *A Mouzell for Melastomus* (1617), in Shepherd ed., 1985.

Spivak, Gayatri Chakravorty, 'The Rani of Sirmur: an essay in reading the archives', *History and Theory* 24, no. 3 (1985), pp. 247-72).

— 'Imperialism and sexual difference' *Oxford Literary Review* 8, nos. 1 and 2 (1986).

— 'Interview with Gayatri Chakravorty Spivak', *Book Review* XI, no.3 (May-June 1987), pp. 16-22.

— In *Other Worlds: Essays in Cultural Politics* (New York and London, Methuen, 1987).

Sri Aurobindo (Ghosh), '. . . this sheer creative Ananda of the life-spirit which is Shakespeare' in Narasimhaiah ed., 1964, pp. 128-38.

Stallybrass, Peter, 'Macbeth and Witchcraft', in John Russell Brown ed., *Focus on Macbeth* (London, Routledge, 1982).

— 'The history of sexuality in the English Renaissance' (unpublished manuscript).

— 'Patriarchal territories: the body enclosed' in Ferguson, Margaret Quilligan and Vickers, Nancy J. eds., *Rewriting the Renaissance* (Chicago University Press, 1986) pp. 123-42.

Staton, Shirley F., 'Female transvestism in Renaissance comedy; "a natural perspective that is and is not"', *Iowa State Journal of Research* 56, no. 1 (1981), pp. 79-89.

Stone, Lawrence, *The Family, Sex and Marriage in England, 1500-1800* (London, Weidenfeld and Nicolson, 1977).

Sunder Rajan, Rajeswari, 'After "Orientalism": Colonialism and English Literary Studies in India', *Social Scientist* 158, July 1986, pp. 23-35.

Swetnam, Joseph, *The Arraignment of Lewde, Idle, Unconstant and Froward Women* (1615) (AMS Press, 1970).

Swetnam the Woman-Hater Arraigned by Women in Coryll Crandall ed., *Swetnam the Woman-Hater: The Controversy and the Play* (Lafeyette, Indiana, Purdue University Studies, 1969).

Swift, Jonathan, *Gulliver's Travels* (London, Methuen, 1965).

T. E., *The Lawes Resolutions of Women's Rights: or the Lawes Provision for Women* (1632) (Norwood, Walter J. Johnson, 1980).

Tapper, Bruce Elliott, 'Widows and goddesses: female roles in deity symbolism in a South Indian village ', *Contributions to Indian Sociology* (new series) 13, no. 1 (1979).

Tawney, R. H., *Religion and the Rise of Capitalism* (Middlesex, Penguin, 1926 rept. 1984).

Tennenhouse, Leonard, 'Strategies of State and political plays: *A Midsummer Night's Dream, Henry IV, Henry V, Henry VIII*' in Dollimore and Sinfield eds., 1985, pp. 109-28.

— *Power on Display* (London, Methuen, 1986).

— 'The Politics of Misogyny; Monstrous Women in Jacobean Tragedy' (unpublished manuscript).

Thapar, Romila, *A History of India Volume I* (Harmondsworth, Middlesex, Penguin, 1966; rept. 1984).

Tharu, Susie, 'The rise of English studies in India' (paper given at Miranda House, University of Delhi, April 1988).

Thiong'o, Ngugi Wa, *Decolonizing the Mind* (London, Methuen, 1985).

Thomas, Keith, 'Women and the civil war sects' in Trevor Aston ed., *Crisis in Europe 1560-1660* (London, Routledge, 1965).

Thorne, Anne, 'Women's Creativity: Architectural Space and Literature' (Unpublished DipArch thesis, Polytechnic of Central London, 1979).

Tillyard, E. M. W., The Elizabethan World Picture (Harmondsworth, Penguin, 1964).

Travitsky, Betty ed., The Paradise of Women : Writings by Englishwomen of the Renaissance (Westport, Greenwood Press, 1981).

— 'The lady doth protest: protest in the popular writings of Renaissance Englishwomen', English Literary Renaissance 14, no. 3 (autumn 1984).

Trauffaut, Francois, Hitchcock (London, Granada, 1978).

Tyrell, William Blake, Amazons: a Study in Athenian Myth-making (Baltimore, John Hopkins University Press, 1984).

Vanita, Ruth, 'Men's power and women's resistance – wife murder in Much Ado, Othello, Cymbeline and Winter's Tale in Chatterji ed., 1986, pp. 23-39.

— '"Ravana shall be slain and Sita freed. . .": The feminine principle in Kanthapura' in Chatterji ed, 1986, pp. 188-93.

Viswanathan, Gauri, 'The beginnings of English literary studies in British India', Oxford literary Review Vol. 9, nos. 1-2, 1987, pp. 2-26.

Wadsworth, Frank, 'Webster's Duchess of Malfi in the light of some contemporary ideas on marriage', Philogical Quarterly 35 (1956).

Warner, Marina, Monuments and Maidens: the Allegory of the Female Form (Picador, London, 1985).

Warnicke, Retha, Women of the English Renaissance and Reformation (Connecticut, Greenwood Press, 1983).

Webster, John, The Duchess of Malfi ed. John Russell Brown (Manchester University Press, 1964).

*— The Selected Plays of John Webster eds. Jonathan Dollimore and Alan Sinfield (Cambridge University Press, 1983).

*— The White Devil ed., Elizabeth M. Brennan in Elizabethan and Jacobean Tragedies (Kent, Ernest Benn, 1984).

*— The Duchess of Malfi ed. Elizabeth M. Brennan (London, A & C Black/ New York, W. W. Norton, 1985).

Weigel, Sigrid, 'Double focus: on the history of women's writing' in Ecker ed., 1985.

Weir, Angela and Wilson, Elizabeth, 'The British women's movement', New Left Review no. 148 (Nov.-Dec. 1984).

Weimann, Robert, Shakespeare and the Popular Tradition in the Theater (Baltimore, John Hopkins University Press, 1978).

Wells, Henry H. and Anniah Gowda, H. H., Shakespeare turned East: a Study in Comparison of Shakespeare's Last Plays with Some Classical Plays of India (Mysore, University of Mysore Press, 1976).

Whigham, Frank, 'Sexual and social stability in The Duchess of Malfi', PMLA, March 1985, pp. 167-85.

White, Allon, 'Bakhtin, sociolinguoistics and deconstruction' in Frank Gloversmith ed., The Theory of Reading (New Jersey, Barnes and Noble/ Sussex, Harvester, 1984), pp. 123-46.

Whittey, Steve, 'English language as a tool of British neocolonialism', East Africa Journal 8 (1971), pp. 4-6.

Williams, Raymond, Culture and Society 1780-1950 (London, Chatto and Windus, 1958).

— Marxism and Literature (Oxford University Press, 1977).

Woodbridge, Linda, *Women and the English Renaissance: Literature and the Nature of Womankind 1540-1620* (Brighton, Harvester, 1984).

Wright, Louis B., 'The popular controversy over women' in *Middle Class Culture in Elizabethan England* (Chapel Hill, University of North Carolina Press, 1935).

Young, Iris, 'Beyond the unhappy marriage; a critique of the dual systems theory' in Sargant ed., 1980.

Index